FLASH MX
AUDIO MAGIC

Brad Kozak, Eric E. Dolecki, Craig Swann, and Manuel Clement

New Riders

201 West 103rd Street, Indianapolis, Indiana 46290

An Imprint of Pearson Education

Boston ▪Indianapolis ▪London ▪Munich ▪New York ▪San Francisco

FLASH MX AUDIO MAGIC

International Standard Book Number: 0-7357-1194-1

Library of Congress Catalog Card Number: *2001093814*

First Printing: August 2002

06 05 04 03 02   7 6 5 4 3 2 1

Interpretation of the printing code: The rightmost double-digit number is the year of the book's printing; the rightmost single-digit number is the number of the book's printing. For example, the printing code 02-1 shows that the first printing of the book occurred in 2002.

Trademarks

All terms mentioned in this book that are known to be trademarks or service marks have been appropriately capitalized. New Riders Publishing cannot attest to the accuracy of this information. Use of a term in this book should not be regarded as affecting the validity of any trademark or service mark. Macromedia Flash MX is a registered trademark of Macromedia Corporation.

Warning and Disclaimer

Publisher
David Dwyer

Associate Publisher
Stephanie Wall

Executive Editor
Steve Weiss

Production Manager
Gina Kanouse

Managing Editor
Sarah Kearns

Acquisitions Editor
Theresa Gheen

Development Editor
Audrey Doyle

Project Editor
Jake McFarland

Copy Editor
Amy Lepore

Indexer
Chris Morris

Product Marketing Manager
Kathy Malmloff

Publicity Manager
Susan Nixon

Manufacturing Coordinator
Jim Conway

Book Designer
Steve Gifford

Cover Designer
Aren Howell

Proofreader
Karen Gill

Compositor
Gloria Schurick

Media Developer
Jay Payne

CONTENTS AT A GLANCE

ABOUT THE AUTHORS

Brad Kozak is the founder and CEO of Grok·Media Technology, a strategic marketing and rich media design agency in Dallas, Texas. Brad began his career as a professional musician and freelance graphic artist. He discovered computer graphic design in the early '80s, teaching himself the PostScript language, and subsequently used what at the time was one of the first PC-compatible PostScript printers, the Apple LaserWriter, to create what was possibly the first desktop-published magazine created on a PC. Spending six years at Micrografx as the creative director and user interface evangelist, he subsequently moved to work for Altsys (now a division of Macromedia) as the senior product manager for Virtuoso, the Windows NT/Sun Solaris/NeXTStep version of FreeHand. Leaving Altsys in 1992, Brad launched his own design agency, specializing in both traditional print and online interactive graphics.

An acknowledged expert in rich media and user interface design, as well as music composition, arranging, and orchestration, his cutting-edge work as a creative director and graphic designer has been recognized by such companies as Macromedia and Allegiance Telecom. His client list ranges from Prodigy, The Sharper Image, Nortel, Samsung, and Hewlett-Packard to a number of Internet startups. Brad currently serves on the Macromedia advisory boards for Fireworks and FreeHand, and he was a lecturer at FlashForward2001/San Francisco, speaking on *Using Flash in Business*. He created the online tutorials for Flash 5/FreeHand 10 Studio. He is currently at work on a new venture for Prodigy, an online interactive magazine/catalog, created entirely in the Flash environment.

Eric E. Dolecki is currently Senior Interactive Designer and Interactive Technology Manager at Boston-based Directech eMerge. Clients include notable high-technology clients such as Teradata, WorldCom, and Connected.

His Flash work appears in the *Macromedia/ Centennial Media Advanced Flash 5 ActionScripting Training* CD-ROM, past issues of *Computer Arts UK* magazine, and he was a co-author of the advanced Flash book *Macromedia Flash Super Samurai*. Eric has won numerous international Flash awards, and he is a regular contributor to several open source Flash sites. Eric maintains a personal site at **www.ericd.net**, which showcases experiments, manages his personal clients' work, and serves as a conduit between himself and those seeking to learn more about Flash. He actively maintains a personal client list.

Craig Swann has been an active member of the Flash community since its early days. He formed CRASH!MEDIA in 1997 as a way to express and explore this non-linear and interactive digital landscape. CRASH!MEDIA is a Toronto-based interactive design agency that specializes in integrating fresh ideas with cutting-edge technology. The company has worked on Flash projects for Coca-Cola, Intel, Alliance Atlantis, Miller Brewing, YTV, University of Toronto, Toronto Symphony Orchestra, The Canadian Gemini Awards, as well as Excite @ Home. Craig's love for all things audio has led to the creation of the award-winning site **www.looplabs.com**, which specializes in the integration of audio within a Flash environment. He has also won a Webby Award, Macromedia Site of the Day, and S×SW Best Streaming Audio site, among other awards.

Manuel Clement is the founder of MANO1.COM. Winner of three Macromedia SOD awards, he speaks around the world at events such as FlashForward, Macromedia Web World, and Flashkit. He has contributed in the past to books such as *Flash Bible* and *Flash Studio Secrets*, and he was one of the chosen designers for the *New Masters of Flash* book.

Manuel is an established and respected member of the community, who has published articles and moderated discussion forums at FlashPad, Flashzone, and were-here. He also runs FutureProducers.com, a huge resource site and community for musicians featuring daily news from the industry, tutorials, reviews, and forums. Passionate about design, technology, 3D modeling, and music, Manuel's client list ranges from Microsoft, the State of Florida, and *How Design Magazine* to Native Instruments, Lynda.com, and the president of France: Jacques Chirac.

ABOUT THE TECHNICAL REVIEWERS

These reviewers contributed their considerable hands-on expertise to the entire development process for *Flash MX Audio Magic*. As the book was being written, these dedicated professionals reviewed all the material for technical content, organization, and flow. Their feedback was critical to ensuring that *Flash MX Audio Magic* fits our readers' need for the highest-quality technical information.

Jim Caldwell is a self-taught and ambition-driven creative developer. He has worked for communications giants such as BellSouth and MCI WorldCom. Currently, he is a senior applications developer with MCI WorldCom. While Jim has been responsible for WorldCom's Intranet applications, his passion is creating new benefits and uses within Flash. Jim is known for making his designs incredibly download-friendly, and most of his projects can be updated without altering Flash files. His own design studio, Innovative FX, LLC (**www.innovativefx.com**), while in its growth stage, is contributing to his success by allowing him to serve clients such as Cisco Systems, Inc. His greatest achievements have been the opportunity to co-author *Flash MX Magic* and to write *Instant Macromedia Flash 5*. Jim has always been a large part of the design community, moderating at forums such as Ultrashock (**www.ultrashock.com**), were-here (**www.were-here.com**), and Flashmove (**www.flashmove.com**). He owes his accomplishments to the many great designers within the community for their lasting advice and support.

Scott Balay, a native of Denver, is a mild-mannered web and graphics guru and co-founder of Eyeland Studio (**www.eyeland.com**), who has worked on projects for Nokia and Procter & Gamble, among others. He has served as a technical editor for numerous books, including *Flash deCONSTRUCTION: The Design, Process, and ActionScript of Juxt Interactive* and *Flash 5 Magic*. After hours, however, while wearing a chicken on his head, Scott makes music experimentally, uses technology to make art, and contemplates the platypus.

DEDICATIONS

Brad Kozak: I'd like to dedicate this book to my wife Elizabeth, and to the memory of those who gave their lives so that the United States of America can remain the single greatest nation on the face of the Earth. It is because of their sacrifice that we live in a world where individuals can pursue their own dreams, just as I am pursuing mine.

Eric E. Dolecki: I would like to dedicate this book to my grandfather, Stanley P. Duda, for being an inspiring pillar of strength and a true bastion of love and devotion in a world that seems to forget more and more about these things everyday.

Craig Swann: I would like to dedicate this book to all the people who chase their dreams, knowing full well that by doing so they become reality. Dream on.

Manuel Clement: I dedicate this book to each person who made the design community what it is today. They created millions of amazing projects over the years, inspiring newcomers to express themselves as well.

ACKNOWLEDGMENTS

Brad Kozak

I could not have written this book without the love, support, council, understanding, and infinite patience of my wife Elizabeth. She is the catalyst that has helped me to achieve everything in my life that is worthwhile.

I would also like thank our kids, Will and Phoebe, for putting up with all the long hours I spent cozying up to my computer instead of spending more time with them.

I would like to thank my co-author, Manuel Clement, for his enthusiasm, talent, and support. Although we've not met face to face (yet) we quickly became friends, trading knowledge, ideas, and concepts for the book. In my experience, collaboration always makes creative endeavors stronger. This project was no exception. Mano, you rock!

I will be eternally grateful to the team at New Riders for not only helping me get this book out the door, but providing me with much-needed support and encouragement, and vital help. Specifically, I'd like to thank my editors, Steve Weiss, Theresa Gheen, and Audrey Doyle. Without their patience and support, I'd still be writing chapter one.

I'd also like to thank Steve Foldvari and the folks at Sonic Foundry. Aside from making some great audio software, they have been very supportive throughout the course of the project.

Finally, I'd like to thank everyone in the Flash community who have been so generous with their time and knowledge. It's unusual in life to find a group of experts that are so willing to freely share what they know. In the Flash world, that's the rule and not the exception. Writing this book is one way for me to give something back to everyone who wants to know more about Flash.

Eric E. Dolecki

I would like to thank my parents for having always been there for me and starting my journey early with that Apple][+. I fondly remember PR#6, peek, poke, and all the rest of it. I would also like to thank the love of my life, Deanna Charpentier, for putting up with all of my numerous deadlines! That can't be easy, and I love you even more for it. I would like to thank Mike Grundivg, Jobe Makar, Max Oshman, Klaus Hougesen, and Guy Watson for always pushing me to improve my craft. You are all great friends and you make those late nights of development a lot more fun. Thanks to my editor Audrey Doyle and also to Jeremy Allaire, Domo, and Troy Evans at Macromedia and everyone on the Flash MX beta team; Joe at Quicktimers.com; Kari Bulkley at Sorenson Media; those fine innovators at Apple Computer; and Theresa Gheen at New Riders.

Craig Swann

First off, I would like to thank my family for all their support, love, and encouragement. I would also like to give a special thanks to both Robert Marks and Lumi Necula for their hard work and devotion. Looplabs would not be what it is today without them.

Manuel Clement

I would like to thank my talented wife, the so-amazing Christine. Go Smartie, I love you! Thanks to my big brother Karim, my mother Arlette (you are a saint!), and the wonderful family I am lucky to be a part of.

Thanks to New Riders and to Brad Kozak, who made this project happen! I'd also like to thank Lynda Weinman and all the other wonderful people I've met over the years.

To all the ones who supported me: Christian Coron, Antonio Munoz, Regine and Romain Fouques, and all my dear friends in Marseille, thank you.

A Message from New Riders

As the reader of this book, you are our most important critic and commentator. We value your opinion and want to know what we're doing right, what we could do better, in what areas you'd like to see us publish, and any other words of wisdom you're willing to pass our way.

As Executive Editor at New Riders, I welcome your comments. You can fax, email, or write me directly to let me know what you did or didn't like about this book—as well as what we can do to make our books better. When you write, please be sure to include this book's title, ISBN, and author, as well as your name and phone or fax number. I will carefully review your comments and share them with the authors and editors who worked on the book.

Please note that I cannot help you with technical problems related to the topic of this book, and that due to the high volume of email I receive, I might not be able to reply to every message. Thanks.

Fax: 317-581-4663

Email: **steve.weiss@newriders.com**

Mail: Steve Weiss
         Executive Editor
         New Riders Publishing
         201 West 103rd Street
         Indianapolis, IN 46290 USA

Visit Our Web Site: www.newriders.com

On our web site, you'll find information about our other books, the authors we partner with, book updates and file downloads, promotions, discussion boards for online interaction with other users and with technology experts, and a calendar of trade shows and other professional events with which we'll be involved. We hope to see you around.

Email Us from Our Web Site

Go to **www.newriders.com** and click on the Contact Us link if you…

- Have comments or questions about this book.
- Want to report errors that you have found in this book.
- Have a book proposal or are interested in writing for New Riders.
- Would like us to send you one of our author kits.
- Are an expert in a computer topic or technology and are interested in being a reviewer or technical editor.
- Want to find a distributor for our titles in your area.
- Are an educator/instructor who wants to preview New Riders books for classroom use. In the body/comments area, include your name, school, department, address, phone number, office days/hours, text currently in use, and enrollment in your department, along with your request for either desk/examination copies or additional information.

INTRODUCTION

"The man that hath no music in himself,
Nor is not moved with concord of sweet sounds,
Is fit for treasons, stratagems, and spoils.
The motions of his spirit are dull as night,
And his affections dark as Erebus.
Let no such man be trusted."

—LORENZO IN *THE MERCHANT OF VENICE* BY WILLIAM SHAKESPEARE

Any visual experience coupled with underpinnings of dynamic and rich audio becomes even more powerful and moving. It can bring about such an astounding array of emotions.

Imagine a major motion picture release, such as *The Fellowship of the Ring*. You hardly even notice the symphonic score that dances behind the visuals, feeding you clues and immersing you into the environment. Take out that score, and the movie loses most of its brilliance.

Flash is a visual medium with the capabilities of delivering dynamic audio. There are far too many Flash sites around the web that have almost no audio experience associated with them. You may hear the occasional techno loop, a streamed in SWF, rollover sound effects, and so on, but you never truly feel enveloped in the experience. This book will help

you deliver sites and projects that create an immersive experience. You will learn audio basics, techniques in editing audio, practices in recording audio, and then you will learn some techniques for deploying your audio in creative and precise ways.

GOALS OF THIS BOOK

The primary goal of this book is to help open doors for those of you just beginning to integrate audio into your Flash projects, and to help those with intermediate audio skills to take their craft to new levels. Because audio assets can be triggered and controlled programmatically, and not simply tied to a frame on a Timeline, the ability to creatively use audio in different ways has grown exponentially since the release of Flash 5. Flash MX adds even more audio control, and if you are a Flash MX user, you'll find some new audio techniques in this book you can learn and build on.

In the end, you will be given the tools and approaches to create truly dynamic audio/visual experiences using Flash (and with the optional help of some third-party applications).

WHO THIS BOOK IS FOR

This book has been written to help

- New Flash users who want to add dynamic and rich audio to their Flash projects.

- Flash users with little to no experience in adding audio to their Flash projects.

- Current Flash users who have a good understanding of ActionScript but have yet to deploy any sort of advanced audio system.

- Intermediate Flash users looking for ways to improve their ability to deliver even more engaging experiences using audio.

Those of you who are currently deploying audio and/or video assets in your Flash projects will benefit from this book's attention to detail and explanations of some of the more advanced techniques. Part IV, "Audio, Video, and Flash," in particular touches on integrating video into your projects, allowing you to add even more dynamic and engaging content into your projects. You will learn how to simulate video within the Flash 5 authoring environment, how to stream video with Flash MX (with an example), and also how to embed Flash 4 controls into a QuickTime movie.

As of this writing, QuickTime 6 has been announced but not yet released. QuickTime 6 promises to bring Flash 5-level Actionscript to it and MPEG-4 streaming support, blowing the doors off the previous Flash 4 controls (Flash track) in QuickTime 5. (A preview version of QuickTime 6 is currently available.)

OVERVIEW

Flash MX Audio Magic was compiled and assembled in a way that walks you through theories, working directly with audio, assembling video, and integrating it into your Flash projects. Each project takes you a step further toward the end goal of providing you with an advanced set of skills in working with audio in the Flash authoring environment.

Here is a breakdown of the book by its projects:

- **Project 1, "Designing with Audio."** Adding sound to animation is what puts the "multi" in multimedia. But there's more to designing with audio than just importing a sound file and looping it ad infinitum. In Project 1, we'll cover how a little pre-planning and goal-setting will make a huge difference in the success of your projects.

- **Project 2, "Recording What You Hear."** It would be wonderful if there were nothing more to recording than plugging a microphone into your PC and pressing the record button. The good news is that recording may require a little skill, but it's not rocket science. We'll review how best to record live music and sound effects, and touch on how to merge sounds as well.

- **Project 3, "Editing Audio."** The difference between adding some sounds and using audio as if it were another actor in your movie frequently comes down to editing. Certainly, editing audio files can save huge amounts of bandwidth, but it can also make the difference between a good audio track and a great one. In Project 3, we'll cover everything from cropping and fading to mixing and adding special effects.

- **Project 4, "Enhancing UI with Audio."** Audio can bring an otherwise staid user interface to life. Or it can drive visitors mad with repetitive, annoying sounds whose ultimate goal seems to be to drive users away. In this project, we'll cover ways to make audio a vital— and welcome—part of a site's interface.

■ **Project 5, "Controlling Audio Playback."** Sometimes the best audio is no audio. Even if you feel that your magnum opus is nothing without sound, sometimes users want—or need—a way to visit your site without being forced to hear it as well as see it. Here, you'll learn how to create audio controls that give visitors the option of muting audio throughout the site.

■ **Project 6, "Creating Looping Backgrounds."** When you need the maximum sound with the minimum impact on file size, loops are the only way to go. But sometimes, commercially available loops just won't cut it. Here's a guide to creating your own loops and building customized audio for your projects.

■ **Project 7, "Creating Backgrounds for Synchronization."** Loops are often a necessary evil when file size is the only issue. When you find yourself in a situation where you can create an entire soundtrack, why not design something original...a soundtrack that you can synchronize with animation, and which will lend a new dimension to your work. Here's how to do it.

■ **Project 8, "Using Background Sound in Flash."** The Holy Grail of theatrical movie audio is now attainable. With the advent of broadband connections and Flash, you too can create audio that can work dynamically as a part of your animation. Here's how to synchronize your sound and make it work.

■ **Projects 9, "Controlling Sounds with ActionScript"; 10, "Streaming MP3 Audio in Flash"; and 11, "Building a MultiSound Mixer."** These projects focus on the underpinnings of ActionScript-controlled audio. By now, you have seen many ways in which audio can be used in Flash projects. These projects will teach you some of the scripting capabilities of Flash MX. You will learn how to control your audio through button, frame, and event actions. You will also learn how to control multiple sounds through applications such as music mixers and sequencers.

■ **Project 12, "Designing Game Architectures."** Build a complex musical memory game in Flash using ActionScript. Record the player's choices using arrays and trigger sounds dynamically. Learn about loading sounds only when you need them and how to create a game interface where sound libraries are randomly assigned to a grid of buttons. This project covers many vital features of Flash, including the Sound object.

■ **Project 13, "Finding Source Material."** In this project, learn how to create your own sounds using Sound Forge Synthesis Tools. You will also read all about copyrights, Internet myths, sample CDs, and online resources. Make yourself comfortable with terms such as oscillator, chorus, and envelope. Find sounds for any Flash project and understand copyrights. All these are essential skills to master when working on any project involving sounds.

■ **Project 14, "Video Planning and Creation."** In this project, you'll learn the Flash 5 technique for simulating streaming video and also learn how Flash MX has reinvented itself to allow for true streaming video. This project covers the core technologies for both techniques, and explains how you can deliver streaming video using both plug-ins.

■ **Project 15, "Flash-Tracked QuickTime."** In this project, learn how to import a QuickTime reference asset, add Flash functionality, and Export or Publish a QuickTime movie with an embedded Flash track. By adding a Flash track to a QuickTime movie, you have another means by which to deploy video assets using the Flash authoring environment. This project covers QuickTime 5's integration, as QuickTime 6 has not yet been released.

DESIGNING WITH AUDIO

"Music expresses that which cannot be

said and on which it is impossible

to be silent."

—VICTOR HUGO

AUDIO MAKES MULTIMEDIA

Audio puts the "multi" in multimedia. Moving

pictures are a wonderful way to communicate,

but they are exponentially more effective when

combined with audio. Want proof? Try turning

off on your television's sound for a while. In

fact, audio is much more of a trigger for

creating ideas than are pictures. That's why

radio was so popular in the days before

television—people could create their own sets,

costumes, and lights in their mind's eye. Adding

audio to Flash MX adds that kind of impact to

any production. This project starts with the

basics of sound design, and then you will apply

what you learn to sound, enabling a web site

user interface.

Project 1

Designing with Audio

by Brad Kozak

GETTING STARTED

This project covers how to conceptualize an audio plan for a web site user interface. Save the Project 1 folder from the accompanying CD-ROM to your hard drive, and install Sound Forge from the accompanying CD-ROM or download it from **www.sonicfoundry.com**.

Open **laffbox.com01.fla** and examine the layout.

This is an early mockup of the entire site. The client wanted us to create something more than a simple HTML site, adding as many bells and whistles (in some cases, literally) as we could to make the site fun.

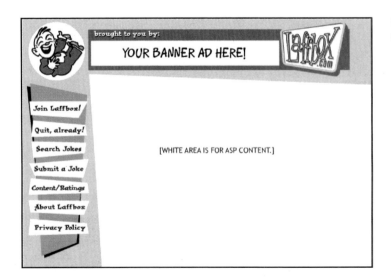

Visualize the layout as it will appear in a browser window.

Sound Design

To demonstrate the audio conceptualization process, you'll use Flash MX (since we know you have it) and Sound Forge (you'll find a free trial version on the CD) to show you some of the processes you'll go through to plan sounds for a corporate web site.

In web site design, it's important to know your client and the client's audience. To help you in that endeavor, we've come up with a list of questions directed toward the client.

Without the answers to these questions, there is no way to make intelligent, informed choices about the use of audio within a site. These questions are designed to paint a picture of the typical user (or range of users) so that you can better understand what the average visitor will want and need from the site. After the questions are answered, you should be able to infer a number of things about the projected users, in particular both the lowest common denominator and mean or average user profile. This information is essential to good site design. (Note that we don't actually create the questionnaires in Flash—it's simply easier to illustrate them for you here, as it means that you won't have to own or open another application to read the sample files. If you're curious, I use Macromedia FreeHand as my preproduction tool of choice.) Keep in mind that you'll probably kick around a number of ideas and perhaps give your client several concept sketches or mockups. We've truncated the visual side of the process here to allow us to concentrate on the audio side of things.

1   Open the list of questions by going to the marker at frame 11 labeled Questions. Select File > Page Setup. In the Layout group box, make sure the Frames drop-down box is set to All Frames. Click OK.

Note: Color is a funny thing in design. I usually make it a practice to design the first mockup in grayscale, simply to make sure the client focuses on the design and not on the colors used. Creating both a grayscale version and then a color version can be a little more work, but I've found that it's worth it in the long run. On this project, for instance, the biggest issue with the client wasn't the button layout, the logo design, or even the use of Flash. Instead, it was a rather protracted discussion about which colors to use. An important point to remember for any project involving more than one opinion is to save all your source files—not just your FLA files, but also the source bitmaps, line art, and audio files you use and modify that make their way into your Flash presentation in one form or another. Keep everything separated out into layers and individual symbols. It is the nature of this business that the day after you ditch your source files, somebody will suddenly have a life-or-death reason why you'll need to make some earth-shattering change that requires—you guessed it—the source files.

2 Print out the questions by going to File > Print. In the Print Range group box, select Pages From and enter **10** to **10**. Click OK.

Let's assume your client has answered the questionnaire. It's important to answer all the questions as honestly and accurately as possible. The more valid the data you have, the greater the chance that you and your client will be on the same page, each with reasonable expectations for the project.

---

website design audio survey

Have the client answer all the following questions as accurately and honestly as possible:

1. Who is the target audience for the site? Specify age range, socio-economic factors, gender, and any other pertinent data.

2. What is the purpose of the site? Specify if the site is to be business-to-business, business-to-consumer, e-commerce, advocacy, entertainment, education, and so on.

3. Will the site be used primarily by users at home? At work? Both?

4. Will the typical user be connecting via dialup or broadband?

5. Will the typical user's computer be audio-enabled?

6. Will the typical user have a recent version of a web browser (IE or Netscape 4.5 or newer, for example)?

7. Will the typical user visit the site occasionally? Often? Regularly? Daily?

8. Will the typical user be a computer novice? Average user? Experienced user? Power user?

9. Will the site need to use a combination of HTML and Flash? Flash exclusively? Generator?

10. Will the site need to link to a database or be otherwise automatically updated?

Fill out the answers to all the questions in the survey. This will help you determine the right way to use sound within the site design.

---

3 Go to the marker at frame 20 labeled Answers. Select File > Print and select the page range from **20** to **20**. Click OK.

So what have we learned? We've learned that the users are all over the map, but we need to build for the likelihood of a dialup connection and provide a way to turn off the sound on demand. The site needs to be easy, fun, and accessible for the average/beginner user and needs to use a combination of HTML and ASP pages but with a menu created in Flash. The site will use frames.

---

website design audio survey

Have the client answer all the following questions as accurately and honestly as possible:

1. Who is the target audience for the site? Specify age range, socio-economic factors, gender, and any other pertinent data.
Upper-middle-class, mostly male, 21 to 55, $40K and up annual income, enjoys humor.

2. What is the purpose of the site? Specify if the site is to be business-to-business, business-to-consumer, e-commerce, advocacy, entertainment, education, and so on.
The site will allow visitors to sign up for a daily email joke service and provide access to a joke server.

3. Will the site be used primarily by users at home? At work? Both?
Both.

4. Will the typical user be connecting via dialup or broadband?
Both.

5. Will the typical user's computer be audio-enabled?
Yes, but we need to work with corporate users who don't have speakers, or turn them off.

6. Will the typical user have a recent version of a web browser (IE or Netscape 4.5 or newer, for example)?
Yes.

7. Will the typical user visit the site occasionally? Often? Regularly? Daily?
Regularly, we hope. At least once or twice a week at the least.

8. Will the typical user be a computer novice? Average user? Experienced user? Power user?
We expect a broad spectrum of users, but they should have at least some experience with computers.

9. Will the site need to use a combination of HTML and Flash? Flash exclusively? Generator?
Hybrid HTML/Flash. We'll drive it via a SQL Server database.

10. Will the site need to link to a database or be otherwise automatically updated?
Yes. The joke server pages and the "joke of the day" will change regularly. The forms functions will need to link directly to the member database.

The answers point you in a specific direction, namely the use of relatively low-bandwidth, friendly audio. A mute button will be an absolute necessity.

Note: There are a couple of questions you might have expected to see but didn't, such as "Does the user have the Flash plug-in installed?" With a greater than 96% penetration rate for the various versions of the Flash plug-in as of this writing, we believe it's become a nonissue.

Some of you might be concerned about the use of frames since this debate seems to rage on. With apologies to such usability experts as Jakob Nielsen, we believe that users are at least clever enough to figure out how to navigate a well-designed site built using frames. Like any technology (including Flash), frames—in and of themselves—are neither good nor evil. It is how a technology is used that determines whether it is useful or useless. A well-designed, frames-based site is infinitely faster and easier to navigate than a comparable frameless site. The trick is to design a site that is logical and consistent.

We now have a picture of the target user and a set of parameters we can use to extrapolate the specs for the site design.

STORYBOARDING

At this point, most artists begin sketching things on paper—usually interface designs, button designs, or page layouts. We recommend that, instead, you start by drawing an organizational chart. This could save you a lot of wasted time because an organizational chart can point out the need for more pages or a different hierarchy.

We've provided an organizational chart for you.

1 Go to frame 30, labeled Orgchart, and print it.

This is a simple organization chart (or "orgchart" for fans of process engineering) that depicts the site hierarchy for Laffbox.com. Note the dark gray group boxes (with white keylines) that depict the two frames within the master frameset.

Creating an organizational chart for the site will force you (and your client) to think logically about site design. Anything that's missing in the site will suddenly become glaringly obvious, as will the perceptions and preconceived notions regarding the way sections are organized into top-level categories.

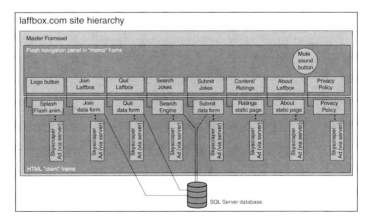

Draw an organizational chart—even if it's just on a piece of paper—before you start committing any design to Flash or HTML.

One hot button for any Flash-enabled site is the use of splash screens. Splash screens, also known as "intros" or "title sequences," are often used to help brand the site and to force the user to focus on the brilliant use of spinning logos and other special effects (sarcasm intended). The problem? Many—or most—of these splash screens take a significant amount of time to load and play. Many users get frustrated and leave before they ever see the main page of the site. Still, they are almost universally popular with web designers and clients (largely because they allow designers to show off their animation skills and clients to show off their spinning logos).

The usability Band-Aid has become the addition of a "skip intro" button that allows the hapless user to stop the animation and proceed into the site. I've always believed that this is an imperfect solution and that there has to be a better way. There is.

As you can see in the organizational chart, in this site design, the menu buttons will come up first, followed by the splash screen playing in the client area only. There is no skip button because the user can immediately click on any button in the site, terminating the animation. This also gives the splash screen some time to load without dictating the need for a preloader sequence.

BANDWIDTH PREPLANNING

Perhaps the most important consideration you can make at this stage is to decide what kind of limitations you will allow bandwidth to make on your site design.

When Flash 2 was released, the fastest computer available was a Pentium I running (as I recall) at a blistering 90MHz. Few had Windows NT, and 128MB of RAM was seen by most as extravagant. Most video cards were of the 256-color, 800×600 variety. Most people connected online with a 28.8 or 33.6 modem. Today, you'd be hard-pressed to find even a low-end system with less than an 800MHz Pentium III or Pentium IV processor, and 128MB is virtually a standard. Most off-the-shelf computers come with video cards that are capable of hyper-realistic 3D rendering with millions of colors, 32-bit with an Alpha mask. Broadband connections are still not in the majority, but within five years or so, even that should reach critical mass. The point? Times change. Things evolve. As a graphic designer, considering your audience and its bandwidth requirements is a fundamental design consideration that will touch every other aspect of your work. Do you build dual low-bandwidth and high-bandwidth versions? Cater to the dialup customers? Ignore them in favor of the allure and demographics of the broadband customers? I don't know. You and your customer are the only ones who can answer that.

1   Open Sonic Foundry Sound Forge. Open the **jackinthebox.wav** file. Familiarize yourself with the zoom in and zoom out controls located on either side of the horizontal scrollbar.

    This is the sound we'll use for the splash screen that will play in the main client area when a visitor loads the site. It is the longest (and largest) file we'll use in the Laffbox.com site.

2   Play the file and listen to the stereo imaging. Notice that the music box is oriented toward the right speaker, and the tympani pedal glissando is on the left.

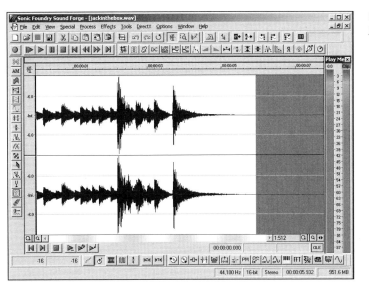

Open the jackinthebox.wav file.

3   Go to File > Properties and look at the General tab.

    This is one, big honkin' file (to use a technical musician's term). It's just about 6 seconds long, and yet it is over a megabyte in size. Granted, it sounds great (at least if you love music boxes and tympani), but it's huge.

    There are two schools of thought as to what to do to fix this problem in Flash. One school—we'll call them the "fix it in the mix" group—recommends that you record everything in CD-quality stereo, import it into Flash, and then let the MP3 compression tool in Flash work its magic. The other school—let's call them the "less work for mother" group—maintains that it is far better to import only what you need into Flash because your audio tools' ability to munge (another technical term) is more sophisticated than that found in Flash.

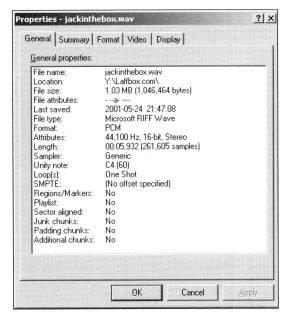

Review the attributes of this file. At 44Hz stereo, it is over 1MB—too large for most Flash movies.

The answer? They are both right. (Huh? What do you mean?) Well... I've done a good bit of experimenting on this topic, and I've found that it's often a "six of one, half dozen of the other" kind of thing. True, if you import big, beautiful files, you'll get beautiful sounds (the antecedent of the "garbage in/garbage out" principle). The downside is that your FLA files will be huge, will take up lots of RAM, and will take forever to load. On the other hand, if you munge your files down to the bare minimum in Sound Forge, you will have little that you can do in Flash to make the sounds sound better.

I recommend a middle course—use stereo only when you absolutely must have it and resample large files down to 22K, 16-bit. Remember, if you are building a CD-ROM in Flash or doing something that requires the best audio fidelity you can provide, all bets are off—bring in everything at the highest resolution you have available. Otherwise, try to economize where you can.

Let's see what we can do about getting this file down to a more manageable size.

4   Go to Process > Resample, select Resample to 22,050Hz with Anti-Alias Filter, and click OK. Save the file as **jackinthebox_22K.wav**.

Resampling is the process of reducing the sample rate (the number of "snapshots" per second taken of a waveform), which reduces the file size. If you have too low a sample rate, the file no longer will reproduce the sound faithfully. The "sweet spot" for online work is considered to be 22K. It's large enough for (more or less) realistic sound, but it's small enough to keep the files from becoming outrageously unwieldy.

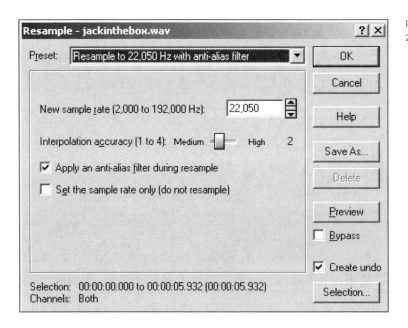

Resample the file down to 22K to save 50% in size.

5 Go to File > Properties and look at the File size. Compare this to the original file's size.

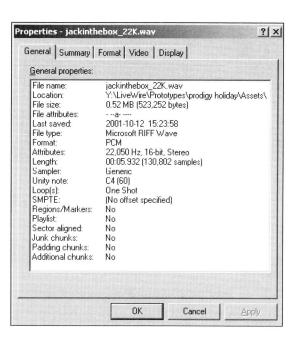

Note that the file size is now .52MB—half of what it was before resampling.

6 Go to File > Save As and change the Attributes from 22,050Hz, 16-bit, Stereo to 22,050Hz, 16-bit, Mono. Call the file **jackinthebox_22Kmono.wav**.

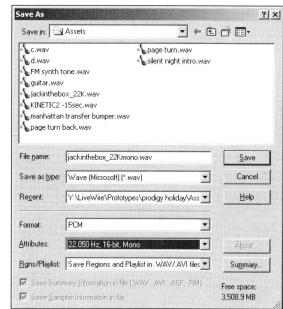

Save the file and change the Attributes from Stereo to Mono. This will again cut the file size in half.

Stereo is wonderful for CD-ROM projects and for projects that you know will be accessed by broadband users. For anything else, it's an expensive luxury. Note that when you convert from stereo to mono, Sonic Foundry will display a message asking whether you want to reload the new mono version of the sound.

Click Yes to hear the new mono version of the sound.

Note: A word about stereophonic sound: It's an unfortunate fact of life that not everyone has access to a broadband connection. Because so much of the world still reaches the Net via a dialup modem, anything you can do to cut down on the size of your files is important. Although stereo mixes obviously sound much better than comparable mono sounds, they come with a 200% file size "price tag" attached. Just because you need to maintain small files, don't despair—you can use the panning tools in Flash to simulate stereo effects with mono sounds. If you are using brief sound cues and effects, you can keep them in stereo, but be sure to weigh the benefits of stereo files versus an increase in file size.

7   Go to File > Properties and note that the file is now just .39MB.

We started with a file that was over a megabyte and ended up with one that is one-quarter of that size. Not too bad! Plus, you'd be hard pressed to justify the difference in quality as worth the extra file size.

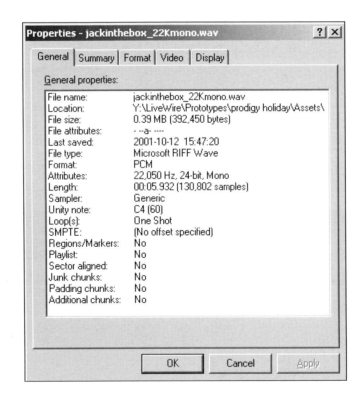

Open the Properties dialog box and review the file size changes.

FILE SIZES AND OPTIMIZATION

Doing your homework and creating files that are optimized before you bring audio into Flash is the first step. Now we'll take a look at how different settings in Flash can affect your sound.

1 Switch back to Macromedia Flash MX. Go to File > Import (or press Ctrl+R) and find and select the **jackinthebox_22Kmono.wav** file you created. Click OK to import the file.

   Note that the sound is not immediately assigned to a frame or attached to an instance of an object on the Stage.

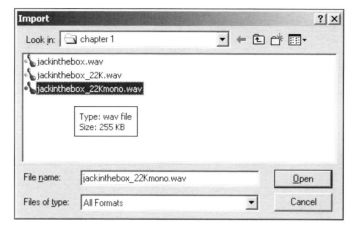

Import the sound file into the Library of Laffbox01.fla.

2 Open the Library either by clicking on the Library icon in the lower-right corner of the main Flash window or by pressing Ctrl+L. Double-click on the **jackinthebox_22Kmono.wav** icon.

   Macromedia Flash offers several configurations for audio compression. The Default setting uses whatever compression scheme (if any) your original audio file used before it was imported into Flash. The ADPCM setting exists for backward compatibility with earlier versions of Flash. Unless you must create a SWF file that can be played by Flash 2 or 3, you can safely avoid ADPCM compression. MP3 compression is the setting of choice for any work you plan to do on the Internet. The Raw setting removes all compression from the audio file. If you plan to master for audio CD and you have no restrictions on file size or load times, the Raw setting might be an appropriate choice.

Open the Library panel and double-click on the jackinthebox_22kmono.wav icon. This will open the Sound Properties dialog box.

3 In the Sound Properties dialog box, change the Compression setting from Default to MP3.

MP3 compression is the compression method of choice because it's simply better at reducing the file size without compromising sound quality. Now your task is to decide on the amount of compression that is appropriate.

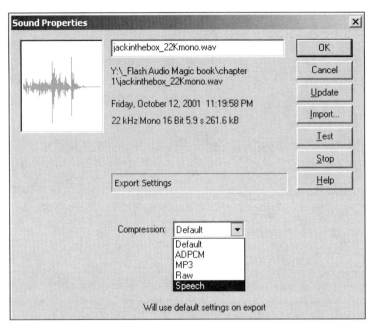

Change the Compression setting to MP3.

4 Click the Test button and listen to the difference in the sound after it has been compressed. Click on different bit-rate levels and click the Test button to compare and contrast the audio fidelity. Note that the final audio file size and the percentage of savings will be listed along the bottom of the dialog box.

Selecting the "right" bit rate is part art and part science. I've seen situations in which two similar sounds required two different bit rates to achieve the same sound quality. Essentially, you need to try to pick the smallest bit rate you can get by with and still maintain an acceptable sound quality. Experiment until you come up with settings that work for you. There's no magic bullet here—just trial and error.

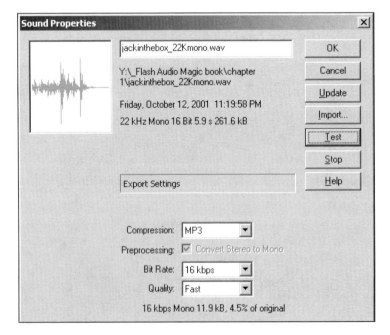

Click the Test button. Listen to the audio file playback and then experiment with different bit-rate levels.

Flash also offers a Quality setting that controls the tradeoffs between compression and quality. The Fast setting gives you the fastest compression but compromises sound quality. The Slow setting provides the slowest compression but the highest sound quality. For online projects, Macromedia recommends that you stick with the default Fast setting. Again, experimentation is the best way to determine what works best for you.

Selecting the Right Music

Choosing the right music for your project is about as completely subjective a pursuit as you can imagine. There are as many different ways to score a rich media production as there are composers and arrangers. The essential choice you should make at this point in your project is to decide between using a looped sound background and a single audio file that will play the length of your production. We'll get into looping and tying animations to music cues later in the book. For now, it's enough to define the differences between the kinds of sound you'll be using.

- **Looped audio.** Flash enables you to import a sound and specify how many times it plays. If the sound is designed to have a seamless start and end, the sound will seem as though there is no beginning and no end—what musicians refer to as a *vamp.*

  Another category of looped audio is what audio engineers call *walla*—essentially a loop of ambient sound that plays in the background. Walla works as a sort of audio shorthand to imply a setting or framework for the production. For instance, if you were creating a presentation with a beach scene, you'd want a walla of surf, seagulls, and other audio cues that you'd expect to hear at the beach.

- **Background or soundtrack audio.** These are usually longer, larger files that ordinarily play for the length of the presentation. The advantage of using background audio is that you have the ability to synchronize visual events to sound cues within the audio file. Plus, you avoid the monotony of a sound that loops ad infinitum. The downside is that the file is invariably larger and therefore makes your SWF file larger than if you use a looped file.

- **Sound effects audio.** These usually are very short files that you synchronize to specific visual cues to add impact. They are well worth the small hit you'll take with your file size. Button sounds and other user interface elements fall into this category.

FINDING ROYALTY-FREE MUSIC

So, where do you find this music? First of all, keep in mind that audio—all audio—is considered somebody's intellectual property and is therefore covered under copyright law. We'll go into the specifics of copyright law in Project 13, "Finding Source Material." For now, it's enough to know that it is screamingly illegal to rip a few bars off a commercial CD you like and use that to create a loop for your presentation.

You can license many copyrighted works for specific use. Typically, these licenses are written to allow the use of the work within a narrowly defined context. For instance, you might purchase the rights to use a recording of a song for three months online with expected user traffic of 10,000 unique visitors per month. This can be painful to negotiate, but the big draw here is that you actually license recognized songs, frequently performed by the original artists. (As I write this, Microsoft has just launched Windows XP with a song licensed from Madonna. That's how this business works.)

If the nature of your project or your budget prohibits spending money on royalties for music, your next best choice is often to license royalty-free music. With royalty-free music, you pay for it once and can use it as often as you like (as long as it is used within the terms of the license). Many sites offer royalty-free music. Many of these sites have begun to offer not only background audio but also audio loops specifically designed for use within Flash.

Equally important is where *not* to find royalty-free music. You won't find it in closeout bins in your local CD emporium, nor will you find it on services like Napster and other download sites. Keep in mind that because you get it for free does not mean you have permission to use it. Audio files are notoriously difficult to track; therefore, it's important for you to maintain as much information as you can regarding how you acquired the sound, just in case someone challenges your right to use the file. If you are in doubt as to your right to use an audio file, your best bet is to use one that you are sure of.

FINDING SOUND EFFECTS

Finding sound effects presents many of the same challenges as finding royalty-free music. Just like music, sound effects come in two flavors—royalty and royalty-free. If you have access to a microphone (or ideally a portable tape deck and a microphone), you can record your own sounds. What makes this interesting is that there are many ways to create sounds. You can record gravel shifting in a box as a substitute for the sound of a cement mixer, or you can use the sound of breaking celery for punches in a fight scene. The next project covers recording techniques in more detail.

HOW IT WORKS

The really wonderful thing about audio is that it can become the equivalent of a cast member in your production. Using the right audio can make the difference between an average production and one that is both moving and memorable. It can be easy, though, to let your audio plans get out of hand, using such elaborate music and sound effects that your file size balloons and your files take too long to load. The best way to avoid this problem is to plan ahead. Using the site survey, the site organizational chart, and a site mockup will help you develop a realistic plan that is well suited to your project's needs.

RECORDING
WHAT YOU HEAR

"I don't know anything about music.

In my line you don't have to."

—ELVIS PRESLEY

RECORDING YOUR OWN SOUND

Recording your own sounds is what separates

a person who uses sound from a person who

really understands it. Unfortunately, digital

recording is as much alchemy as it is science.

There seem to be as many ways to convert

audible sound into bits that can be reproduced

by a computer speaker as there are tools to

help you do it. This project demystifies the

process and gives you some insight into the

best way to record and edit sounds on

your own.

Recording What You Hear

by Brad Kozak

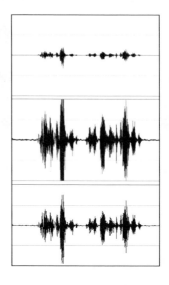

GETTING STARTED

Copy the Project 2 folder to your hard drive from the accompanying CD-ROM, and install Sound Forge and Vegas Audio from the CD-ROM. This project covers how to record live sound effects.

1   Open Sound Forge and create a new (blank) file. Set the sample rate to 22,050Hz and the bit-depth to 16-bit. Unless you have a stereo microphone, set the channels to Mono. The New Window dialog box will give you the chance to preconfigure the basic file parameters before you begin recording.

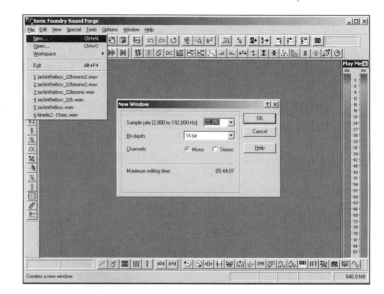

Go to File > New and create a new sound file.

2   The new, empty file appears in Sound Forge.
    Familiarize yourself with the main controls, particu-
    larly the ones that are similar to those found on a cas-
    sette recorder. If your screen looks different from the
    one in the illustration to the right, go to View >
    Toolbars and browse through the other toolbars in
    Sound Forge. Configure your window by dragging
    and dropping toolbars to suit your workflow.

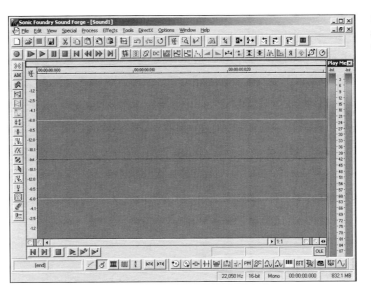

Drag and drop toolbars
against the sides of the application window to dock them.

3   Click the round, red Record button on the toolbar.
    This button will open the Record dialog box. Set the
    Mode to Automatic Retake (Automatically Rewind).
    Click the Monitor check box, which will enable you
    to check your recording levels.

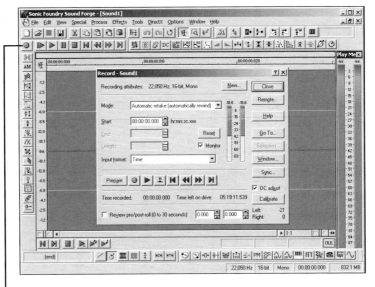

Record button

Click the red Record button
on the toolbar to prepare to
record.

RECORDING AUDIO

If your hardware is properly set up and configured, you should now be ready to start recording. You should see some green in the Play meters, indicating that you are getting an input signal. If you make some sounds within range of your microphone, you should see the levels change in your VU meters. Ideally, what you want to see is a gain level that averages in the yellow range, only occasionally moving into the red range. Much more, and you'll see the meters indicate a condition known as *clipping*, where there is too much input signal for the recorder to handle. Clipped recordings are distorted, so you want to get your levels as "hot" as possible without clipping. If your audio signal is of widely varying levels, you might have a hard time with the dynamic range—the soft passages won't record well, and the loud ones will distort. You want to go for sounds that have a relatively modest dynamic range that will record as hot as possible without overloading the audio and clipping.

Now is probably a good time to explain how meters correspond to what you hear. Two kinds of meters are used in audio work: VU and dB meters. They both measure audio power when recording, and they both use logarithmic scales to convert the power into a visual display of some kind. Think back to your high school math class, and you'll probably remember that a logarithmic curve describes the increase in power needed to raise a value to the next higher unit of measure. Commonly, audio uses a logarithm of 10. Without going into a lot of detailed math, suffice it to say that a power increase with a factor of 10 displays as an increase of 10 units on an audiometer. Therefore, −30dB equates to 10 times the power of −40dB. So, what's a dB? For that matter, what's a VU? The short answers are that dB stands for "decibel" and VU is a handy way of saying "volume unit." They are similar yet different units of measure for sound. You've probably noticed that all audio meters use 0 as the highest power level before a signal begins to distort (proving that computer geeks aren't the only ones who love to arbitrarily come up with different jargon and measuring scales). VU and dB only differ in the way they measure audio power.

For our purposes, you can think of a dB meter as a tool for measuring "impulse" audio power because it responds quickly to every instant of the audio signal. dB meters calibrate zero to a level with 3% Total Harmonic Distortion (THD).

Note: Think of the dynamic range of an audio recording using the metaphor of a room. In any room, you have a ceiling and a floor. For our purposes, the floor is the point below which you can't hear anything but noise. The ceiling (which in decibel terms is measured as 0) is the absolute limit of the loudest reproducible signal. Any sound that is louder than the ceiling gets clipped, or cut off. Now all that energy has to go somewhere, and it does. It folds back into the waveform and causes the distortion that is the main characteristic of clipped sounds. The best way to avoid clipping is to carefully limit the dynamic range of the audio signal you want to record. You can do this organically (in other words, don't play, sing, or talk too loudly or softly) or electronically (using a compressor or limiter).

In the analog realm of magnetic tape, occasional peaks above 0 (the maximum volume unit) don't cause a problem because the point at which magnetic tape becomes saturated is a variable. In digital recording, however, 0 represents an absolute maximum, and any signal beyond 0 gets literally clipped. Essentially, this means that digital audio has absolutely no headroom. It's essential then to set the sampling recording level. If you don't know the maximum level you can expect, leave at least 3 to 6 decibels of headroom.

VU meters measure average audio power. They tend to respond slowly, analyzing audio volume over time. VU meters calibrate zero to a level with 1% THD in the audio signal.

Because we are recording digitally, the concept of headroom is finite rather than variable. Because of this, dB meters will give you a much better read of your signal strength (and will tell you if your signal is too hot).

1   Note the Record and Playback buttons in the Record dialog box (as opposed to the Record button on the main toolbar). When you are ready, click the red Record button. Record your sound. When you are done, click the Stop button (which automatically replaces the Record button when you begin recording). Your sound now displays as a waveform in the window behind the Record dialog box, and the Record dialog box stays onscreen. A really useful feature of the Sonic Foundry user interface is that the Record dialog box enables you to play back the sound you've just recorded without closing the dialog box. If you are satisfied with the recording, click the Close button. If not, you can erase what you recorded and start over without having to close and reopen the Record dialog box.

At this point, you should have a sound recorded (but not saved) within Sound Forge. Note the two horizontal lines that run at the midpoint (–6.0dB) between the top and bottom of the waveform display area. (If you are looking at a stereo recording, you'll see two sets of waveform displays, one each for left and right sounds.) They are equidistant from the –Inf. Line (which represents "infinity" or, in technical terms, "silence"). What you are looking at is a visual representation of the volume levels of the sound you just recorded. Optimally, you should see your sound levels reach these two horizontal lines as much as possible without going beyond them for any

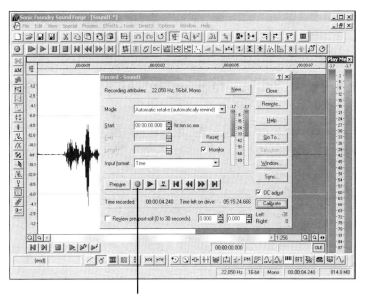

Record your audio by clicking the Record button in the Record dialog box.

Record button

appreciable amount or time. You don't want to see a lot of waveform going past these lines, nor do you want to see a waveform in which the loudest portion never reaches the horizontal lines. Think of these −6.0dB lines as an ideal median for your audio levels.

Take a look at the samples of the same waveform in the figure to the right, recorded at different levels.

So, what do you do to control a wide range of dynamics? The best thing to do, as far as getting a good recording to start with, is to use tools that will compress or limit the dynamic range. A *limiter* is an electronic device that will automatically reduce the volume level of a sound if it goes above a predetermined level. Think of this as the same thing that happens when you are listening to television and you reach for the remote to turn the volume down when a commercial comes on that is appreciably louder than the program you were watching; then you turn the volume back up when the commercial is over. The difference is that the limiter performs this trick thousands of times faster than any human can. A *compressor* works like a limiter, but it also increases the volume of the softest sounds, reducing the highs and pumping up the lows to limit the entire range of dynamics. When used with discretion, this can make a remarkable yet almost undetectable difference in your audio recordings. Most recordings that feature slapping and popping bass lines use compression to control both the high and low volume levels. You can find limiters and compressors in everything from a guitar effects pedal to a stereo rack-mounted unit for professional audio recording.

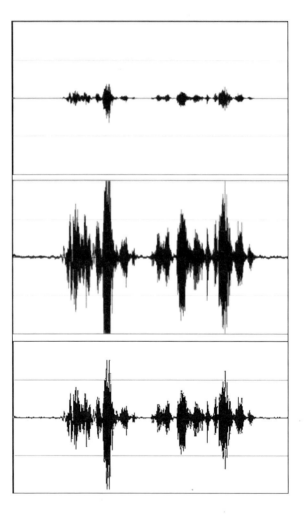

Review the three waveforms, which represent recording levels that are too low, too high, and just right. Goldilocks would be proud.

What can you do about an audio clip that, for one reason or another, cannot be limited or compressed? There are two main techniques you can use to fix imperfect samples. You can use a number of built-in Sound Forge effects and tools, including the compressor and limiter effects, and the normalize volume levels to fix your samples. Here's how this works.

2 For a sound clip that was recorded at too low a level, go to Process > Volume. Use the slider control to increase the volume level. Use the Preview button to listen to the result before you click OK to preserve the change. Optionally, you can use the preset for a 6dB (200%) boost.

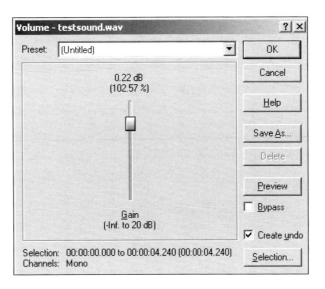

Open the Volume panel and adjust the slider (or use the +6dB preset) to increase the volume level of the sample.

3 For a clip that has a wide range of dynamics, go to DirectX > Sonic Foundry Track Compressor. Choose the preset that is most appropriate. In this case, Limit levels to −6dB (hard limiter) will remove the extreme peaks in the waveform without changing the rest of the file.

With waveforms that have a wide variety of dynamic levels, you might find that using one of the compression presets provides better results.

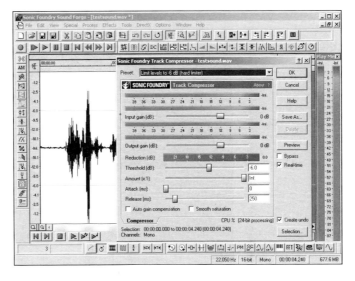

Open the Sonic Foundry Track Compressor and change the Limit levels to −6dB (hard limiter) preset. This will reduce the volume of only the portions of the waveforms that are louder than −6dB.

SAMPLE RECORDING CONFIGURATIONS

So, what about the recording equipment itself? Virtually everyone who records digitally has his own favorite gear to record. Of course, *what* you are recording makes a huge difference. Recording the spoken word in a home office requires different equipment than recording sound effects in the field or live music in a nightclub. We've put together three configurations—a kind of "good…better…best"—that should cover most recording situations you might encounter. Keep in mind that these are not endorsements of any particular manufacturer's gear, and what we recommend might not be appropriate for your situation. Having issued these standard disclaimers, here are some solutions for your recording needs:

- **Basic Setup.** You can't get much more basic than a decent sound card with a microphone plugged directly into the backplane. Most 16-bit sound cards have a 1/8-inch microphone input jack, and many computer manufacturers bundle microphones with their systems. I've had surprisingly good results with just this kind of setup. It's essential to isolate the microphone from extraneous sounds, including the noise of the computer fan, central air/heat, ceiling fans, and so on. Generally speaking, inexpensive microphones don't include extras like windscreens, isolation mounts, and the like. What works well is a small block of foam rubber under the microphone stand, coupled with a heavy-duty windscreen.

  Many music stores carry devices that stop *sibilance*— usually consonants like "s," "t," "p," and "k" that result in dynamic spikes in recorded sounds. These devices are usually a combination of a clamp, an adjustable gooseneck shaft, and a double-ring configuration that holds taut a double layer of what is, in reality, nylon-stocking material. You can make your own by stretching a section of nylon hose over an embroidery frame hoop. Place the hoop between the business end of the microphone and the speaker or singer's mouth. This will help reduce sibilance and therefore will cut down on "hot spots" in your digital recordings. This is a very inexpensive way to record. If you are going to go this route, remember the axiom "garbage in/garbage out." Strive to make your recordings as clean as possible. That way, you'll have significantly less work to do to clean them up.

- **Midlevel Setup.** The best rule to observe here is to remember that a system is only as strong as its weakest link. Start with a good microphone and a pre-amp/mixer that will enable you to record directly to your sound card. Upgrading to a sound card with a higher sampling rate and S/PIDIF inputs will enable you to increase the quality of the sounds you record. In fact, this way, you can utilize newer consumer technologies like DVD-RAM recorders and can transfer audio without the obligatory signal loss that comes from digital-to-analog-to-digital conversions.

- **Advanced Setup.** If you want to get serious about recording, you need to crack open the case of your PC and add a dedicated card for recording digital audio. The M-Audio (**www.m-audio.com**) Omni Studio is a card/external interface box combo that includes software to let you record just about anything—vocals, guitars, keyboards, you name it. Add a high-quality microphone like the Audio-Technica model 4033 (**www.audiotechnica.com**), a good general-purpose microphone for vocals and instruments, an M-Audio CO3 format converter box, and a compressor/limiter like the Alesis 3060 rack mount compressor (**www.alesis.com**), and you're ready for everything but live recording.

- **Remote Recording.** Consider this a bonus configuration. Many times, to get the best sound effects, there's no other way to get them but to go out and record them where they happen. This means you must have gear that is both portable and flexible. Most pros recommend that you purchase a portable digital audio tape (DAT) or mini Disc recorder. (Make sure you get the pro models because the consumer products have circuits built-in that prevent you from copying one digital signal to another digital recording device.) A good DAT will set you back anywhere from $450 (used) to several thousand dollars. To go along with this, get a good-quality condenser microphone (like the Audio-Technica AT3031) for fieldwork. To transfer the DAT audio to your computer, you'll need a format converter box like the aforementioned CO3 by M-Audio. This rig will enable you to record remotely and then bring the DAT recorder back to your computer to transfer the digital audio files directly to the PC without converting them to an analog signal.

RECORDING SOUND EFFECTS

The art of recording sound effects can be approached from two distinctly different points of view: recordings of real sounds and recordings of things that are essentially simulations of sounds, commonly known as "Foley" work in the motion picture business.

Recording real sound effects is no more sophisticated than getting a microphone and recording gear into position to record the sound you want. For instance, if you need the sound of an automobile starting and driving away, all you need to do is to set up a microphone and recorder in your driveway and record what you hear. It *can* be that simple, although there are those who will insist that you'd need a variety of microphones, a mixer, and a multichannel recorder to get the perfect ambience. Again, the key to recording sound properly is keeping extraneous sound from the microphone. In the case of recording sound outdoors, you'll need some serious windscreens and a way to isolate the microphone from the rest of the system, usually with some sort of shock mount.

Foley effects bring an element of creativity to sound design. There are a host of ways to use common things you might find around your home to convincingly simulate sound effects. For instance, you can simulate rain by putting dried popcorn kernels inside a tube (cardboard or PVC pipe) and letting them fall from one end to the other. A mallet striking a large gourd (like a pumpkin or watermelon) can sound convincingly like a skull being caved in. (Okay, that's kind of disgusting, but it's the way this is really done.) With a little imagination and some experimentation, you can create a host of sound effects for next to nothing.

RECORDING LIVE MUSIC

Let's get this out of the way up front: Unless you have the permission of the musicians, entertainers, venue, and promoters, *it is illegal to make a recording of a live musical performance*. That doesn't stop most people. The Grateful Dead made careers out of allowing bootleg tapes to be made at their concerts. In the real world, however, using a recording that you make of live music is no more legal than using a song you've ripped from a CD with an MPEG encoder. In short, it is a violation of United States copyright law (**www.loc.gov/copyright**) to use recordings of live or prerecorded music without the artist's permission.

Let's assume you have permission to record music at a live event. There are two ways to record the sound and get the results you want. One way is to take a signal directly from the audio mixer (board). If you are working with the sound crew, this isn't as remote a possibility as it might seem. Keep in mind that mixing for audio recording and mixing for live sound reinforcement are two different animals. For instance, it's rare that the mix you get from the board will include all of the drums and bass that the audience hears—much of that sound may well come from the on-stage amplification or acoustic sounds of the instruments themselves. This makes for a less-than-ideal situation unless you have the rare opportunity to set up a dual-mixer configuration so that you can employ a discrete mix for the audience and a second one for your recording.

A much more likely scenario would be for you to set up two microphones near the front of the stage, running them to a recorder so that you hear essentially what the audience does. If you want to get adventuresome, you can mic the PA speakers as well and mix down a combination of the main speakers and the ambient sound you get from the front of the stage.

Microphone choices are always an issue in these situations. My preference is to use electret condenser mics because they have a wide frequency response and tend not to color the sound the way many other types of microphones do. The important thing if you are recording in stereo, however, is to use identical mics for your stereo mix.

SAMPLING AUDIO

I could refer you to the first paragraph of the preceding section, but I think this bears repeating: It is illegal to record and use copyrighted works. Realistically, this means that sampling an eight-bar phrase off your favorite CD to use as a background loop is illegal unless you have written permission from the copyright holder. What you might not know is that it is technically illegal to record even one note of a commercial CD. Several years ago, a musician sampled Phil Collins' snare and kick drum sounds to use in his own work. Collins had such a distinctive sound that it was immediately apparent where the sounds had originated. This pushed the ethics of sampling individual sounds into the area of copyright law (see **www.law.berkeley.edu/journals/btlj/ articles/04_1/McGraw/HTML/text.html**).

Realistically, most people don't get too bent out of shape over the sampling of a single note. However, you should be aware that sampling anything can be a problem. To make matters even murkier, it *is* legal to sample virtually anything as long as you substantially change it before you use it. Think about Andy Warhol's pop art—his painting of the Campbell's soup cans was not a violation of Campbell's copyrights because he changed the form and medium of the original work. (If Warhol had used Campbell's art to create soup cans, that would have been a different story.)

What does this mean to you? It means you can sample some audio tracks and use them, as long as you process the sounds and change them radically enough that your version no longer resembles the original. The legal litmus test has always been "Does it cause confusion in the marketplace?" If you modify your sound by changing the tonality, adding effects, and so on, you can probably get by without any problem.

MERGING SOUNDS IN VEGAS AUDIO

I think Sound Forge is an amazing application, but there is one thing it doesn't do that you might need to do from time to time—merge two or more sounds into one WAV file. Fundamentally, Sound Forge is a digital version of a stereo tape deck. You *can* merge sounds, but it takes some luck, some skill, and a lot of patience to get it right. This is largely because Sound Forge makes what is called a *destructive merge*—any adjustments you need to make must be done by undoing your merge and then reapplying it.

As luck would have it, Sonic Foundry makes an application that is the digital version of a multitrack tape deck—Vegas Audio. Vegas Audio is designed to enable you to take two or more sounds and merge them. It doesn't have the sophisticated sound-shaping tools found in Sound Forge because Sonic Foundry designed the two applications to work together.

1   Open Vegas Audio. In the Sound Explorer panel at the bottom of the interface, find the Project 2 folder.

   As in Sound Forge's ACID Pro, the Explorer panel in Vegas Audio lets you preview audio clips before you open them in the application. This is an amazingly convenient feature. (If only all developers put this much thought into making a product that's easy to use.)

2   Drag each of the audio (WAV) clips from the Explorer panel up to the working area. Drag the **Echo Clacker.wav** file a second time to create two copies.

   As you drag the sound clips up to the working area, you'll notice a dragable representation of the waveform. You can drag the sound clip from left to right to adjust when it plays. You can also stretch the clips to loop multiple times. Experiment by sliding the clips from side to side. Click the Play button to listen to how the tracks mix down together.

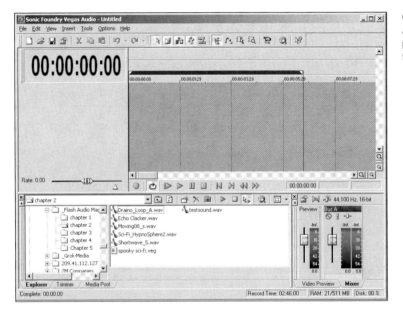

Open Sonic Foundry Vegas Audio and use the Explorer panel to find the Project 2 folder.

3   Use the Magnify buttons on the horizontal and vertical scrollbars to zoom in and out so that you can see
more of the tracks and get a more detailed look at the
waveforms.

Note the toolbar just under the menu in Vegas Audio.
Find and click the Envelope Edit tool. This will enable
you to right-click on a track and add an envelope—
controlling either the volume or the stereo pan.

4   Open the file called **spooky sci-fi.veg** in Vegas
Audio. You'll see the settings for the volume and
panning envelopes.

5   Right-click the **Shortwave_5.wav** track and create a
volume envelope. I chose to fade this sound in and
out. Add points on the envelope by right-clicking at
the appropriate point on the line and adding a point.

6   Do the same for the **Sci-Fi_HypnoSphere2.wav**
file. On this one, I chose to create a slow, tapered
fadeout (see **Sci-Fi_HypnoSphere2Fade.wav** on
the accompanying CD-ROM).

7   Stretch the Loop Region markers to extend the loop
to encompass all the audio clips used. Go to File >
Save As and save the file as a WAV (Microsoft)
(*.wav) file. You can now open the file you created
in Sound Forge.

To get the effect we want with the two Echo Clacker
files, I staggered them slightly, added panning
envelopes, and adjusted them to pan the sound on
one track to the extreme left and the other to the
extreme right. The result is that you hear the sound
effect ping-pong back and forth between the speakers.

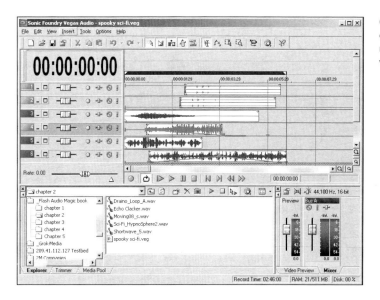

Open spooky sci-fi.veg and
examine the track arrange-
ment as well as the pan and
volume envelopes.

How It Works

Recording is part science, part art, and part alchemy. The best way to make great
recordings is like many things in life—practice and experimentation are the keys.
There is much you can learn from just making recordings and comparing them to
similar, professionally recorded files. I'd also recommend that you read the documentation that comes with both Sound Forge and Vegas Audio. Both applications
are user friendly and easy to pick up without cracking the user manuals. However,
there are many powerful features that you might miss unless you study the documentation. Now let's move on to editing audio files in Sound Forge.

EDITING AUDIO

"After silence, that which comes nearest

to expressing the inexpressible is music."

—ALDOUS HUXLEY

EDITING ESSENTIALS

It's been observed that the greatest jazz improv soloists share one trait—they tend to play very economically, not wasting any notes. They play only what is essential. What they leave out is as important as what they put in. Editing audio is a lot like playing a solo. The key to editing is to leave in what is needed and leave out everything else. This approach makes for smaller files, faster loads, and better communication with your audience.

Project 3

Editing Audio

by Brad Kozak

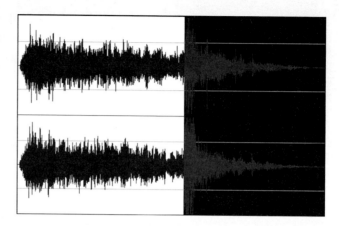

GETTING STARTED

Copy the Project 3 folder from the accompanying CD-ROM to your hard drive.
Install Sound Forge from the CD-ROM if you haven't already. Open Sonic Foundry
Sound Forge and choose File > Open. Change the directory to the Project 3 folder on
the your hard drive. Make sure Auto Play is checked in the Open dialog box and click
on each filename.

CROPPING IN SOUND FORGE

This section will talk about how to optimize samples by eliminating the "dead air"
often found at the beginning and end of audio samples.

Sound Forge will preview each sound for you.

1 Select **TympaniUp_raw.wav** and open the file.

Note that this is a 22K, 16-bit, stereo sample saved in Microsoft's WAV format.

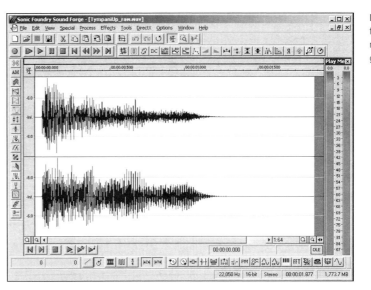

If you maximize the sound file's window, you can see more of the waveform with greater detail.

3 Go to Process > AutoTrim/Crop. Select the Trim Silence from Ends Preset and set the Fade In to 0. Click the OK button.

This will help minimize the overall file size of the sample by eliminating the dead air in the file before you import it into Flash. If your sample has any reverb, echo, or room ambience, it's best to leave a little silence at the end of the sample.

4 Go to File > Save As and save the file as **TympaniUp.wav**, changing the file's Attributes from 22,050Hz, 16-bit, Stereo to 22,050Hz, 16-bit, Mono.

You should change this to mono unless there is a compelling reason to maintain stereo separation in a given sound; it takes half the memory and file size to work with monophonic samples.

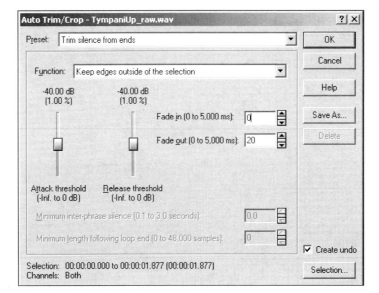

Select AutoTrim/Crop to automatically remove unnecessary silence from the beginning and end of your audio files.

Most computers come with a reasonably good-quality sound card and speakers that sound better than most boom boxes. The fact that many computer systems can now reproduce sound accurately comes at a price, however. To add CD-quality sound to your Flash projects, you would need to record your audio files in a 16-bit, 44Hz, stereo format. Because stereo files are literally twice as large as mono files (and because 44Hz files are twice as large as 22Hz files), you can see that your files can expand in size dramatically if you insist on higher-fidelity files. Between building files that will work for both dialup and broadband users and never really knowing on what kinds of computers your work will be played, most Flash developers find it advantageous to keep sound files as small as possible. Converting stereo to mono is a good way to start.

Note: When computer manufacturers first added sound capabilities to their systems, they followed much the same path as automobile manufacturers did. In other words, they installed underpowered monophonic units with the cheapest speakers they could find. A funny thing happened, however. Computer gamers clamored for higher fidelity, better speakers, and more wattage. Gaming is responsible for what became a large and vibrant (no pun intended) part of the computer industry—third-party sound cards and speakers.

5   You will see a dialog box that asks if you want to reopen the file with its changes. Answer Yes to see the new, monophonic version of your file.

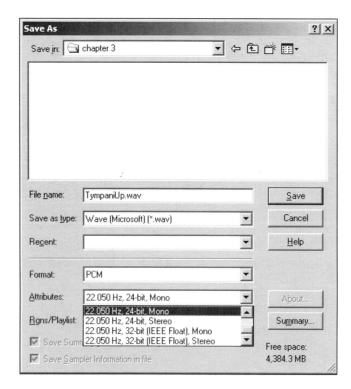

Save audio files as mono rather than stereo whenever possible. This alone will save 50% on file size for each audio clip.

FADING IN AND OUT

Sometimes it's more appropriate to fade in a sound or to allow it to fade out. You can accomplish this in two ways—either by modifying the audio sample in Sound Forge or by creating an envelope in Flash. The Sound Forge method permanently changes the sample; this is useful if you plan to have the same fade every time you use the file. The Flash method is more appropriate if you want to loop the audio file or use the same sample in different ways within your Flash movie. Here we'll take the same clip and demonstrate both methods, starting with the Sound Forge method.

1   Open Sound Forge and choose File > Open. Change the directory to the Project 3 folder on your hard drive. Select **lafftrack_raw.wav** and open it.

2   Note the red marker at the 3-second point in the file. Double-click on the waveform after the marker and press the Delete key. Next, click on the waveform at the point that's approximately one-half second before the end (where the volume begins to grow louder).

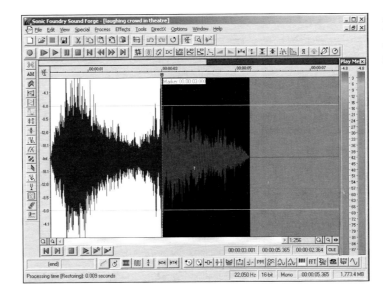

Adjust a selection by moving the cursor over the starting or ending point of the selection, pressing, and then dragging left or right.

3 Select the rest of the waveform from that point to the end. Select Process > Fade > Out.

4 That's it. You've created a fade out in Sound Forge. Save the sample as **lafftrack_fade.wav**.

Now we'll fade out the same sample for use within a Macromedia Flash movie.

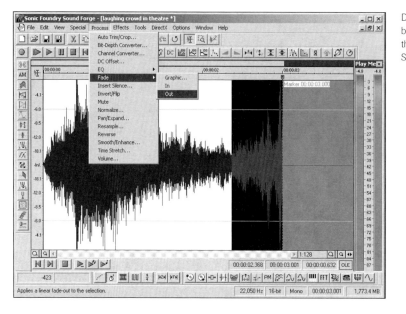

Double-click in the waveform between the red marker and the end of the waveform. Select Process > Fade > Out.

5 Start Flash, open a new file, and select File > Import. Select both **lafftrack_raw.wav** and **lafftrack_fade.wav** and click the OK button in the Import dialog box.

6 Use the horizontal scrollbar to find frame 125. Click on it to move the playhead to frame 125 and then press the F5 key. Your movie is now 125 frames long. Select frame 5 and press the F6 key to create a keyframe. Select frame 75 and create a second keyframe there.

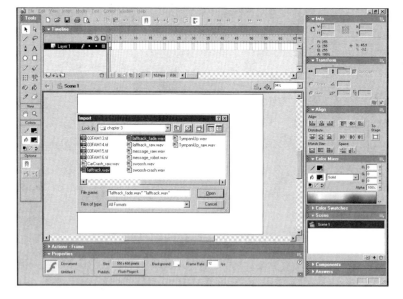

Import more than one file at a time by holding down the Ctrl key (Cmd for Macs) and clicking on the files you want to select.

7 Double-click the keyframe at frame 5. This will open the property inspector. Select **lafftrack_raw.wav**. Double-click on the keyframe at frame 45 and then select **lafftrack_fade.wav**.

8 While you have frame 5 selected, click the Edit button in property inspector. Click the Zoom Out button (in the Edit Envelope popup) twice.

Notice the tick marks on the Timeline—they represent seconds. Note that there is a white box in the upper-left corner of each (L and R stereo) of the waveform displays, with a line that extends out across the waveform.

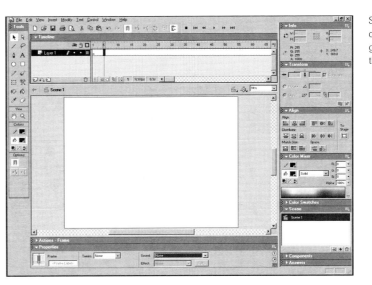

Select a keyframe and then open the Sound panel to trigger an audio clip directly from the Timeline.

9 Click on the line above the second tick mark and again above the third tick mark. Drag the box created over the third tick mark down to the bottom of the waveform display. You will need to do this for both the left and right waveform displays.

10 Rewind and play the movie.

Effectively, you have now created within Flash the same fade out that you created in Sound Forge. The difference is that you have the original waveform intact when you edit in Flash. The decision of which method to use depends on whether you need to use the entire waveform elsewhere in your movie. Generally speaking, it is more efficient to import only the portions of the audio clips you need in Flash. You can use the same techniques—hard-coding in Sound Forge or using the Edit tools in the Audio dialog box of Flash—not only to fade out but also to fade in or even to vary the volume in the middle of an audio clip.

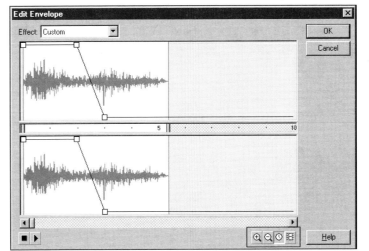

Adjust the volume and create a custom envelope to fade in or fade out each sound within the Flash sound edit control. Note the four buttons at the bottom of the Edit dialog. Use them to zoom in or out, or to convert the Tmeline from a time-based to frames-based reference.

Tip: It's good programming practice to isolate all sounds played on the Timeline to an individual layer (or layers) and not insert the sound along with a graphic object. This makes the audio easier to find and easier to modify when you need to adjust the frame you use to trigger the sound.

MIXING EXISTING AUDIO

One of the best ways to create new sounds is to edit existing sounds, using small portions or "samples" from a variety of files to create a new sound. Sound Forge lets you edit audio files quickly and easily.

1   Open Sound Forge. Go to File > Open and then open **CarCrash_raw.wav**.

Listen to the sound—we will use only the "crash" portion, eliminating the "skid" sound.

2   Click in the middle of the stereo tracks just before the large volume spike in the sound. Then drag the cursor to the right, selecting everything after that initial selection point.

The background of the selected portion of the wave-form will turn black.

3   Audition your selection by clicking the Play Normal button at the bottom of the audio clip's window.

4   Hold the mouse over the first part of the selection.

The cursor will change into a double-headed arrow when you mouse over the start of the selection.

5   Adjust the precise point where the selection begins. Use the Magnify tools and sliders to zoom in for a closer look. The horizontal controls affect the amount of time visible; the vertical controls affect the capability to view the softest sounds in a clip. The narrow button between the horizontal and vertical Zoom In and Zoom Out buttons is a slider that will let you dynamically change the zoom ratio.

6   Select Edit > Trim/Crop to delete all but the selected portion of the sample.

When you play this audio clip, you should notice that the loudest portion sounds distorted. This is clipping

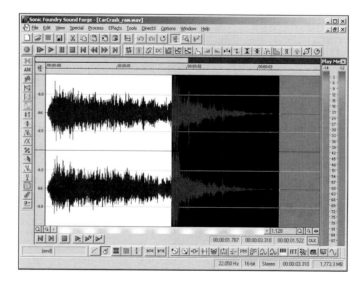

Click on the dual magnifying glass icons in the horizontal and vertical sliders to zoom in or out.

(that is, the sound is exceeding the capability of the system to play it back without distorting the sound). Look at the waveform display carefully. Notice that the loudest part actually runs all the way up to the edge of the display area (and past it, in fact). What you see is a visual display of what happens when you have too much sound (volume) and not enough headroom. You can use Sound Forge to correct the problem.

7 Go to DirectX > Sonic Foundry Clipped Peak Restoration and select the No Attenuation, Limit Clips Preset. Save this file as a 22K, 16-bit, mono WAV file with the name **CarCrash.wav**.

8 Open the file **swoosh.wav**.

Sometimes you'll want to have more than one sound play at the same time. Although you can overlap sounds with multiple layers in Flash, you can reduce your overall file size if you merge the audio files in an editor to create a single audio clip to import into Flash. Sound Forge was designed to be strictly an audio-editing application, but on occasion, you can use it to merge sounds if you'd rather not fire up a multitrack application to perform a relatively simple edit.

Note the marker and the red dotted line. We've pre-determined that this is where we'd like to trigger the second sound. What we're going for here is a "swoosh" sound, followed by a crash.

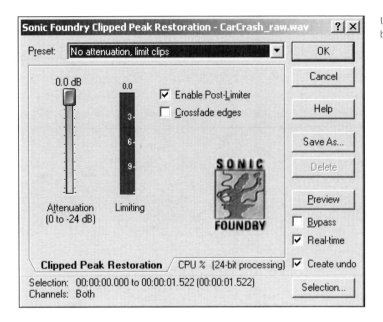

Use the attenuation dialog box to control clipping.

9 Go to the Window menu and select Cascade to see all the audio clips currently open in Sound Forge. Double-click on the waveform of the **CarCrash_raw.wav** file. Now drag it over on top of swoosh.wav so that the starting point of the CarCrash_raw sample coincides with the marker.

The position of the CarCrash_raw waveform is indicated by a block of diagonal line shadings.

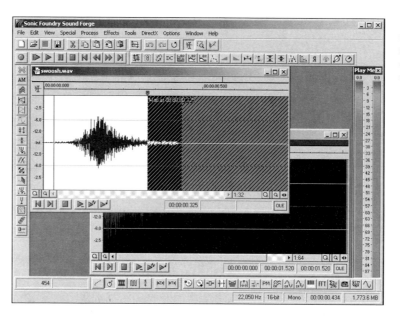

Use markers to create a precise merge point for blending sounds. Drag a selection from one audio clip to another to merge sounds.

10 Select the Normal Mix (No Fades) Preset in the Mix dialog box and click OK. Click the Rewind button and then play the newly mixed WAV file. Save this file as **swoosh–crash.wav**. With a little trial and error (and judicious use of the Undo function), Sound Forge can mix two sounds into one.

Note: As long as you don't mind experimenting and using the Undo feature of Sound Forge, dragging one clip onto another is an easy way to merge two clips. For much greater control and ease of use, consider using Sonic Foundry's Vegas Audio, an application designed for multichannel mixing. Vegas Audio works much like the Timeline in Flash, enabling you to maintain a number of discrete tracks that contain individual audio clips and then mix them together to create a single audio file. This is comparable to what Flash enables you to do with vector graphics, mixing them into a SWF file.

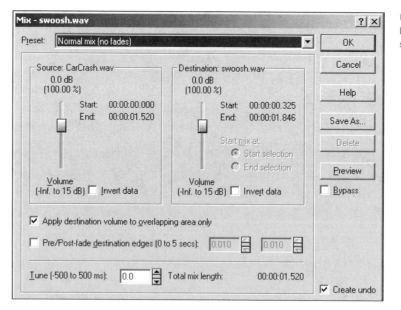

Use the Mix dialog box to blend waveforms and create a single mixed-down audio clip.

ADDING SPECIAL EFFECTS

There really isn't a limit to the types of things you can do to an audio sample. The key is to experiment, trying different ideas until you come up with ways to create the kind of effect you want. This section will cover a few ways to change raw samples and, in the process, will show how other, more involved changes can be made.

1 In Sound Forge, open the file **message_raw.wav**.

First, we'll convert this voice into something a bit more robot like (or go from monotone to robotic, if you want to get particular).

2 Go to DirectX > Sonic Foundry ExpressFX Delay and select the Robot Preset. Click the Preview button in the dialog box. Now select some of the other presets.

Sonic Foundry's Preview function enables you to hear all the presets, as well as any modifications you make, in real time.

3 Choose an effect and click OK. Play the result. Now go to Edit > Undo.

Sonic Foundry's nondestructive editing enables you to undo multiple changes, as many levels as you have capacity within your computer to hold.

4 Go back to DirectX > Sonic Foundry ExpressFX Delay and select the Robot Preset. After applying this effect, go to DirectX > Sonic Foundry ExpressFX Equalization and roll off all the Bass (–25.0dB).

5 Open the Sonic Foundry Dynamics tool and select the Limit levels to the –6dB setting.

This is a wonderfully useful tool you can use to automatically adjust a variety of clips to the same maximum volume level.

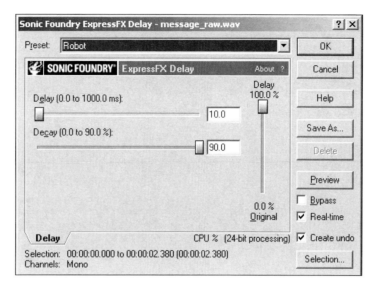

Use ExpressFX Delay either with its presets or with custom controls to adjust virtually every aspect of the audio clip's delay characteristics. The Preview button enables you to hear the effect before you okay changes to the audio clip.

6 Use the Auto Trim/Crop tool to get rid of the dead air at the beginning and end of the clip.

Now it's time to experiment with DirectX > Sonic Foundry Track Compressor.

7 Start with the Limit levels to –6dB Preset (hard limiter).

This tool is perhaps the best way to adjust your samples so that they do not clip. You can also experiment with the different compressor settings, which are particularly useful if your sample has extreme differences in its dynamic range. Note that there are several tools in Sound Forge that do similar things in different ways. For instance, there are two graphic equalizers at your disposal. You should experiment with all the effects to familiarize yourself with what they do and how they do it.

8 If you need to adjust the duration of the sample, go to DirectX > Sonic Foundry ExpressFX Time Stretch and then choose Time Compress 85% of Original.

9 Because this is a spoken-word sample, select Speech in the Mode drop-down box. Click the Preview button. Now try the Time Expand 110% of Original Preset. You can also adjust the sliders or spinner controls to adjust the duration to a specific time.

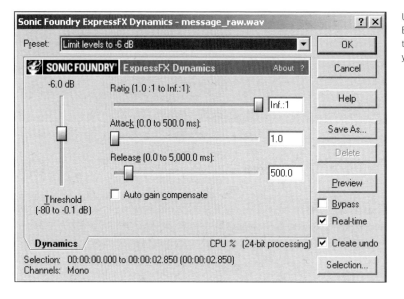

Use the Sonic Foundry ExpressFX Dynamics plug-in to limit the dynamic range of your audio clips.

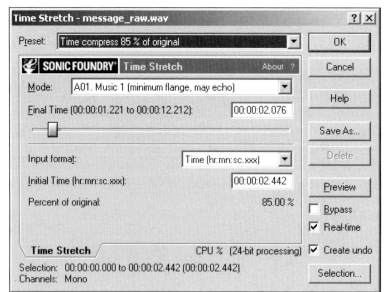

Use Time Stretch to adjust the duration of an audio clip with precision and accuracy.

10 Now go to Effects > Pitch > Bend. Choose the Whole-Tone Scale Preset.

The controls in this dialog box function exactly like the ones that control the volume envelope within Flash.

11 Preview this effect and then try dragging the pitch bend line to see how this affects the result.

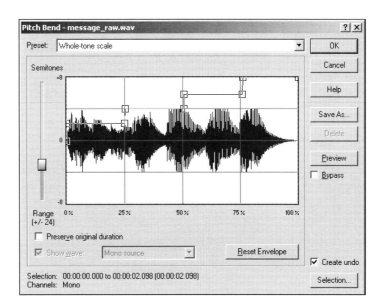

Using Sound Forge pitch controls, you can bend sound effects and transpose sounds to a lower or higher pitch without changing the duration of the audio clip.

HOW IT WORKS

Sound Forge is a flexible, robust application for creating and editing samples. It includes both automated and manual controls for adjusting, manipulating, and modifying virtually any sound you can create.

Although Sound Forge is designed to enable you to work with one channel (or two stereo channels) of audio, you *can* mix two audio samples together if you are willing to take the time to experiment (and use the Undo function liberally). Alternatively, you can use Sonic Foundry's Vegas Audio, which is designed to enable you to create multi-track sounds and mix them down to a single mono or stereo sample.

Essentially, your goal should be to create the cleanest audio files you can, with a signal that is as "hot" (loud) as possible without clipping (distorting). Along the way, you might find that you have to reduce the dynamic range of the audio clip to have it play back without distortion. Also, you should try to avoid the two extremes—clips recorded not only too loudly but also too softly. As you've discovered, clips that are recorded at too high a level sound distorted. What you might not realize is that recording audio well under the optimal setting is not an acceptable solution. If your audio clip is recorded with too little volume, you will have to increase the volume level to hear it. Unfortunately, increasing the volume also increases the noise level. All clips have a certain amount of noise in them. Audio engineers refer to this as the "floor" (just as headroom is also referred to as the "ceiling"). Your goal as an audio engineer should be to record and edit each of your waveforms so that they have the best audio fidelity you can manage.

Regardless of how effective the tools you have at your disposal might be, the cleaner the sample you start with, the better your final results will be. Because Flash MX can compress sounds upon export, you can actually export CD-quality audio samples. This is not really necessary for most Flash work, especially work you intend for distribution across the Internet. Frankly, because of bandwidth concerns and the quality of the average user's speaker system, I rarely use anything more than 22K, 16-bit, stereo sound, and I usually resample it down to mono before importing into Flash. Of course, a lot depends on your target requirements for your SWF file. If you are designing a piece for a CD, or your client wants the best possible audio quality, by all means, import CD-quality sound. You can always compress it as you export to a SWF file. On the other hand, if you're designing for the web, there's little reason to burden your hard disk with a lot of extra data in your FLA. Keep in mind that a CD-quality stereo WAV file will cost you 400% more space on your drive than will a comparable 22k mono file.

As I alluded to in the introduction to this section, you might find that "less is more" when it comes to audio. For instance, let's say you are trying to create the ambience of a lake at dusk. Realistically, you might hear crickets chirping continuously and all sorts of creatures making noises—so many that you'd be hard pressed to re-create the sound without going out into the field and recording the ambient sound live. I suggest that you might find it better to use individual sounds and use them in such a way as to *imply* an outdoor scene rather than attempting to accurately reproduce every ribbit and chirp.

The next time you watch a television show, listen carefully to the sound effects and in particular to the way the sound works in scenes shot outdoors. You'll find that in a city scene, for instance, the sound designer will include some ambient sounds of cars, horn honks, and so on, but there will be far fewer sounds than you would actually hear on the street. If the soundscape were completely accurate, you'd never be able to hear the dialogue. In the movie business, this is referred to as *walla* (go figure).

Several years ago, I purchased one of the first General MIDI sound modules—a gadget that enabled me to play digitally recorded samples of all kinds of instruments like a computer-controlled player piano or music box. It had a very real-sounding, nylon-stringed (classical) guitar sound. I meticulously wrote the notes that I played on a finger-picked guitar part on one of my songs and recorded it with a MIDI sequencer. For some reason, the sound was accurate—but almost *too* accurate. It sounded sterile and lifeless. After playing around with the sound module for a bit, I discovered that one of the effects it contained was nothing but the sound of a finger squeaking on a guitar string. It dawned on me then what my MIDI track needed. Again, I worked out exactly when I tended to hear string squeak as I played the part on the guitar, and then I replicated that using the string squeak MIDI sound. That was the missing element—from then on, my guitar sounded real. You only noticed it when it was missing. That's what walla does for your work. It provides the background audio cues that make things sound real.

Walla must be used with discretion. You never want it to overwhelm or distract from the focus of your work. It's kind of like the setting for a jewel in that respect. This same "less is more" technique can be useful in your own Flash work regardless of the project. If you can *imply* something with a brief sound effect, it can be much more evocative and effective than if you attempt to accurately re-create an entire aural experience.

ENHANCING UI
WITH AUDIO

"Art is a re-creation of reality according to an

artist's metaphysical value-judgments."

——AYN RAND – INTRODUCTION TO THE

35TH ANNIVERSARY EDITION

OF *ATLAS SHRUGGED*

USING MOVIE CLIPS TO CREATE SOUND

Flash is a lot like an onion; it has many layers,

each one a little different from the last. When

you first began working with Flash, you likely

saw it as a collection of drawing tools that

included some easy ways to animate objects on

a stage. Think of that as the first layer. You

encounter the second layer when you start

animating using Movie Clips. The third layer

involves using ActionScript to do most of your

animation programmatically. In this project, you'll

be exploring the second layer, exploiting Movie

Clips to create user interface sounds, and you'll

use a couple of techniques that start you on

your way toward exploring the third layer:

control exclusively by ActionScripting.

Project 4

Enhancing UI with Audio

by Brad Kozak

GETTING STARTED

In this project, you'll build flexible, programmable buttons using Movie Clips. Remember the onion analogy? In the first layer, you created buttons with Button symbols, where you get a single frame each for your up, over, and down states. But what if you want to create a button that displays different animations for more than just an over or down state? That's where Movie Clips come in. In this project, you'll learn how to replace Button symbols with animated Movie Clips. This will add incredible flexibility to Flash and will enable you to make buttons that have all kinds of specific behaviors, such as rolling in, rolling out, pressing, and releasing. Before you start on the project, copy the contents of the Project 4 folder from the accompanying CD-ROM to your local hard disk for easy access.

CREATING MOVIE CLIPS

Forget buttons. While the button class of symbol is useful for very simple jobs, if you want more than up, over, and down states, you must learn how to use a Movie Clip as a button. First, you'll create a Movie Clip that has sections delineated by frame markers. Each of these sections will correspond to different button "states"—up, down, rollover, rollout, release, and so on. This will enable you to potentially animate any kind of reaction to what the mouse is doing within your button. You then program the Movie Clip "button" using an onClipEvent mouse handler that effectively tells the Movie Clip to behave (in respect to mouse movements) just like a button. Why go to all this trouble for a button? Because this way, instead of a static image for each button state, your buttons can come to life when you interact with them. Now creating a Movie Clip button may sound a little complicated, but after you see it in action, you'll find that it's not only a very easy thing to create, but incredibly flexible, too.

1   Open Flash and choose File > Open. Navigate to the Project 4 folder you copied to your hard drive. Select **menu_basic.fla** and open the file.

2   Press Ctrl+L to open the Library panel and double-click on the buttons folder. If necessary, double-click on the buttons folder to expand it. Double-click again on the b_join anim Movie Clip.

Based on the storyboards you created in Project 1, "Designing with Audio," you'll see markers defined for several button states that will define how the button will respond to the cursor. (If you'd like to see the original concept layout/storyboard again, open the file in the Project 4 folder called **laffbox.com04.fla**.) You might notice few minor changes to the original concept to improve the look and feel of the site.

Note: There is a way to add motion to a simple button, if you don't need the additional control you get by using a Movie Clip as a button. You simply create the animation you want for a particular button state and then save the animation as a separate Movie Clip. Open the button and drag that new Movie Clip containing the animation into a single frame of the button. For example, to animate the onRollover and onRelease states (or within the button, the Over and Down frames), you create a button with your artwork for the up state, then create separate Movie Clips for the Over animation and the Down animation, and then drag them into the button and place them on the Over and Down frames, respectively. This will give you the animation effect, but you won't gain any of the additional functionality you get when you use a Movie Clip symbol instead of a Button symbol to create your button.

3 Back in the menu_start.fla file, click the Scripts layer on the Timeline and create a blank keyframe on the frame just prior to the rollover marker (frame 7). Repeat this process, creating blank keyframes on the frames immediately preceding the rest of the markers.

You'll use the blank keyframes to hold ActionScript commands that will tell your Movie Clip exactly how you want it to behave when the user rolls the cursor over the button trigger area.

Note: It's good programming practice to isolate all Timeline scripts to an individual layer, just as you've learned to do for audio clips. This makes it easy to find scripts on a Timeline and to move/copy/paste individual frames. You'll save a lot of time this way, especially when you need to go back and make changes to a project you thought was finished.

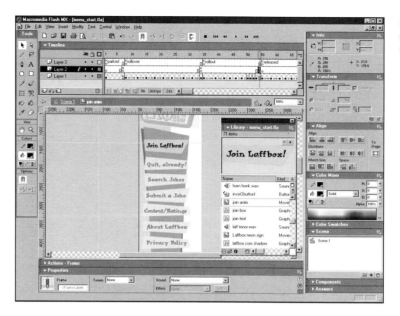

Insert blank keyframes on the scripts track just before each marker.

4 In the last frame of the parked section, insert a stop() command using the Actions panel.

When you use an instance of this Movie Clip as a button, the parked section will be used as the up state—in other words, when the cursor is not hovering over the button's hit area, and is therefore "at rest."

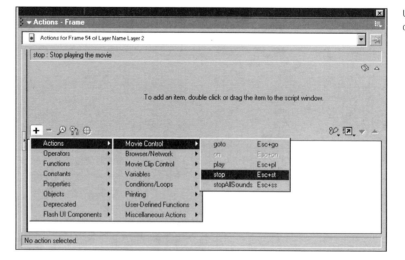

Use the Actions panel to add commands to keyframes.

5 On the last frame of the rollover section, insert the following ActionScript command:

```
gotoAndPlay ("rollover");
```

What you're doing here is setting up a loop. When the invisible button tells the Movie Clip to gotoAndPlay the rollover marker, the command you just entered will cause it to loop indefinitely (unless you program the button to issue a rollout command to the Movie Clip when the user moves the cursor off the invisible button trigger; stay with me here… it gets easier).

This command will cause Flash to repeat the rollover animation sequence when the user keeps the cursor over the Movie Clip button. The sequence will repeat until the user clicks or moves the cursor off the button.

If you're in Expert mode, all you have to do is type in the commands. Don't have them all memorized? No problem. Just click on the + button near the top-left corner of the dialog box, and the pop-up menu provides an easy way to insert commands into your work. The left-side panel that lists the different kinds of ActionScript commands can be hidden and revealed by pressing the button on the dividing bar between it and the ActionScript code window. I usually keep it closed because I find the + button to be more convenient and because this gives me a lot more room to see long lines of script.

Note: Back in the days of Flash 5, Movie Clips couldn't accept mouse handler commands. This gave rise to a clever little work around known as the "Invisible Button Trick." Now that Movie Clips can respond to mouse movement, there's no need for this; however, you do need to understand one important difference in how Button symbols and Movie Clip symbols work. The fourth frame of a Button symbol is always reserved for the "hit" zone—a shape that defines what's "hot" and what's not (in other words, the area that responds to mouse movement). There is no equivalent in a Movie Clip. Therefore, you must make your own "hit" zone within a Movie Clip. If your animation takes place all within the same area encompassed by whatever object is on the first frame of your Movie Clip, you're probably okay. If not, or if the object on the first frame is a text object (or something that is not a solid geometric shape) then you'll have to create something that defines the hit zone. Just create a layer in your Movie Clip and label it **hit zone**. Then either create a new symbol or drag some object (I keep a generic box around in the Library for this very purpose) and make sure it stays put. Then set the Alpha value of this symbol to 0%. As long as it's there throughout the Movie Clip's Timeline, it will act as the symbol's hit zone.

Tip: It's at this point that you'll likely want to make a decision: ride with training wheels or go for the gusto and go without. I'm referring to the Actions panel's two modes: Normal and Expert. Normal mode's fill-in-the-blanks way to write ActionScript is designed for beginners, while Expert mode is for those who are comfortable typing in commands directly and want to work quickly. Both modes offer a drag-and-drop list of ActionScript commands and both have hierarchical drop-down menus with all the ActionScript commands at your disposal. The real difference is that with Normal mode, you have no choice but to use the individual text entry and combo box fields for each command, whereas Expert mode allows you to modify your scripts by typing directly into the ActionScript code display. For newbies, Normal mode is a kind of security blanket, but that security comes at a price: It can slow you down once you get comfortable with ActionScript. I'm assuming you have some experience with ActionScripting already. If and when you want to code as fast as possible (or when you just get frustrated with the limitations of Normal mode), I recommend that you switch to Expert mode and give it a whirl. (Just click on the menu icon in the upper-right corner of the Actions dialog box on its title bar. You'll see a drop-down menu of choices, allowing you to toggle between the two modes.)

6 On both the last frame of the rollout section and the last frame of the released section, insert the following ActionScript command:

```
gotoAndPlay ("parked");
```

This command "parks" the button when the user clicks and releases it, returning it to its neutral state. Think of it this way: To make an animated button, it's not enough to come up with cool animations.

PRETZEL LOGIC

Stop for a moment and take a look at the animation supplied for the buttons. Play the Movie Clip (you're not ready to test the movie, as everything's not yet wired). Notice anything? This is an extreme example of what you can do with a button, at least as far as the released state goes. But having a button fall off the page brings with it some design challenges—challenges that will force you to sit down and think things through in order to make the button behave the way you want it to.

You have to think things through so that you know what will happen when you roll over the button, roll out, click, roll out after you click, and so on. If you don't think this through before you begin coding, I guarantee that you'll see some unexpected results when you test your work.

Logic can be a tricky thing. Making buttons work can be as well, simply because you have to think in a very literal fashion. In this case, think about the rollout behavior. Any time you roll out, you've told Flash to execute the rollout

sequence. That's great, but what if a user decides to rollout while the released sequence is playing? As it is, the button will abruptly stop falling, magically reappear in place, and play the released animation. If you think this sounds a little whacked, consider the buttons on a VCR.

There are several kinds of tape transport buttons on a standard VCR—let's call them single function, multifunction, and multistate buttons. The Stop button is usually a single state button. It does one thing (stop the tape) no matter what else is going on when you push it. Some tape decks have a Stop/Eject button. This is a multifunction button, as it performs two functions, depending on if the tape is in motion or not. If the tape is moving, it stops the tape. If the tape is not running, pressing the button ejects the tape. The Fast-Forward and Rewind buttons are examples of multistate functions. If the tape is not running, these buttons fast forward or rewind the tape, respectively. If the tape is playing, however, they do what's called cue and review—essentially playing the tape faster while is runs across the playhead.

The next chapter covers creating multifunction buttons, in the context of building a Mute/Unmute button. For now, consider how mouse behavior will affect how a single button's animation will play under given circumstances.

Moving the mouse outside the hit area would ordinarily trigger the rollout sequence. If the user has just clicked the button, triggering the rollout sequence would interrupt the released animation and keep it from completing. Because there's no way to make the user keep his mouse still until the animation sequence finishes, you have to come up with a way to tell Flash to only execute the rollout sequence *if the button is not currently playing the released sequence*.

To put this in plain English, you want to find a way to tell the button "Do *this* when the cursor rolls over you and *that* when the cursor rolls off, *unless* you detect that the user clicked the button. In that case, do *something else*." To accomplish this feat of logic, you'll create some if statements that will trap the behaviors. To make the if statements work, you'll need to set up a variable (or flag) that tells Flash—in this case anyway—whether the button has been clicked.

1   On the main Timeline, click on the first frame.
Open the Actions panel. You will see some code
already placed in the window. Ignore this code. Place
the edit cursor on the first (empty) line and select
Objects > Core > _global from the Actions toolbox.
Set the variable name to **_root.OnClickFlag** and
the value to **1.** After you make the edit, you should
see the following text in the ActionScript window.

A variable is a placeholder you can use to store and
retrieve information. This particular variable
functions like the flag on a mailbox. It has two
settings—0 and 1. This is the Flash equivalent to
off/on, false/true, or no/yes. You can do two important things with variables: set them and get them.
In other words, you can flip the switch, and you can
check it to see if it's on or off.

You've now created a variable in Flash called
OnClickFlag and set its value to 1. (You'll use 1 to
equal *on* and 0 to equal *off*.) You've also just set up
your first bit of Boolean logic (extra points if you use
this to impress your friends).

2   To save a lot of time (not to mention a lot of typing),
close this file and open one with some of the code
preconfigured. Open **menu_scripted.fla**, and click
on the Scripts layer in the main Timeline.

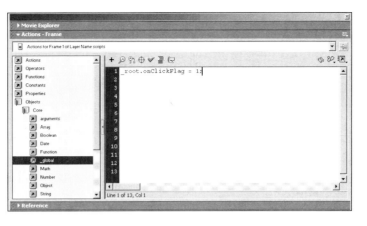

Drag commands, objects, and
functions from the Actions
toolbox to jump-start your
ActionScript code.

```
_global.OnClickFlag = 1;
```

Note: There are two kinds of variables in Flash—local and global. Local
variables are used within Movie Clips or selections of ActionScript code,
and they have no effect beyond their location. Global variables can be
used from anywhere within a Flash movie. You can specify where you
want to place a local variable by using the dot notation path. The
variable here uses the _root designation to indicate that it sits on the
main Timeline. To call it from outside the main Timeline, use its full path:
_root.onClickFlag. A global variable allows you to refer to it using its
name only. If this had been declared as a global variable using the
"global" tag, you could call it from anywhere within the movie by simply
using it's name: onlClickFlag. The only tricky thing about local versus
global variables comes if you try to use the same name for both. Don't
do that. That way lies madness. Trust me.

```
/*   DEFINE VARIABLES
        this variable controls the behavior of the main buttons,
        specifically when you click on the button and then roll
        out before the animation sequence has completed.*/
_root.onClickFlag = 1;
//END VARIABLES SECTION
```

The first thing you'll notice is that, where there was once a vast wasteland of white pixels, there's now a huge amount of code. Follow along one section at a time, so you can understand what's going on.

This first section is not much different from what you saw previously, except that we've taken the time to comment the code. When you add comments to your code, it provides a road map for you to follow, should you need to go back some time later and modify your work. There are two ways to add comments to Flash. Single line comments always begin with two forward slashes:

```
//  this is a comment.
```

Multi-line comments start with /* and end with */, like this:

```
/*    this is a longer comment. By using
      the slash-asterisk method, you don't
      have to start each line with two slashes. */
```

The next section adds some important new kinds of ActionScript—user-defined functions:

```
// USER-DEFINED FUNCTIONS
//define menu button rollover behavior
function rollOverMe(myClip) {
      if (_root.onClickFlag) {
            myClip.gotoAndPlay("rollover");
                  return;
      }
}
//define menu button rollout behavior
function rollOffMe(myClip) {
      if (_root.onClickFlag) {
            myClip.gotoAndPlay("rollout");
                  return;
      }
}
// define menu button clicked behavior
function clickMe(myClip, myURL) {
      _root.onClickFlag = 0;
      myClip.gotoAndPlay("released");
      //    getURL(myURL, "_client");
            return;
}
// END USER-DEFINED FUNCTIONS
```

If you don't come from a programming background, creating functions might be a little intimidating, but it's really fairly easy. Here's what's going on: You define a function by giving it a name and specifying any arguments you want it to include. An *argument* (for our purposes, anyway) is just something within the function that serves the same purpose as a variable—it's something you can change or specify when you use the function. Think of the built-in getURL() function in ActionScript. The getURL part is the name. The part inside the parentheses is the argument. In the function called rollOverMe, you are going to create what amounts to a variable name for the only argument. The reason you need an argument here is to apply the function to a Movie Clip to be specified later. If you like, you can think of user-defined functions as being the ActionScript version of a macro—reusable code that you can customize to your own needs.

So what does this little jewel do for us? Well in plain English, this function says, "If the onClickFlag is true (equal to 1), go to the rollover marker in the Movie Clip we specify and play the animation."

Tip: ActionScript provides several ways to write code—most notably a verbose way and a shorthand way. The statement if(myVariable == 1) can also be written as if(myVariable) because Flash assumes that what you want to say is, "If myVariable tests as true." If you need to test for a statement being false, you would write it as either if(! myVariable) or if(myVariable != 1). This is also a cool way to avoid one of the most frequent causes of bugs in ActionScript code—confusing the equals symbol "=" with the symbol used for testing equality "==" (they are *not* interchangeable.)

This is way cool. It may not seem like much now, but you will be able to expand the code within this function and then have each of the menu buttons use the same code. Effectively, this means that you can shorten the length of the ActionScript in the movie by several orders of magnitude. Notice that the clickMe function has not one but two arguments: The first one is a placeholder for your Movie Clip name. The second one provides a way to specify a different URL name each time you use this new function. An in-depth discussion of creating functions is beyond the scope of a book on audio. If you want to unlock the power of ActionScript, start by learning how to create your own functions.

Note: Back in the old days of Flash 2 and 3, ActionScript was a neat little way to add some basic functionality to what was really just an animation tool. With Flash 4 and 5, Macromedia got serious about providing a real programming language. With the release of Flash MX, it's fair to say that Flash has become every bit as much of a programming tool as it is a graphics application. Not only has the ActionScript language grown more robust, but the way you can use it has become much more streamlined. In earlier versions of Flash, one of the frustrating things was that your code could be all over the place: You could have little bits of ActionScript tucked away in strange places you'd never think to look. Starting with Flash 5, it became possible to move your code away from the objects themselves and consolidate all (or at least most) of it in one place. This makes it considerably easier to maintain and update your code. It also makes Flash work much more like other programming languages. Of course, Macromedia has taken great pains to make almost everything in Flash MX and ActionScript backward-compatible with earlier versions of Flash. However, you'd be foolish not to take advantage of the new ways of working with ActionScript, because they can make your programming work a lot more efficient.

Notice that in the clickMe function of the preceding code, the onClickFlag's value is changed to 0. Once this variable is changed to 0, neither the rollOverMe nor the rollOffMe sections will do anything. Of course, unless you flip the variable back to 1 at some point, the rollOverMe and rollOffMe functions will stop the animations from playing. The logical point at which to flip the flag back to 1 is after the rollover sequence plays within the Movie Clip you will use as the physical representation of the button. The logical place to put the code to reset the variable is in the Timeline of the Movie Clip itself.

3   Open the Library if necessary, and double-click on the b_join anim symbol. Click on frame 91 of the Scripts layer. Add a statement to change the onClickFlag variable back to 1.

For now, we've commented the getURL line by using two forward slashes. This turns any line in ActionScript into a comment. It's a useful technique when you want to deactivate code without deleting it. Since you don't have a site created yet, with a join.asp page or a frameset with a frame designated client, this keeps you from seeing a parade of error messages every time you test the movie. You'll remove the "//" from this line before you're finished.

Note: New programmers take heart! If "debugging" is the act of removing bugs from code, then "programming" must be the act of putting bugs in the code. Or as an unknown programmer once offered: "If architects designed buildings the way programmers write code, the first termite to come along would end civilization as we know it."

To make the if statements work they way you expect them to, you'll have to add some code that sets the onClickFlag from on (1) to off (0) at the appropriate points within the animations.

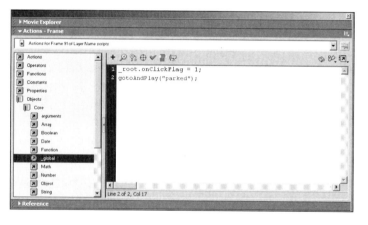

Add a statement to reset the onClickFlag variable, so that your buttons will animate properly each time you roll over them.

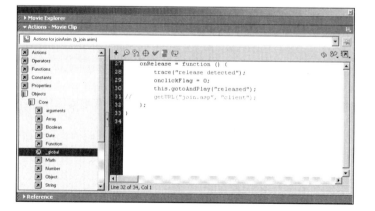

Use two forward slashes (//) to deactivate any line and effectively turn it into a comment.

4   You'll need to repeat this process for each of the button Movie Clips.

So…what you've done is set (or, in this case, reset) the flag that determines the rollover or rollout state. This is needed to turn on the rollover and rollout behaviors after a user has clicked the button. Make certain to check the Expression box next to the Value edit field; otherwise, Flash will misinterpret and convert the variable to hold text as opposed to a binary value. What does this mean in English? Simply put, you have created a "behavior" that you want to see when a user rolls over a button, one for when the user rolls off the button (or technically, out of the button's hit zone), and one for when the user clicks on the button. But what happens when the user clicks on the button and then rolls out? That's why you need the flag—so that Flash will only play the rollout animation sequence when the user has *not* clicked the button.

Let's recap. You've added some ActionScript to a Movie Clip so that you can use it to display animations for various button states. Now it's time to add some audio, adding ActionScript to that Movie Clip that will make the buttons "talk" as they move.

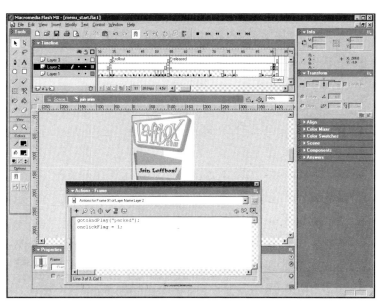

Click the Scripts layer of the main Timeline and code in the Actions panel to "wire" your application.

Audio P.O.V.

If you've played around with audio in Flash before, you've more than likely just attached a sound to a Timeline, or perhaps to one frame of a button symbol. That's cool, but there's so much more you can do with sound, and so many more ways in which to do it. There are really three ways to control audio in Flash. The first and most obvious way is to attach a sound directly to the main Timeline or the Timeline of an object. The second way is to create a kind of remote control for audio—a separate Movie Clip that you use as an audio placeholder, then make calls to its Timeline to trigger sounds. The third method is to use the Sound() controls within ActionScript to control audio programmatically. But which way is right for you?

Attaching audio directly to an object's Timeline is simple, fast, and effective, as long as you don't want to do anything but play sounds. If you want to control the volume of the audio, pan it, fade it out, or anything along those lines, attaching the sounds directly won't work. For that, you must control the sounds using ActionScript. The third way of controlling sounds (through making calls to a separate Movie Clip within your movie) is kind of a hybrid of the first two techniques. The big advantage of this method is that you can easily synchronize sounds against a Timeline. In previous versions of Flash, this was often the best way to control sound, simply because using the ActionScripting methods forced you to completely load each audio file before it would begin to play. All that's changed in Flash MX—you can even stream MP3 files from an external source.

Note: Because you can use ActionScript to control sounds, it might occur to you that it's possible to put the code just about anywhere within your movie. Where you put it should be governed by two factors—logic and flexibility. It's logical to put the code for a button on the button object itself. That may or may not be the best place for it, depending on how you want to maintain your code. You can also place the code on the Timeline within the button animation. This might make it a little harder to find when it comes time to modify the code, but it makes sense if you are using several separate audio clips that need to be synchronized to animations within the Movie Clip. Here, you'll learn both ways, just so you can see how both work.

Because of something planned for the next chapter (a Mute/Unmute button), you will use some limited ActionScripting to control the audio. Keep in mind, this same technique will work with the method 2 mentioned above. You'll use ActionScript here because it's a relatively easy way to get into using the Sound() controls in ActionScript.

1   Open the Library panel. Double-click on the sounds folder to expand it. Click on the short laff.wav audio clip, then click on the Library popup menu button (in the upper right-hand corner of the dialog) to see a list of options. Select Linkage.

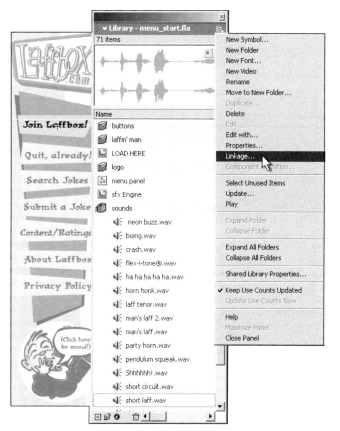

Right-click on any Library Object icon for a quick way to see a list of options you can choose.

2 In the Linkage Properties dialog, check the box labeled Export for ActionScript and the one below it labeled Export in First Frame. Change the Identifier to **shortLaff** (note the initial capital letter and the lack of spaces in the name).

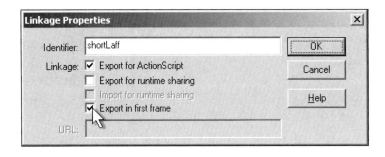

Select the Export in First Frame option to ensure that the sound will load immediately and be ready to play when you need it.

3 Press the OK button to close the dialog. Repeat this process with the following sounds:

What's all this then? Well, to use ActionScript to call a symbol, the script must be able to refer to an instance name for the symbol. What you're doing here is telling Flash to load these sounds in the first frame (that's the "Export in First Frame" part) and giving them a unique name. By the way, avoid names that begin with numbers or contain spaces because Flash tends to react to them, shall we say, "unpredictably."

Symbol Name	Linked Name
crash.wav	crash
flex-i-tone®.wav	flex-i-tone
neon buzz.wav	neonBuzz
party horn.wav	partyHorn
pendulum squeak.wav	pendulum
Shhhhhh!.wav	shhhhhh
short circuit.wav	shortCircuit
swoosh.wav	swoosh

Now you need to add some code to the main Timeline to load and play the sounds at the appropriate time. First, you'll use the _new Sound ActionScript command to create what amount to placeholders for each sound. Then you'll load the sounds into the placeholders.

Note: Sound synchronization is something of a tradeoff in Flash. Logically, you would assume that setting everything to Sync would give the best results, but that is far from the case. It fact, it's best to use the Sync setting only when absolutely necessary because it tends to both distort audio clips and increase your file size, sometimes dramatically. Event sound is no panacea either; however, because Flash must load event sounds into memory in their entirety before it can begin playing the audio clips. That's why it's important to select the Export in First Frame option when using linked sounds, so that the audio is loaded and ready to go when you want to use it.

4   Click on the Scripts layer in the main Timeline.

5   Edit the code so that it is identical to the following:

Again, let's take a look at the changes to the code, line by line. There are two lines of code needed for each sound we use. The first line specifies a name for our placeholder and establishes it as a sound, for instance

```
overSound = new Sound();
```

The next line loads a sound into the placeholder:

```
OverSound.attachSound("shortLaff");
```

The key is to make sure that you first set up a specific placeholder for the sound, then associate the sound you want with that placeholder. Note that you're still not playing the sound—you're just preparing it for use in the movie. The reason you have to go through all this is that only the sounds placed on a Timeline are automatically included when Flash builds a SWF file. Anything in the Library that doesn't appear on a Timeline is left out of the SWF. By creating a linkage and then attaching the sound to your code via ActionScript, you can overcome that limitation and use sounds in the Library that are not attached to a Timeline. You might notice that some of these place-holders are defined as part of the _global space. That's because they will be called from somewhere other than the main Timeline.

Now you have to modify the user-defined functions so that they will actually trigger the sounds you've set up.

```
//AUDIO CLIP DEFINITIONS
/*  here, we use the NEW constructor to configure the sound
for use with each of the buttons. The idea is to create a
sound placeholder, then attach a sound to it. Note that you
must give each audio clip a "Linkage" name to use here. */
overSound = new Sound();
overSound.attachSound("shortLaff");
outSound = new Sound();
outSound.attachSound("flex-i-tone");
releaseSound = new Sound();
releaseSound.attachSound("pendulum");
overLogoSound = new Sound();
overLogoSound.attachSound("neonBuzz");
outLogoSound = new Sound();
outLogoSound.attachSound("shortCircuit");
_global.releaseSound2 = new Sound();
_global.releaseSound2.attachSound("swoosh");
_global.releaseSound3 = new Sound();
_global.releaseSound3.attachSound("crash");
_global.muteSound = new Sound();
_global.muteSound.attachSound("partyHorn");
_global.unMuteSound = new Sound();
_global.unMuteSound.attachSound("shhhhhh");
//END AUDIO CLIPS
```

6 Scroll down the code until you see the user-defined functions, and change the code so it matches the following:

```
// USER-DEFINED FUNCTIONS
//define menu button rollover behavior
function rollOverMe(myClip) {
        if (_root.onClickFlag) {
                myClip.gotoAndPlay("rollover");
                        overSound.start();
                        return;
        }
}
//define menu button rollout behavior
function rollOffMe(myClip) {
        if (_root.onClickFlag) {
                myClip.gotoAndPlay("rollout");
                        outSound.Start();
                        return;
        }
}
// define menu button clicked behavior
function clickMe(myClip, myURL) {
        _root.onClickFlag = 0;
        myClip.gotoAndPlay("released");
//       getURL(myURL, "_client");
                releaseSound.start();
                return;
}
```

All you've done is add a start() command to each of the functions to trigger the appropriate sound. Because you have a somewhat complex sound plot for the released sequence for each button, you should trigger only the first sound from the main Timeline. Because you want the other effects (the sound of the button falling and the sound of it crashing) to be synchronized with the animations, you'll have to make some changes to the buttons themselves. (This means that not all the code will reside in the main Timeline, but sometimes it just can't be helped.)

7 Double-click on the joinAnim instance of the b_join_anim Movie Clip on the main Stage. Create a keyframe in the Scripts layer at frame 74, and add the following code to that keyframe:

```
releaseSound2.start();
```

8 Create a keyframe in the Scripts layer at frame 77. Add the following code to the new keyframe:

```
ReleaseSound3.start();
```

This triggers the "swoosh" and "crash" sounds along with the proper animations. Because you're triggering the sounds on the Timeline, the sounds should synchronize with the animations, regardless of the speed of the client computer.

WRAPPING IT ALL UP

Based on what you've done so far, there really no reason to avoid attaching the sounds directly to the Timeline and go the ActionScript route. In the next chapter, however, you'll see why you did this, because you'll be adding a Mute button that will allow you to simultaneously turn on and off all the sounds at will. What you've done here doesn't begin to scratch the surface of what you can do with audio in ActionScript, but this method will give you the flexibility to add things like a volume control, should the occasion call for it.

What's left? Nothing much—you just need to make the same changes to the other buttons. Since there's really nothing left to do but to copy and paste code, why not cut to the chase and open **menu_final.fla**. Test it to see what the panel looks like with the buttons working. You might also want to check out the code we've added to control the Laffbox.com logo button. Notice how the arguments in the start() function in the onRollOver handler loops the sound clip, and the stop() command in the onRollOut interrupts the loop and shuts down the sound associated with the onRollOver handler.

HOW IT WORKS

The beauty of ActionScript is that it enables Flash to control one object with another. This one fact opens up a world of possibilities for user interface design. Essentially, it enables you to create reusable objects and pieces of code, effectively making any design modular in nature.

In this project, you created a Movie Clip with markers and scripts that provide animation sequences for a number of possible behaviors, or "states," for a button. You then learned how to configure audio clips to be called dynamically, using ActionScript, and subsequently added code to the button that would include sound effects. Add all this up and you get a sophisticated button control.

There is one "gotcha" left, however. What if some users don't want your buttons to make noise? To discover a relatively easy way to give your users the capability to turn sound on and off a will within your interface, turn to the next riveting project in our audio adventure, Project 5, "Controlling Audio Playback."

CONTROLLING AUDIO PLAYBACK

"Imagination is more important

than knowledge."

—ALBERT EINSTEIN

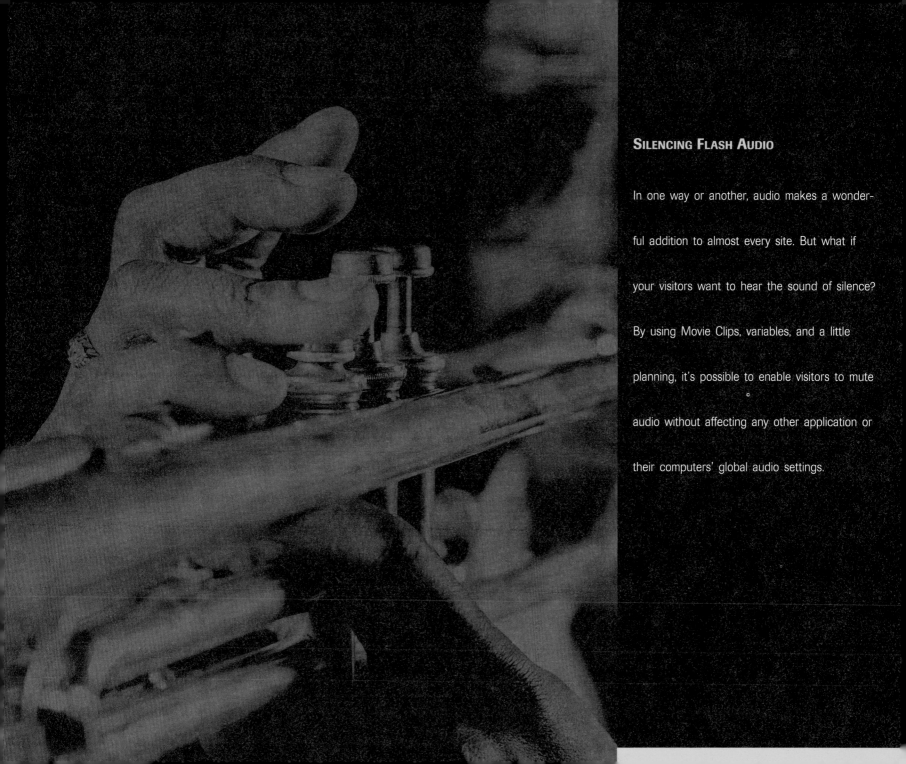

SILENCING FLASH AUDIO

In one way or another, audio makes a wonder-

ful addition to almost every site. But what if

your visitors want to hear the sound of silence?

By using Movie Clips, variables, and a little

planning, it's possible to enable visitors to mute

audio without affecting any other application or

their computers' global audio settings.

Project 5

Controlling Audio Playback

by Brad Kozak

GETTING STARTED

Before you start this project, copy the Project 5 folder from the accompanying CD-ROM to your local hard drive for ease of access.

CREATING A MUTE BUTTON

In this section, you'll create a button that will serve as a toggle for muting audio.

1   Open Flash and choose File > Open. Change the directory to the Project 5 folder on your hard drive. Select **menu_start.fla** and open the file.

2 Double-click on the cartoon symbol of the laughing man, just under the lowest button. (You might want to zoom in to make the area fill your Stage.)

Notice that the symbol has but one frame, but a number of layers that perform essentially the same graphic function within the symbol—two laughing men, two balloons, and two speaker icons. You'll use this symbol not just as a button, but also as a special kind of button—a multifunction button that will change graphics to indicate the state of the audio playback. When you're done, you'll have a button that serves as both a Mute and an Unmute button.

The idea behind this is deceptively simple. The two cartoon guys and the two balloons are actually Movie Clips in and of themselves. Each is set up so that it rocks back and forth. There are four combinations of the three pairs of symbols that will go into creating the multistate button. For the purposes of discussion, they're described as "sound on – up," "sound on – rollover," "sound off – up," and "sound off – rollover." When the overall movie first appears on your screen, you'll see the sound on – up state of the button. When you roll over it, you'll see the sound on – rollover state. When the user clicks the button, the sound for all the buttons will be muted, and the button display will switch to sound off – up. If the user rolls over the button now, they'll see sound off – rollover. Clicking the button again will switch the sound on, and the display back to sound on – up.

How do you accomplish this? By using a bit of ActionScripting and a variable that is monitored each time you call a sound.

Now you'll create some code that will turn these individual Movie Clips within your button on and off. First, take a look at the existing script that is on the Scripts layer of the main Timeline.

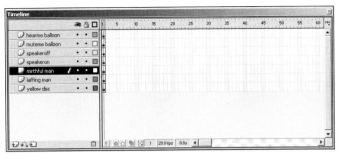

Open the laughing man cartoon button. If you drill down further, you'll discover that the cartoon man and balloons have synchronized, built-in animations.

3 Click on the Scene 1 tab to return to the main Stage. Open the Actions panel, then click on the Scripts layer in the main Timeline. Find the first section comment marked "//DEFINE VARIABLES."

4 Add the following line at the end of that section, just after the other variable declaration.

Add ActionScript to a global variable on the first line of the frame script to control the audio playback.

```
/*    this global variable tracks the status
of the mute button, where 1 = on
and 0 = off. */
_global.audioFlag = 1;
```

Now you need to add a user-defined function to handle how the Mute button reacts to mouse events. As you did in the previous chapter, take a closer look at this code, section by section.

5 Scroll down to the end of the section labeled "// USER DEFINED FUNCTIONS," and type in the following code just *before* the "// END USER DEFINED FUNCTIONS" comment:

You're doing what you did before, by creating user-defined functions to respond to onRollOver, onRollOut, and onRelease mouse events. What's unique here is that instead of asking Flash to jump to a spot on a Timeline and play an animation, you're making specific parts of the Movie Clip visible or invisible. This works because the Laughing Man button is really a Movie Clip that contains several other Movie Clips. As you'll see, this makes it possible to create a multistate button whose graphics are state-dependent.

```
// define the multi-state MUTE button user-defined functions:
// define the rollover behavior:
function audioRollOver(myClip) {
    if (audioFlag) {
        _root.manloader.muteMe._visible = 1;
        unMuteSound.start();
    } else {
        _root.manloader.hearMe._visible = 1;
    }
}
// define the rollout behavior:
function audioRollOut(myClip) {
    trace("audioFlag = " + audioFlag);
    if (audioFlag) {
        _root.manloader.muteMe._visible = 0;
    } else {
        _root.manloader.hearMe._visible = 0;
    }
}
// define the release behavior:
function audioRelease(myClip) {
    if (audioFlag) {
        myClip.lMan._visible = 0;
        myClip.mMan._visible = 1;
```

continues ▶

continued

```
                myClip.muteMe._visible = 0;
                myClip.hearMe._visible = 1;
                myClip.noSound._visible = 1;
                myClip.speakerOn._visible = 0;
                stopAllSounds();
                _global.audioFlag = "0";
        } else {
                myClip.lMan._visible = 1;
                myClip.mMan._visible = 0;
                myClip.muteMe._visible = 1;
                myClip.hearMe._visible = 0;
                myClip.noSound._visible = 0;
                myClip.speakerOn._visible = 1;
                muteSound.start();
                _global.audioFlag = "1";
        }
}
```

Note: When creating a Movie Clip that is to be triggered as a button, you usually will create a default button state and then create states for rollover, rollout, release, and potentially several other states. The button you're creating here is a little different. It's a *two-state* or *toggle* button. When it's completed, it will function exactly like a Pause button on a tape recorder—press once to Pause and press again to continue.

6 Insert the next section of code just *before* the section labeled "// SETUP BUTTON CONTROLS":

```
//   CONFIGURE INITIAL MUTE BUTTON STATE
/*   This code configures the initial state of
        the MUTE button, regarding which portions
        of the internal graphics are visible and
        which are invisible at run-time.*/
_root.manloader.muteMe._visible = 0;
_root.manloader.hearMe._visible = 0;
_root.manloader.lMan._visible = 1;
_root.manloader.mMan._visible = 0;
_root.manloader.noSound._visible = 0;
_root.manloader.speakerOn._visible = 1;
//
```

You need to turn off some of the Movie Clips and leave others on when you first launch the movie. This code provides that initial setup. This is the part of the code that actually wires the Movie Clip button to all those wonderful little functions you've defined.

You are creating three user-defined functions to associate with the mouse events onRollOver, onRollOut, and onRelease. The code in each of these functions accomplishes two tasks, the first of which should be familiar from Chapter 4. First, it evaluates the state of the audioFlag variable. What's new is that you are now drilling down into the Button Movie Clip and setting the visibility of certain Movie Clips within it. Why? Because you want the little cartoon guy to constantly rock back and forth. When you roll over the button, you want to make a text balloon popup. The balloon has text that is related to the state of the button. If the audio is not muted, the button will read "Click Here to Mute!," but if the sound is muted, the text balloon should read, "Click here for Sound!"

Now seems like an excellent time to discuss variables. Variables are high on my list of really useful things in Flash. There are two basic kinds of variables—local and global. They differ primarily in scope—that is the extent of what they can control. Essentially, a local variable is used within an instance of a Movie Clip. When that clip is no longer on the main Timeline—directly or as a part of another Movie Clip—the variable ceases to exist. Global variables are extremely useful because they can be set and inspected from anywhere within your movie. Why not use only global variables? You would lose the big advantage of local variables—you can use the same variable name in several areas, and they can peacefully coexist.

Variables are useful as flags—on/off, yes/no, 1/0—and as placeholders for counting loops, storing current values, and so on.

I mentioned previously that there was a reason for declaring that onClickFlag on the main Timeline outside the boundaries of any code that would make it function as a local variable. I did this specifically so that I could make the variable perform more than one function at the same time. The original function of that variable was to prevent the onRollOver and onRollOff sequences from firing if the user has clicked a menu button, at least until the onRelease animation has finished playing. Because I've kept the variable from being limited to a local scope, it also keeps the other buttons from animating while the clicked button does its thing. This saves me from having to create an array to keep only one button onRelease animation from playing at a time.

Note: You might be wondering, "Why is the onClickFlag setup using _root instead of _global?" Well, the straight answer is that I've found the _global feature to be a little unpredictable when it comes to variables. Because Flash allows you to create a variable with nothing more than a simple statement like "myVar = 1," Flash seems to have trouble determining if you are checking a global variable or declaring a new local variable every time you refer to a variable by its name, sans path. The _root designation is a leftover from Flash 5, but I've found it to be bulletproof. In the spirit of "who cares if it's pristine—I want it to work," I offer you the _root.myVar as a workable solution.

Take a close look at the rest of the code on that frame, especially the "_visible" lines. These four lines of code specifically target the two cartoons and two balloons within the Movie Clip button. This allows you to change the Movie Clip elements from visible to invisible. Had you needed to, you cold have used set property instead of _visible. This would have allowed you to change the Alpha (transparency) value from 100% (opaque) to invisible (0%), or anything in between. If you wanted to get really elaborate, you could write a script to fade objects in and out. For now, keep things simple and just make each object visible or invisible.

In order for you to understand exactly what you're doing here, it might be useful to take advantage of an old programmers technique called *pseudo code*, where programmers write out in English what they want the code to do. Here's how that might look:

At the moment you load the movie, define how the button will react to mouse movement. When the mouse clicks (releases) over the button, check the state of the audio flag. If it's on, set it to off. Otherwise, turn it on.

When the mouse rolls over the button, check the flag and leave room to define what happens if the flag is on or if it's off. Do the same thing for when the mouse rolls off the button.

Make sense? Now you just need to fill in the blanks—specifically *what* happens in each one of those if/else conditionals.

Without belaboring the obvious, here's what is going to occur: You'll turn on one of the cartoon guys and turn off it's mate. You'll do the same thing for the pair of balloon clips and the sound icons.

7   Finally, add the following code just prior to the
    comment "// END BUTTON CONTROLS":

    You have two things going on here—in each section,
    you're changing the Alpha properties of specific
    symbols within the Movie Clip button, and you're
    attaching sounds and playing them. I've added in a
    few trace statements that check the state of the
    audioFlag as an aid to debugging.

8   Go to Control > Test Movie and try the button out.

    If everything is functioning properly, the button
    animations should work, and the sounds attached to
    the button should work as well. What won't work yet
    is the actual muting of the other sounds. For that,
    you'll have to add some code to the original, user-
    defined functions.

```
// MUTE button controls:
manloader.onRollOver = function() {
        audioRollOver(this);
};
manloader.onRollOut = function() {
        audioRollOut(this);
};
manloader.onRelease = function() {
        audioRelease(this);
};
//
```

Setting Up the Variables

The first thing you'll need to work on is to isolate the
Sound functions in each button within an if statement
that checks for the condition of the audioFlag.

Here's the way the code looks now:

```
// USER-DEFINED FUNCTIONS
//define menu button rollover behavior
function rollOverMe(myClip) {
        trace("rollover var. = " + _root.onClickFlag);
        if (_root.onClickFlag) {
                myClip.gotoAndPlay("rollover");
                        overSound.start();
                        return;
        }
}
//define menu button rollout behavior
function rollOffMe(myClip) {
        trace("rollout var. = " + _root.onClickFlag);
        if (_root.onClickFlag) {
                myClip.gotoAndPlay("rollout");
                        outSound.Start();
                        return;
        }
}
// define menu button clicked behavior
function clickMe(myClip, myURL) {
        _root.onClickFlag = 0;
        myClip.gotoAndPlay("released");
        //    getURL(myURL, "_client");
        trace("audioFlag = "+ audioFlag);
        trace("global audioFlag = "+ _global.audioFlag);
                releaseSound.start();
                return;
}
```

And here's the way the code should look, once you've added the if conditionals:

The only difference is that you've bracketed the call to the audio clip with an if statement that checks the state of the audioFlag variable.

You'll need to bracket the two audio clips you call within the Movie Clip button's Timeline, too.

```
onClipEvent (enterFrame) {
     onRollOver = function () {
          trace("rollover detected");
          trace("onClick flag = "+ onClickFlag);
          if (onclickFlag == 1) {
               this.gotoAndPlay("rollover");
               if (audioFlag == 1) {
                    overSound = new Sound();
                    overSound.attachSound("shortLaff");
                    overSound.start();
               }
          }
     };
     onRollOut = function () {
          trace("rollout detected");
          if (onclickFlag == 1) {
               this.gotoAndPlay("rollout");
               if (audioFlag == 1) {
                    outSound = new Sound();
                    outSound.attachSound("flex-i-tone");
                    outSound.start();
               }
          }
     };
     onRelease = function () {
          trace("release detected");
          onclickFlag = 0;
          this.gotoAndPlay("released");
//        getURL("join.asp", "client");
     };
}
```

1   Double-click the instance of the Join Laffbox! button
    on the Stage. Click in the Timeline on frame 74 of
    the Scripts layer. Add an if conditional so that the
    code now looks like this:

```
if (audioFlag) {
        releaseSound2.start();
}
```

2   Do the same thing for the code at frame 77:

```
if (audioFlag) {
        releaseSound3.start();
}
```

3   Remember that you still need to update the other
    buttons in the menu. You'll need to modify the code
    controls the Laffbox.com logo button. Here's what
    the new code should look like:

```
// LOGO button controls:
logo.onRollOver = function() {
        if (audioFlag) {
                overLogoSound.start(0, 15);
        }
};
logo.onRollOut = function() {
        if (audioFlag) {
                overLogoSound.stop();
                outLogoSound.start();
        }
};
logo.onRelease = function() {
        //      getURL("welcome.asp", "client");
};
```

4 Or you can bag all that, and just open **menu_final.fla** and see the complete code in all it's glory.

Tip: Inserting comments in your ActionScript code is such a good idea that it's a shame Macromedia didn't find some way to force users to do so. Why are they so useful? Imagine this: You've just completed your magnum opus in Flash. You receive all sorts of awards and great press. Six months fly by. You now must revisit your original source code for some much needed updating. You failed to comment your code. There is much wailing and gnashing of teeth as you attempt to reconstruct why you did what you did in various and sundry portions of the file.

Now envision your job if you had provided comments in your code. You update your work in record time. There's dancing in the streets, joy in your heart, and a song on your lips. It's your choice. Whenever I'm working on a project that requires any real, conscious thought (about the ActionScript, anyway), I comment my code. You should, too.

HOW IT WORKS

The "gotcha" when creating an audio-rich site is that the sounds can quickly go from cool to annoying, and from there they can go straight to "How do I shut this thing up?" If you are building a site with audio, perhaps the most important button you'll add to your design will be one that enables visitors to turn off the sound.

Setting up a simple global variable (think of it as a flag), you can then use the variable's on/off state to control whether Flash plays—or doesn't play—an audio Movie Clip while you trigger an animation. By controlling all the audio via the Sound() controls in ActionScript and defining an AudioState variable, all you then need to do is check the state of the variable as a part of the script that triggers a button action. This simple principle can be expanded throughout your Flash work—and its application is not limited to controlling audio.

The trick to setting up a useful variable, believe it or not, is finding the right place to put it. If you put it somewhere within a loop, the variable will constantly reset itself to its original state. If you hide it in some Movie Clip that is not called right away, your variable might not have been instantiated (loaded into memory and run), and the routine that calls it won't be able to find it. The best place for variables is the first frame of the main Timeline. If you are declaring a variable you want to call or check from a variety of places in your movie, be sure to look at the new Flash MX _global variable designation.

After you have the variable working, the invisible button triggers the actions of three Movie Clips simultaneously—the audio Movie Clip, the cartoon man, and the speaker icon that serves as a button state indicator. You check the global AudioState variable each time you roll over, roll out, or click on the invisible button to determine whether you should play a sound and which animation you need to display. Along the way, you change the state of that variable to match the current status of the Mute button.

Probably the most difficult part of creating something like this is getting your mind wrapped around the logic of it all. It can be useful to create a kind of if-then-else diagram for toggle buttons. The button you created here really has only four states, but it can get a little hairy when you consider all the possible conditions under which those states can be triggered.

To keep things straight, I've found that three things really help. First, I try to keep the instance and marker names meaningful. This keeps me from doing a lot of guessing when I'm creating the button scripts. Second, I write down a list of the markers and instance names in the Movie Clip. This saves me from having to jump from editing the button script back into the Movie Clip several times. Third, I often draw a Movie Clip hierarchy just so I can make sure I'm addressing the Movie Clip properly. This not only is helpful when I'm writing code, but it also can be a useful debugging tool when I make my inevitable syntax error (or two).

Years ago when I was a kid, my father used to play a verbal game with my sister and me that he created, with the intention of forcing us to use our brains and our verbal skills. He would ask us to tell him—precisely—how to do something simple, like open a door. The trick was, he would follow our instructions literally—but attempt to do everything wrong that he could while still following our instructions. Oh, yeah…and we couldn't use our hands at all. You have no idea how frustrating it is to try to tell someone how to do something when the person is trying very hard to misinterpret everything that most people take for granted.

Computers are a lot like that. You have to tell them exactly what you want to do with absolutely no ambiguity. A computer will rarely follow any implied instructions…you must tell it what you want it to do in every conceivable circumstance or live with the result. Anything you can do that will help you visualize what you want and translate that into the language computers understand will make it that much easier to achieve the results you want.

The techniques you've used here are fundamental to creating modular, Movie Clip–driven Flash files. By using this method, you can create complex buttons, enable visitors to mute or hear audio, and perform a host of other functions.

"Pardon my redundancy."

—W.C. FIELDS

CREATING LOOPING BACKGROUNDS

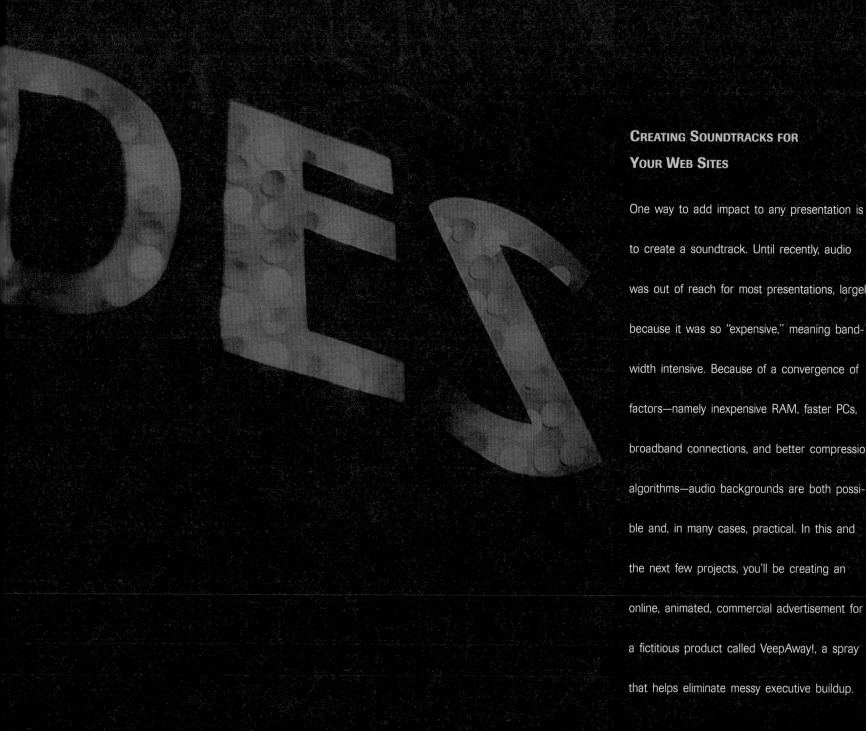

CREATING SOUNDTRACKS FOR YOUR WEB SITES

One way to add impact to any presentation is to create a soundtrack. Until recently, audio was out of reach for most presentations, largely because it was so "expensive," meaning band-width intensive. Because of a convergence of factors—namely inexpensive RAM, faster PCs, broadband connections, and better compression algorithms—audio backgrounds are both possible and, in many cases, practical. In this and the next few projects, you'll be creating an online, animated, commercial advertisement for a fictitious product called VeepAway!, a spray that helps eliminate messy executive buildup.

Project 6

Creating Looping Backgrounds

by Brad Kozak

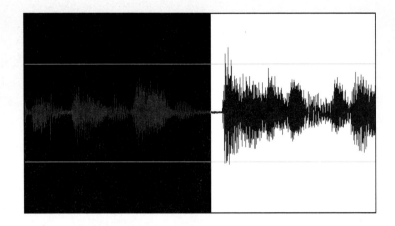

GETTING STARTED

Copy the Project 6 folder from the accompanying CD-ROM to a folder on your
local hard drive. If you don't already have a typeface called Alberta installed on your
computer, drag the file named **Alberta.ttf** from the Project 6 folder into your Fonts
folder (found in your Control Panel). Install the Demos of Sound Forge and of ACID
Pro from the CD-ROM.

WORKING WITH ACID PRO

This section will introduce you to Sonic Foundry's ACID Pro and provide an
overview of how it works. One of the first rules of show business is to make what is
difficult look easy and what is easy look difficult. (Remember this the next time you
watch some entertainer at work.) Sonic Foundry has created an application that makes
it very easy to do two things that are technically quite difficult: synchronize multiple
audio clips so that they appear to work well together and transpose the pitch of clips
without changing their tempo.

82

1 Open ACID Pro. In ACID's Explorer window, navigate to the Project 6 folder on your hard drive.

ACID Pro is a pretty amazing application. It has an intelligent, intuitive user interface and is designed to be invaluable for professional musicians and novices alike. As a case in point, to audition a sound clip before you use it, simply click on it in ACID's Explorer window. You'll automatically begin to preview it.

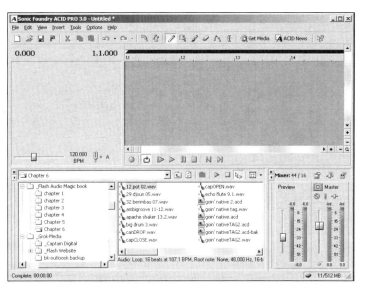

Open ACID Pro and find the Project 6 directory in the ACID Explorer window.

2 Click on the clip called **12 pot 02.wav**. Note that the clip begins playing, and you can observe the levels in the Preview VU meter.

Note: Sonic Foundry's ACID comes in a variety of versions. This book discusses the Pro version because it has the largest number of features and the most flexibility. Other versions are available, from the entry-level, free version called ACID XPress to ACID Techno and ACID DJ (which include specific music loops for their respective musical genres) to ACID Music, the version that includes a feature set that lies somewhere between ACID Techno and DJ and the unlimited flexibility of ACID Pro. All versions are available in a 30-day free-trial demo. ACID XPress (the free, entry-level tool) lets you experiment before diving into one of the more advanced tools.

The audio preview feature and ACID's use of drag-and-drop make it easy to search through your available Library of loops and samples.

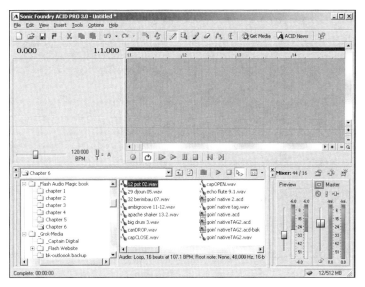

Click on clips in the Explorer window to audition them. Click on the **12 pot 02.wav** clip and listen to it.

3 Drag the 12 pot 02.wav clip into the work area. You'll see ACID add a new track while the name of the clip appears to the right side of the work area. Now click next to that track label (within the work area) and drag your cursor to the right. Keep dragging to the right until you see a small notch in the top and bottom of the waveform strip. This indicates the end of the loop and the point at which the loop starts to play again.

To see the entire waveform, you might need to press the minus button on the right end of the horizontal scrollbar several times. As you zoom out, you'll notice that the major tick marks in the timescale at the top of the work area represent beats in each bar of music. The smaller vertical line divisions represent either beats or, when zoomed in, subdivided beats.

You'll want to familiarize yourself with a couple of buttons. First, the Tape Transport buttons are at the bottom of the work area. Notice that you have a Loop Playback button (the flattened circular arrow), a Play from Start button (the vertical line with the arrow pointing right), a Play button, and then, of course, Pause, Stop, Rewind, and Go to End buttons. A Record button is just to the left of the Loop Playback button.

Now you can use the controls to play the sound you just added. To make the loop controls work, you must first indicate the beginning and end of the loop.

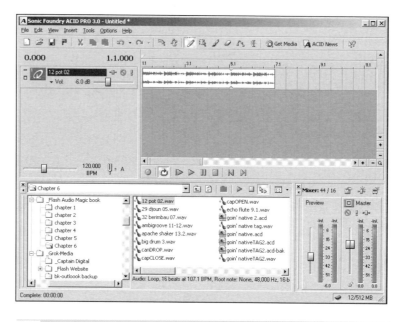

Drag the **12 pot 02.wav** clip to the work area. Now click on the left side of the work area on that first track and drag to the right. You'll see the waveform appear.

Note: If you are unsure about what any button in ACID does, just move the cursor over it and leave it there for a couple seconds. You'll see a balloon with text (a.k.a. "teach text") pop up next to the cursor with a brief description of the button. Any keyboard equivalent is also indicated.

4   Just above the numerical ruler (and just below the toolbar) are two small triangular markers. Click on the right triangular marker and drag it to the right so that it sits several beats past the end of the audio clip.

5   Play the loop. You'll hear your sound start at the beginning and drop out just before the loop ends.

If you click the Loop Playback button, the loop will play over and over until you stop it. (You'll be doing this a lot. If you are married or have a roommate or even thin walls, now might be a good time to consider investing in some headphones.)

Note: You've probably noticed by now that this is a very ethnic-sounding clip, and you might be wondering just what kind of music you'll be creating. The soundtrack and effects you'll be assembling will be used for an electronic commercial (what we call an "eMercial") for a fictitious product called VeepAway! I came up with the concept of VeepAway! when I worked at a large software company that was suddenly teeming with vice presidents. You couldn't turn a corner without bumping into one of them. As you might realize from your own corporate experiences, nothing gums up the corporate works like too many middle-level managers. VeepAway! is a specially formulated spray designed to repel midlevel executives. (Okay, it's really a label wrapped around a can of Glade, but perception *is* reality.) The concept for the eMercial centers on the "corporate jungle" and survival of the fittest—or, in this case, survival of the one who thought to bring along VeepAway! You'll use an all-percussion soundtrack to play up the Darwinian natural-selection concept and to make the eMercial more exciting.

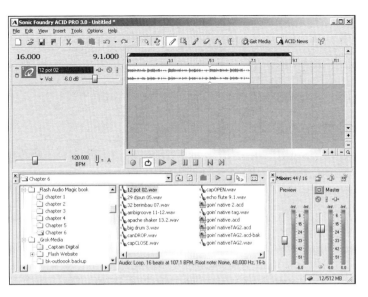

Drag the small Loop Region end marker to the right. End it on the fourth beat (in other words, align it to the 16th beat, or where the time indicator reads 9.1).

6 Now it's time for another "Julia Child" moment. Open the file **goin' native.acd**.

You'll immediately notice a couple of things. First, because of the Loop Region you've defined, ACID ignores whatever is past the end Loop marker. Next, zoom in and scroll down to track 8, the sound called timbali 19.wav. You can use the + buttons on the vertical and horizontal toolbars, or you can cut to the chase and click on the Magnifying Glass tool. This tool lets you click and drag and select a region to zoom into, just like you can in Flash. Look closely at track 8. Notice the small −12 in the lower-left corner of the track? This indicates that you've transposed this loop down 12 half-steps (or one octave, for you musicians in the audience).

7 Click on track 8. Note the three button controls on the left panel, just above the horizontal slider that controls the track volume. You'll be concerned with the last two buttons—the Mute button (which looks like the international "No" symbol used on street signs) and the Solo button (an exclamation point). Click on the Solo button.

If you've never played with an analog or digital mixing board, Mute and Solo do just what you'd expect—Mute turns off the track in question, and Solo turns off all the tracks except the one(s) you're soloing. These two buttons work hand in hand to save you a lot of time when you're trying to isolate a track in the mix.

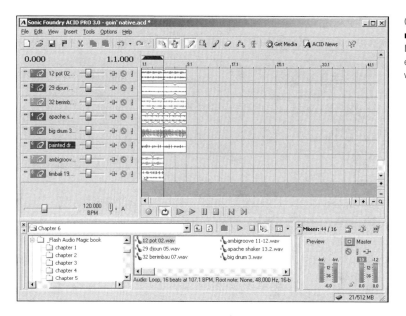

Open the file **goin' native.acd**. Note that the Loop Region is actually shorter than the length of all the waveforms. Play the loop.

8 Play the loop. As you play the loop, with the wave-form selected, press the + key on your numerical keypad. For every time you press it, you'll hear the pitch of the timbali track rise a half-step. If you like, go all the way up 12 half-steps. This is the natural sound of the clip. It was too high-pitched to blend in with the rest of the clips. To prove this point, click the Solo button again and listen to all the tracks together. If you want to make the timbali track more prominent in the mix, move the horizontal volume slider to the right.

If all you wanted to do was learn how to merge loops together to make a loop for your Flash audio backgrounds, you're done. Just go to the File menu, select Render As, and save the loop as a WAV file. (Be sure to select the check box for Render Loop Region Only.)

If you want to experiment with loops, this is a good way to start. You can get a lot more complex with loop creation (which you are about to do). First, it's a good time to consider the pros and cons of using loops in Flash.

On the pro side, loops are easy to create, take up relatively little bandwidth, and can be configured to repeat endlessly, saving you the time and effort of composing, editing, or creating a piece of music that offers variation throughout your Flash production.

On the con side, loops can drive your audience mad. Insane. Ready to burn the designer (you) in effigy and conveniently forget the effigy. I believe that loops are best left to situations in which you can layer them to give the appearance of variety or for creating what's known in professional audio circles as *walla* or what most people would refer to as "ambient back-ground noise." If you want to create an animated

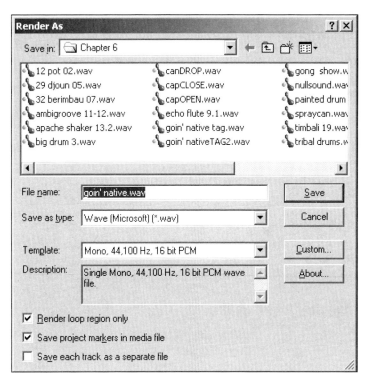

Select File > Render As and save the loop as a WAV (Microsoft *.wav) formatted file. You can save it as either a mono or stereo file. Be sure to check the box labeled Render Loop Region Only.

cartoon set on a city street, a loop of city sounds—car noises, crowds of people, horns, and so on—can be a very effective way to set your scene. On the other hand, if you plan to create a four-bar riff in ACID that will play throughout a 15-minute corporate demo, you will find your audience looking for the mute button inside of two minutes—tops.

USING ACID LOOPS

In this section, you'll use some loops in various ways inside Flash.

If you want background sound, a loop is the easiest, most efficient way to get there. Depending on the length of your loop and the compression you choose, you might add very little to your overall file size. Making short loops is a tradeoff, however, because the shorter the loop, the more obvious (and repetitive) it becomes.

1   Open Flash. Open the file **veepaway-looped.fla**. Move the playhead (the red rectangular marker on the frame count ruler near the top of the Timeline) to frame 12.

Note that the Stage displays a cyan bounding rectangle and a crosshair indicating the origin of that particular instance of the symbol. You'll also see a circle on the Stage, which serves as an indicator of a symbol that has nothing in its first frame.

If you were to move the playhead back to frame 1 and click the Play button, you would discover that there is not much that shows up on the Stage at this point. There's a reason for this—this movie is built almost entirely out of Movie Clips. Now, because this is a book on Flash and audio, it's a little out of scope to talk at length about the nuts and bolts of how to build Movie Clips. What we *would* like to do, however, is talk about *why* you should use Movie Clips in your work.

Flash is a lot like an onion. (Stay with me—I'm going somewhere important with this.) When you first start learning Flash, you work with vector art, learning the drawing tools and how to create symbols you can tween. Think of this as the first layer. I've seen some Flash files from developers that stop with this first layer of our hypothetical onion—they have 30 or so layers on their main Timeline. This makes the movie unwieldy, not to mention very difficult to edit.

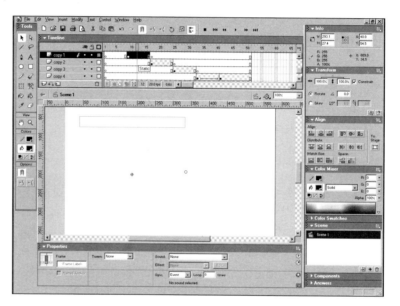

Click on the keyframe at frame 9 on the copy 1 layer.

A Movie Clip is a special kind of symbol that features its own Timeline that runs independently of the main Timeline. In other words, you create movies within movies that can have their own independent behavior. This might not seem like much at first glance, but I promise you it's *huge*. In the VeepAway! movie, we've created individual Movie Clips that control each line of text, with a separate clip for each "page" or screen of text. This alone significantly cuts the number of individual layers needed on the main Timeline.

The real value of using Movie Clips does not lie in layer reductions, however. Movie Clips can function independently. Ultimately, you'll learn how they can "talk" to each other, creating a situation in which one clip can trigger another one so that their behaviors become interdependent. This enables you to create situations in which you have one Movie Clip wait until another has reached a certain point before it continues. It's kind of an "I'm going to tell you to start and then wait here. You let me know when you're finished so I can go on" behavior.

This is enormously useful because it means that these behaviors can become dynamic with the addition of some interactive buttons. When you've mastered the concept and use of Movie Clips, you'll be ready for the third layer of the onion—creating animations via ActionScript without using motion tweens or even placing instances of the symbol on the Stage. You'll get more into that a little later. For now, you might want to explore the veepaway-looped.fla movie and learn how the Movie Clips function within the main Timeline.

Note: This is an online commercial (what we've dubbed an "eMercial") for VeepAway!, a format that gives you a number of advantages over traditional banner ads. Now, the techniques you will learn in this section apply to any kind of ad, demo, or presentation, even something as small as a banner ad. Because we're talking about advertising, let's stop for a moment and consider the nature of advertising on the web.

To date, almost all advertising over the web has been what we refer to as *invasive* advertising—ads that compete with content. To watch the ad, your attention is diverted from the subject matter of the page on which it resides. Think about ads on television and radio. Ads and content alternate, and each gets a shot at your undivided (as opposed to undevoted) attention. We call this kind of advertising *interruptive* because it briefly interrupts the content for a commercial message. Most ads in magazines (at least the expensive, prominent ones that work) follow the same rule—a full-page ad gets more attention than one that shares the page with copy.

We believe that full-page (or full-screen) ads make a lot of sense. For that to work, however, you have to rethink how these ads are used online. The web is an amazing way to communicate, but it has not been used (at least so far) in such a way that the advertising has had as much impact as ads in magazines, on radio, or on television. We are currently test-marketing an online magazine created entirely in Flash that features full-page, interactive, full-motion ads that we call eMercials as the advertising format of choice. Should this succeed to the extent that we believe it will, you'll see a lot more full-screen ads as this electronic magazine format becomes more popular. The net effect of all of this on you will be that your Flash skills will become all the more in demand. That's not a bad deal for both advertisers and Flash developers.

You'll find that a number of the Movie Clips are invisible, at least at first. When there is nothing in the first frame of a Movie Clip Timeline, Flash displays a very small circle at the point on the Stage that represents the origin (X = 0, Y = 0) of the object/instance. If you click on the circle, you'll see a crosshair appear inside the circle, indicating that you've selected it. When you select an object that has an Alpha value of 0% in the first frame of that particular instance, you'll see a crosshairs and a rectangular bounding box (a cyan-colored rectangular outline) that indicates the origin (the crosshairs) and the position of that first object (even though it's invisible).

2   With the Pointer tool selected, double-click either on the crosshair or inside the cyan-outlined rectangle. Alternatively, you can click right-click once on the object. You'll see a pop-up menu where you can choose Edit in Place.

Notice that you now have changed Timelines. You're now in the Timeline for the symbol called text1—the first of the movie clips that display the sequentially loaded lines of text. You can immediately tell that you're not in Kansas anymore by looking at the tabs just under the main toolbar. Note that you see a Movie Clip icon with the word "text1" next to it, just to the right of the Scene 1 icon and text. This is a visual clue. It's also an easy way to get back to the main Timeline. Just click on Scene 1 and you're there. Notice on frame 51 in the Scripts layer that there is an ActionScript command that instructs the clip called sprayCan to begin playing.

This is how one Movie Clip can send a message to another, effectively letting any Movie Clip control another one. The last frame of this Movie Clip has two commands—first, it instructs the main Timeline to continue playing, and second, it stops itself from

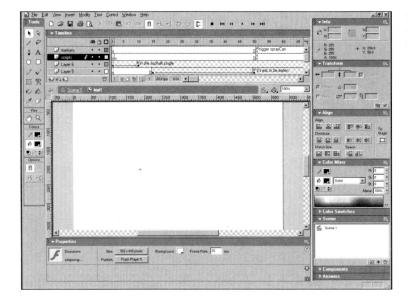

Double-click inside the cyan-outlined rectangle or on the crosshair.

looping back to its own beginning and playing again. Get familiar with this technique because understanding it is critical for using audio (not to mention virtually every other advanced technique) in Flash.

Okay, we've thoughtfully already imported a loop for your listening pleasure. It's called ambigroove 11-12.wav, and it is one of the many sample audio loops you can download for free from the Sonic Foundry web site.

3   Click on the Scene 1 tab under the main toolbox to get back to the main Timeline. Create a new layer just under the Scripts layer. Name it **audio**. Insert a keyframe on the Audio layer under the marker copyblock1. Select that new keyframe and open the Sound panel.

> **Tip:** If you double-click on the new keyframe you've just created in the Timeline, you'll automatically open up both the Sound panel and the Frame Actions panel.

The easiest and most basic way to use background audio in Flash is to trigger a looped sound on the main Timeline. To do that, you'll first explore what looping is and how it works within Flash. For the moment, let's assume you are working with a loop you've purchased and defer talking about loop creation for just a little while longer.

4   In the Sound panel, select the clip **ambigroove 11-12.wav**. Keep the Sync setting as Event. Set the Loops number to 999.

> **Tip:** Movie Clips in a main Timeline will play back only when you test or export the entire movie to SWF format. If you play the movie from within the Flash development environment, the Movie Clips will play their first frame only. This is an unfortunate side effect of the Movie Clip independent Timeline feature because it tends to confuse newbies. The thing to remember is that you can always press Ctrl+Enter and test your movie before you commit to any destructive changes.

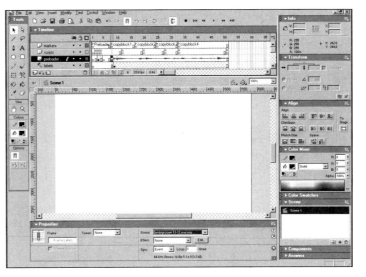

Add a new layer to the Timeline and add a keyframe under the copyblock1 marker.

For all practical purposes, setting the Loops number to 999 will make your sound loop forever. But will it increase your file size? Anybody? Somebody? No. If you use Event sound and loop it, Flash simply records one iteration of your loop into memory and repeats it for as many times as you've told it to. On the other hand, if you use Stream as your Sync type, you have just increased the size of your file by roughly the size of the original audio clip times the number of loops that will play before your Timeline runs out. Ow! That can lead to some hugely bloated files.

The reason is that, to synchronize the sound to your Timeline, Flash goes in and slices up your sounds into segments that are the same length as your frame rate. If you set your frames to 20fps, you get a bunch of little sound files that are all 1/20 of a second long. Now, you never see these files in your Library— Flash handles this internally. One of the great mysteries of Flash is why some sounds work just fine when streamed, and others sound like they've been run through a Waring blender. At any rate, there is absolutely no need to stream a looped audio file. Ever. It defeats the purpose. Don't bother. You need to use streamed (synchronized) sound when you choose audio backgrounds that play throughout the piece without looping (more on this later in this exciting project).

Go ahead now and play your file by exporting it (Ctrl+Enter). It sounds pretty good, if a little monotonous. So what can you do to fix that?

Fun trivia fact: The blender was invented by a musician named Fred Waring, who wanted to create a healthy meal-on-the-go for his singers. He believed that pureed vegetables and fruits would be the ideal drink. As a measure of how humanity can take a noble invention and pervert its original purpose, the most popular use for blenders has been to create milkshakes, malts, and other frozen dessert drinks.

5 In the Sound panel, click the Edit button and launch the Edit Envelope panel. Note that you will see your waveform in a Timeline with a line that represents the volume of the clip.

Okay, what you've got here is a view of the entire looped clip. Click the Zoom Out button a bunch and watch what happens. As you zoom out, you'll see the first copy of the waveform, followed by seemingly endless (well, 998 of them) copies of the original waveform. If you click on the button with the film-strip icon, your Timeline will change from displaying seconds to frames. Notice the horizontal line at the top of both the left and right channels, the one that terminates to the left in a small outlined box.

6 Click on the point at which the loop first repeats. Note that the effect has just changed from None to Custom. Now drag the first outline box (it's a handle—bet you already knew that) down to as low as it can go. Do the same for the other channel. You'll end up with something that looks a lot like this figure.

Now you have a wonderful fade-in over the course of the first loop. Adjust to your taste. This will provide you with a bit of drama as the music begins to crescendo. Of course, it happens really quickly, so you might want to move the second control point farther away from the first handle. That's where the frame counter (as opposed to the timescale) can come in handy. If you know the frame count (assuming you're not using Movie Clips that stop and start the main Timeline, as you did here), you can accurately predict how long to make the sound build from silence to maximum volume.

This is the way that 99.9% of the people use sound in Flash. But journey on and you'll become one of the elite few who know how to make audio do much more in Flash.

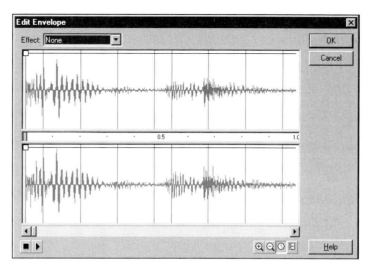

Use the buttons at the bottom of the Edit Envelope panel to zoom in and out and to switch between an elapsed time versus a frame count view.

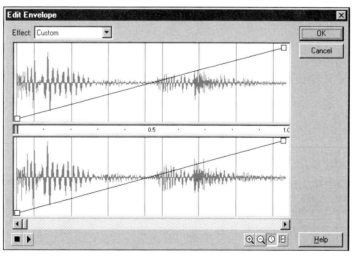

Add a control handle by clicking on the horizontal volume indicator at the point between the first iteration of the loop and the first repeat. Select the first handle on the line and drag it to the bottom. Repeat for the other channel.

CREATING YOUR OWN LOOPS

Music (presuming you are using music and not ambient sound, in which case you're off the hook) has three essential elements—rhythm, harmony, and melody. You can think of these as drums, guitars or keyboards, and lead vocals or soloists. For the purposes of creating a loop, the most important of these three elements is rhythm. Specifically, Western music has what is called *beats*—rhythmic pulses. Most music uses four beats to make up a *bar*. (In computer terms, this is somewhat analogous to the concept that 8 bits make up a byte.)

The key to creating a loop that works is to find a point at which the pattern repeats—sort of a natural break point. Because Western music is usually—but not always—based on the unit 4, the natural breakpoints usually occur after 1 bar, 2 bars, 4 bars, or 8 bars. Now, 8 bars of music might be a pretty substantial loop, but it is also a loop that doesn't become instantly repetitive. Most loops that you can buy from commercial suppliers run 2 or 4 bars. When you are creating your own loops, it's up to you to determine the right length. If you are working from a longer piece of music (hopefully, licensed or royalty free), your loop points will largely be dictated by the music. The important thing to remember is that the beginning and end of the sound must seamlessly fit together. Otherwise, you'll have a noticeable hiccup every time the loop repeats.

1   Open Sound Forge if it's not already open. Open the file **Groove Master Le Roi.wav**. (Okay, I'll admit it. I was watching *Pulp Fiction* for the umpteenth time when I created this file.) Play it from the beginning.

Note that you won't be using this file in the VeepAway! spot, but because you're using kind of a Jungle Drum theme there, I thought this example would be more obvious. I'm a big believer in repurposing assets, especially those I create for my own use. The Jungle Drum theme was derived from a music bed I originally created for my web site: **www.grokmedia.com**.

Let's assume you need a loop instead of what you have here—a 15-second file with a beginning, middle, and end. Listen to the file one more time and watch it as the indicator moves across the waveform. Do you see some natural beats in the file that might be an obvious place to set a loop point? For the purposes of this example, you'll use the first four bars and loop them.

2   Go to the Options menu and select Selection Grid
    Lines. Select an area from the beginning of the WAV
    file to the approximate midpoint, just before the
    largest volume spike in the file.

    Notice that the white vertical grid lines seem to
    "automagically" line up with the volume pulses
    (beats) in the file. Now you want to play the selec-
    tion, but you want to loop it. Click the Play Looped
    button, which is just to the right of the Play button at
    the bottom of the waveform window.

3   Listen to the clip as it loops. Hear the beat in your
    head, snap your fingers, do whatever is necessary to
    determine whether you have the end loop point
    properly defined.

    If you don't, you'll hear a very slight (or sometimes
    not-so-slight) glitch in the regularity of the beats at
    the loop point.

4   Use the Zoom In buttons next to the horizontal
    scrollbar to enlarge the selected area. Move the cursor
    over the end of the selection until you see the cursor
    change to a double-headed arrow. Adjust the end-
    point of the selection until it falls just before the beat
    (volume spike) in the file.

    With a little patience, luck, and perseverance, you'll
    nail it with a perfectly matched loop. (Kind of fun,
    isn't it?) Note that there are some specialized tools in
    Sound Forge, such as the Loop Tuner (found in the
    View menu) that will enable you to fine-tune your
    loops to an incredibly granular degree. This is usually
    not a problem, so we'll leave that for those of you
    who are so inclined to go for extra-credit experimen-
    tation. (There will be a test at the end of the
    semester. Just kidding.)

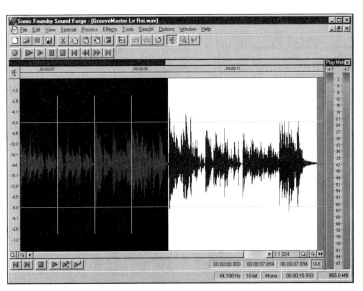

Go to Options > Selection
Grid Lines. Select the first half
of the waveform to a point
just before the large volume
spike in the middle of the file.

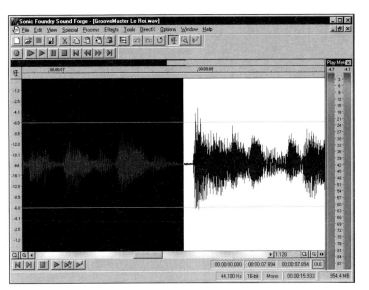

Zoom in and adjust the endpoint of the selection until it
comes at the end of one beat
and the beginning of another.

5 With the loop area selected, go to Edit > Trim/Crop (Ctrl+T). This will delete any area outside of your selection. Save your new loop under a different name—say, **Groove Master loop.wav**.

You've just completed the creation of your own loop.

> **Tip:** Just so you are perfectly clear on this, you cannot legally make a loop out of commercially available music unless the copyright holder has agreed to license it to you or sell it to you on a royalty-free basis. In other words, don't go sampling the latest CD of the Blonde Teen Sensation of the Month Club and expect to be able to use four to eight bars of one track as a loop in your next project. If the prospects of getting caught and punished don't faze you, consider this: Of the $15 you pay for a pop CD, less than 50 cents of the sale price usually ends up in the artist's pocket. When you rip a CD with the intent to use someone else's work for your own project without compensating that person, you are ripping off the artist whose work you enjoy. Unless your project is strictly for personal use (not to broadcast to the world over the web, for profit, or even for your work portfolio), don't do it.

USING LAYERED LOOPS

Now that you've learned to use loops as well as create them, let's explore the possibilities of layering loops within Flash.

The concept of layering loops is one that, when used intelligently, can bring a new level of variety and depth to your work. The concept is simple. Start with one loop playing in the background and then trigger other loops to play throughout the rest of the piece, perhaps to loop briefly, or even to play as a nonlooping sound. Now, you can't really expect to pull this off by using a rhythm section clip (like Groove Master loop.wav) and trying to layer a guitar solo over it. This technique works best when you are working with sounds that have no discernable beat (think New Age ambient music) or sounds into which you can safely layer different rhythms so as to achieve a polyrhythmic feel (as you are about to do with the VeepAway! spot). This is a way cool technique when used properly. When it's misused, however, it's the aural equivalent of a 16-car pileup on the I-30 Mixmaster (and we all know how painful *that* can be).

1 Open **VeepAway.fla** in Flash.

Remember how this file uses a *lot* of Movie Clips? Well, you are going to use a combination of loops and one-shot sounds and trigger them from inside the Movie Clips. To do this successfully, you need to understand how Movie Clips work and how Event sound differs from Streaming sound in one other important way.

When you trigger an Event sound by placing it on a Timeline—*any* Timeline—you cause the waveform to begin playing until it runs out of audio. In other words, even if you run out of Timeline (or you stop the Timeline from playing), the sound will continue playing until the loop count is exhausted or the one-shot file has completed playing. When you set an audio file to play as a streaming event, it is tied to the frame count. If your Timeline stops before the sound file is finished playing, *the sound file playback stops right along with the Timeline*. You can use this idiosyncrasy to your advantage by combining this knowledge with that of Movie Clip manipulation.

Movie Clips are important because they're addressable—you can "talk" back and forth with them via ActionScript. This is important because you can make one Movie Clip tell another to start or stop playing, jump to another frame, and so on. Now I'm a big believer in creating modular designs—both from a reusable code standpoint and from a project management standpoint. In upcoming chapters you'll take this philosophy to it's ultimate conclusion and control sound with reusable ActionScript functions.

Tip: Now, I'm going to tell you about a very cool little secret that shouldn't work but does. (Be veeeewy quiet...heh, heh, heh....) If you stream one sound in your movie, all the other sounds that play at the same time will synchronize without forcing you to convert them from Event sounds to Streamed sounds. I told you earlier that the stream setting can, on occasion, really distort and generally degrade your Streamed sounds. There is a relatively easy way to get around this. Just open Sound Forge and create an empty (silent) sound file that is the same duration as your frames-per-second setting. In other words, if you're running 20fps, create an empty sound file that is 1/20 of a second long. Import this sound to your main Timeline and set it to stream, looping it 999 times (or more if your movie is longer than 999 frames). That's it. Now any other sound you put into your movie will have the benefits of streaming without the associated overhead and sound problems. You'll notice that this is already done for you in the VeepAway! file. (You're welcome.)

Tip: In my "day job," I see a lot of Flash files from a lot of companies. Most of these are very difficult to edit quickly because they often do things like put ActionScript commands in the same layers as symbols. This makes it all but impossible to move the code independent of the instance of the symbol with which it shares a cell in the Timeline. A much better solution is to always have a separate layer for markers, a separate one for nothing but ActionScript code, and if you are using audio directly, a separate layer (or layers) for sounds. Do this on every Timeline in your movie—the main Timeline and Movie Clips alike. To further modularize your work (and make it much easier to modify/update/manage), consider creating a separate Movie Clip just for audio. You will then place an instance of this Movie Clip somewhere on the Stage (it will be invisible when you export your movie to SWF) and use ActionScript commands to trigger the sounds.

2 Use the vertical scrollbar to scroll the page down just a little. Notice the legend outside of and above the active Stage area that says SFX ENGINE. (If you don't see it, make sure you are on frame 9 or later in the main Timeline.) Note that next to this text is a small circle. Double-click on that circle.

This is a very simple Movie Clip. You first set up an empty section labeled parked. You create this parking zone so that you can send the playback marker to this frame and know that the other sounds won't start playing without a little help and instruction from our ActionScript commands.

The rest of the SFX clip is composed of nothing more complicated than a series of markers that correspond to the first frame of an audio clip. A few frames later, you put in an ActionScript stop() command and then start the next sound group. Remember that the only way to play the entire sound when you trigger it is to make sure it's an Event sound or to add in extra blank frames to encompass the entire duration of the audio clip. It doesn't matter if these sounds are configured to loop or to play as one-shots. The beauty of this concept is that you can then call any sound from anywhere via ActionScript commands, specifically from another Movie Clip. Also notice that there really are no commands other than stop within the SFX Movie Clip. It makes no difference where the frame indicator ends up after you trigger a clip remotely because you will always explicitly state which clip to play (as opposed to using the more general play() command that simply starts a movie playing without regard to where it is currently on the Timeline).

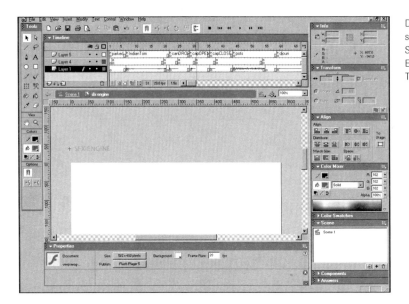

Double-click on the circle that serves as a marker for the SFX ENGINE Movie Clip. Explore the SFX ENGINE clip's Timeline.

The keys to addressing this Movie Clip are as follows:

- You must have an instance of it on the Stage at the point when you want to "talk" to it with ActionScript.

- You must give the instance a unique name. Without this name, you'd never be able to address one of two or more symbols on the Stage that share the same Library name.

Now that you have the audio files in place and have a named instance of the Movie Clip on the Stage, the only thing left to do is to call the Movie Clip from within another Movie Clip. Here's how that works.

3 Go back to the main Timeline. (Click on the Scene 1 tab.) On the main Timeline, find the copy 1 layer. Click on the occupied frames in the main Timeline. You'll see a cyan-outlined box and crosshairs appear. Double-click inside that box (or directly on the crosshairs). On the second frame in the text1 symbol, note that there is a script on the Scripts layer. Click on that frame in the Timeline and open the Frame Actions panel. It should read something like this:

```
root.sfxEngine.gotoAndPlay("IndianTom");
```

Now you can begin to see the power of using Movie Clips in this fashion. You can trigger any sound as often as you like by "remote control" from wherever you like.

Experiment within the three text clips in the VeepAway! movie. Try changing sound clips. Note that some of the clips you trigger are one-shots that are synchronized to specific events in other Movie Clips. A great example of this comes in frame 25 in the can anim. Movie Clip, where you'll find an ActionScript command in the script channel in the frame with the marker sprayIT. This command triggers an animation sequence instead of a sound clip. If you look inside the sprayCan clip, you'll find that it calls some audio clips, too. If you think back to the first project in the book, the construction techniques you used here are similar. The real difference is that you did it more for ease of code maintenance rather than as a way to provide mute button functionality.

HOW IT WORKS

Looping is a very useful technique for adding audio in situations in which file size is a concern. Looping can be used effectively for ambient sound effects as well. Consider looping another tool to use along with one-shot sounds and sounds controlled via ActionScript. Just don't make the same mistake that so many Flash users have made to date: thinking that looping audio is enough to keep your audience enthralled with the brilliance of your audio plot.

CREATING BACKGROUNDS FOR SYNCHRONIZATION

"You wish to see; Listen. Hearing

is a step toward vision."

—ST. BERNARD

ORIGINAL MUSIC IN FLASH

What separates most audio experts who use

Flash from the rest of the Flash community is a

background not in audio engineering but in

music. Thanks to tools like ACID Pro, even

people without musical training can create

compelling, original music. This project will

explore how to use ACID Pro to create original

music for your Flash work.

Creating Backgrounds for Synchronization

by Brad Kozak

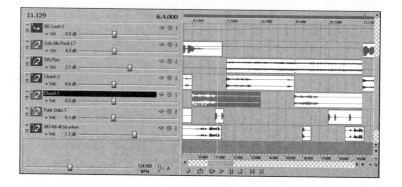

GETTING STARTED

Copy the Project 7 folder from the accompanying CD-ROM to your hard drive and install the demo of ACID Pro from the CD-ROM (if you haven't already).

CREATING MUSICAL PHRASES

In this section, you'll use ACID Pro to build a soundtrack, and you'll explore some of its more advanced features along the way.

Music is made up of building blocks—notes, rests, dynamics, timbres, and tonalities—much like books are made up of letters, words, punctuation, sentences, paragraphs, and chapters. To learn songwriting, composition, and arranging/orchestration, musicians learn how to use these building blocks in a logical, rule-based fashion. They learn scales and chords as well as how to create rhythmic patterns and musical phrases. Many nonmusicians find this to be a somewhat confusing and intimidating process. Applications like ACID Pro take a lot of the grunt work out of the process of composing and arranging and make it possible for nonmusicians to create real, original compositions. ACID is also quite useful for professional musicians as well because it provides a quick way to create grooves and rhythm tracks that can then be augmented by overdubbing live performances onto the ACID mix.

To understand how ACID works its own particular kind of magic, you need to understand a little about tempo and tonality.

So how does ACID Pro work? Consider this "left field with a hockey stick" simile: Garanimals. Remember Garanimals? They were color- and style-coordinated kids clothing that you matched up by their "animal" tags. As long as you chose the same animal for your pants, shirt, and whatever else you were wearing, you would know that everything "went together." The ACID series of applications takes this kind of approach with audio. You have collections of loops that are designed to work well with each other. ACID adds some tags within the loops that coordinate tempo and tonality so that the clips work well together—seamlessly, in fact. It's so simple to put together tracks in ACID that I'm frankly surprised everybody doesn't do this and forego using commercially available, one-size-fits-all clips.

Let's take a few clips, put them together, and see what happens.

- **Tempo.** The speed of the rhythmic pulses (beats) in a given composition. For now, just recognize that all the instruments need to agree on a common tempo for whatever song they are recording or performing.

- **Tonality.** A generalized term for "key center" that dictates both the chords you will use in a composition and which chords (and notes within the key center's scale) will function as the "home base." Think of it like this. If you are playing in the key of C and your guitar player decides to play everything in the key of E, your composition is going to sound much like the aural version of a train wreck. You want everybody in the same key center; otherwise, you will have a lot more dissonance (notes played together that sound as if they shouldn't be played together) as opposed to harmony.

1   Open ACID Pro. In ACID's Explorer window, change the folder to the Project 7 folder on your hard drive.

You will see a folder called ACID Loops that contains an assortment of audio clips in ACID's Explorer window. Sonic Foundry has provided this library of clips for your use from the company's extensive collection of loop libraries. *Please note that you won't use all the clips in this folder.* We've included more than you need for this exercise so that you'll be able to experiment with them and create things on your own. Note that there are several directories in the ACID loops folder, organized into instrumental categories.

In every composition, you have to start somewhere. I've always found it useful to lay down a groove first and then build the song on top of the groove. The bass player and drummer work together to create the groove, so you'll start with one of each.

2   Double-click the Bass folder. Click the first clip and listen to it. Do this for each of the clips in the folder to familiarize yourself with them.

The eMercial client from Project 6, "Creating Looping Backgrounds," has decided that it is not sure about using the all-percussion audio track created in that project. The client has asked for something with an "urban sound" to it.

This mythical customer has expressed a preference for the urban funk sounds of the 1970s. (Hey—*I'm* the one writing this project, so *I* get to pick the style of music. If you'd rather cut a track that sounds like something off of MTV2, be my guest.)

To begin with, you'll select a bass loop and then find a drum riff to match.

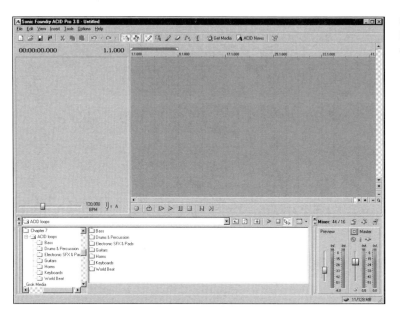

Open ACID Pro and find the Project 7 directory in the ACID Explorer window.

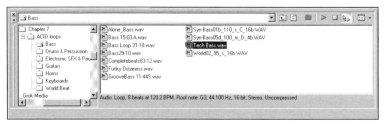

Click each of the audio samples in the Bass directory to preview them.

Tip: No matter how much you know about music, you are sure to run into a client who has different tastes, different preferences, and a different idea of what music matches up with a particular description. Music is a fluid, dynamic, living thing. What is urban or funk or industrial to one person might be described in a completely different way by someone else. The best way to understand what your client really wants is to ask for specific examples. If the client says "urban sound," for instance, that could mean anything from Tower of Power to Staind. Getting specific examples will save you a lot of time.

3 Open **Tech Bass.wav** by dragging it onto the work area in ACID Pro.

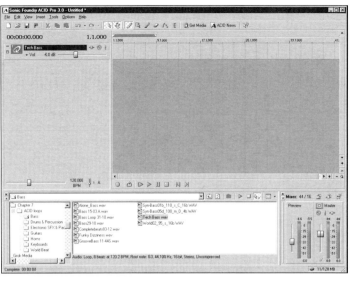

Click Clips in the Explorer window to audition them. Drag Tech Bass.wav to the work area.

4 Select View > Time Ruler > Show Time Ruler. Make sure it is set to display Seconds. Move the cursor into the work area next to the Tech Bass track label and then drag the cursor to the right. Note the time scale at the bottom of the work area—drag the right edge of the clip to align as closely as possible with the 30-second mark. You might need to zoom in by clicking the + button next to the horizontal scrollbar to align the end of the clip with the 30-second mark. Press the spacebar to listen to the track.

The spacebar functions as a start/stop button. Listen to the track. So far, it's nothing but a really busy bass track.

5 Change folders in the ACID Explorer window to the Drums & Percussion folder. Drag the **Funk Master 02.wav** loop into the work area and repeat the process you went through in step 4 for this track.

So far, so good. You've got a bass part and a drum part that match up. Now you need to do something with it. Let's add some saxophone.

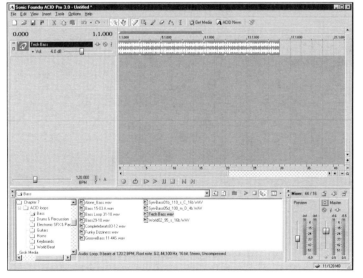

Click in the work area next to the sound clip label and drag to the right to place an instance of the sound in the track mixer.

6 Change to the Horns folder and drag the **Solo Alto Rock E7.wav** loop onto the client area. This time, instead of starting on the first beat, click and drag from the beginning of the fifth segment (labeled 3.1.000 on the upper Timeline) and drag to the right until you see a small notch appear at the top and bottom of the track. Stop at the point at which the notch appears.

You've now placed one entire loop of the alto sax clip in the work area. Go ahead and play this to get an idea of how it sounds.

It's nice, but you've got a long way to go to change this from a simple cut-and-paste job into something that sounds like real musicians playing together. Next you'll add some lead guitar.

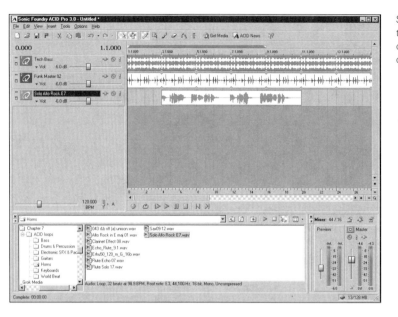

Starting with the beginning of the second bar, click and drag to the right to reveal one complete loop pattern.

7 Change to the Guitars folder and repeat the process using the **60's Pyro.wav** clip. After you drag the clip into the work area, put an instance of it in the Timeline by starting it where the alto sax clip ends. It's only four units (or two bars) long, so it will end before the song does.

Okay, you now have the basic instrumentation that you need for the piece. You'll still need to add a few instruments, though.

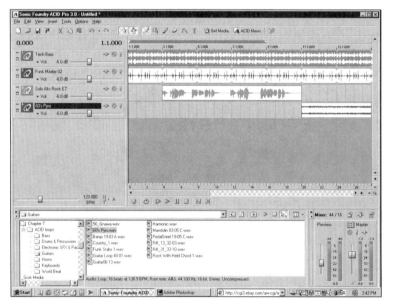

Add the 60's Pyro guitar clip, setting it to play one complete pattern immediately after the sax clip.

ADDING INSTRUMENTS

Just as the bass and drums function as the foundation of the rhythm section and establish the groove, two other instruments commonly provide support to round out the harmonic canvas and provide what writers would call "subtext" to the music. In most popular music, these instruments are the keyboards and rhythm guitars. You'll also be adding a brass section for some added punch. Before you do that, however, it's probably a good time to talk about musical form.

Music follows patterns. (No, really?!) These patterns are usually either 8 or 12 bars in length. Within the context of a 30-second piece of music, you won't have time to create multiple verses, refrains, and the like, but you still need to adhere to the 8-bar structure. You still need some kind of intro section, and then you need to break the rest of the piece down into 8 bar forms. With only 30 seconds to fill, you'll have time for a 2-bar intro, an 8-bar section, a 4-bar section, plus a 1-bar ending. (Now, I know what you're thinking. That doesn't add up to 8 bar segments, now does it? In point of fact, it does fit into the 8-bar form because you can also use logical divisions of the 8-bar form for intros and endings [also known as "outros"].)

You'll have the sax play the first 4 bars and then give the rest of the first 8 to the solo guitar. (If you tried to have these two instruments play at the same time, it would become too "busy.") Professional musicians refer to this as *trading fours*, and it's a time-honored tradition in music improvisation. Think of this as a conversation between two musicians—the guitarist and the saxophonist are "talking" back and forth with each other. We're listening in on their conversation.

1 Open the file **Groove-O-Matic BASIC.acd**. Note
that, depending on where you copy the WAV files,
you might have to help ACID look for the directory.
This is usually only necessary the first time you open
a file.

Notice that a couple of things have been added in
this file—notably the tracks BD Crash 1 and BD
Crash 3. These "one-shot" (nonlooping) tracks are
being used to punctuate the entrances of the soloists
and to help define the bar-form of the piece. Notice
also that the first two bars of the song have been
given to the bass as a solo. (I play bass and drums,
among several other analog instruments. I like bass
and drums. So sue me.) Finally, notice that the last
4 bars have been divided into 2-bar segments, one for
the sax and one for the guitar.

One thing you might notice about the sax and guitar
parts is that each instance doesn't necessarily start
playing at the beginning of the clip; instead, it might
start in the middle. This is important because it
means you can use portions of clips to cut and paste
new sounds from an existing clip. There's an easy
way to do this—just hold down the Alt key and click
and drag inside the instance of a clip. This will let
you set the point at which you begin to play the clip.

You've come a long way, but you have a lot more to
do to make this track really sing. For instance, you
need to learn about three important features in ACID
that enable you to do a lot more than just drag and
drop tracks onto the Timeline. First let's learn how
to split sounds and change the starting point in the
loop instance.

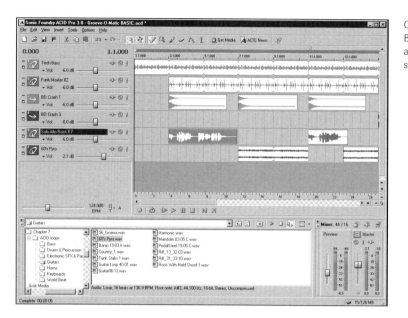

Open Groove-O-Matic
BASIC.acd. Note that the sax
and guitar parts are split up
so that they "trade fours."

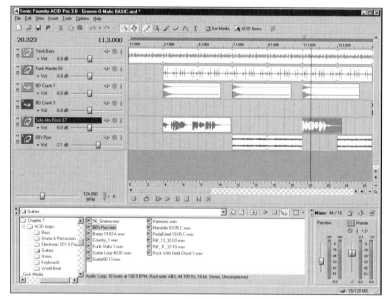

Hold down the Alt key and
click and drag inside a clip
instance to change the point
within the clip where it starts
playing.

To create a little more dynamic intro, you're going to have to "slice and dice" the bass and drum clips. You need to be able to split (and join) clip instances and use pieces and parts of a clip to create new sounds.

2   Place the time marker between the first and second bars (at 3.1 on the upper Timeline). Right-click the Tech Bass track and choose Split at Cursor.

This splits the bass track into two instances. You'll now zoom in so that you can insert just one beat of silence between the two instances.

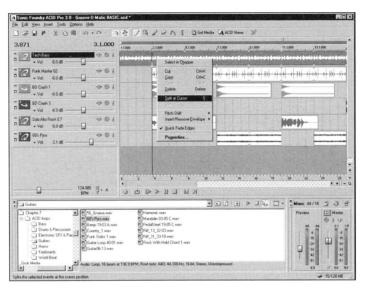

Move the time marker to the point at which you'd like to split an instance, right-click it, and select Split at Cursor.

3   Click the + button next to the horizontal scrollbar three times. This will zoom in and reveal more granular detail in the guides. Move the endpoint of the first instance back one unit. Play the track.

Now you'll add some snare drum.

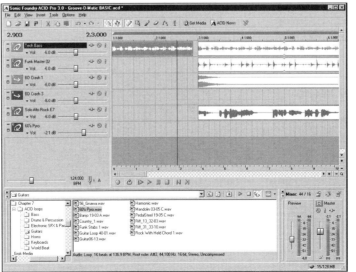

Click the + button next to the horizontal scrollbar three times to zoom in. Move the end of the first bass clip instance back one unit.

4   Drag a new instance of the Funk Master 02 clip
    somewhere in the introduction—just one or two
    units wide. Press and hold down the Alt key and then
    click and drag inside the instance either left or right.
    Click the Solo button (the Exclamation Point icon)
    on the Funk Master track to mute all the other
    tracks. Make sure the time marker is set just before
    the clip and press the spacebar to start and stop play-
    back. Adjust the clip with the Alt key/cursor drag
    technique until you get just the snare drum hit to
    play within the clip.

    The goal is to change the starting point of the clip
    within the instance. You want to isolate the snare
    drum hit and create a mini clip of just the snare.
    You'll then duplicate and use that clip to make it
    sound as if the drummer is playing a 16th note
    pattern on the snare.

5   Press and hold down the Ctrl key and drag the clip
    instance to the right. This will duplicate the instance.
    Make seven copies so that you simulate the drummer
    playing a 16th note pattern on the snare.

    Now all you have to do is to Ctrl-drag to make as
    many copies as you'd like. Drummers rarely play
    everything at the same volume, however. It would be
    nice to add some dynamics to this effect. It's easy to
    do in ACID.

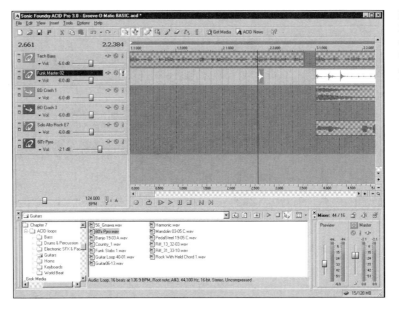

Press and hold down the Alt
key and then click inside the
clip and drag it left or right
to find the snare drum hit.
Adjust the width of the clip
to isolate the snare drum.

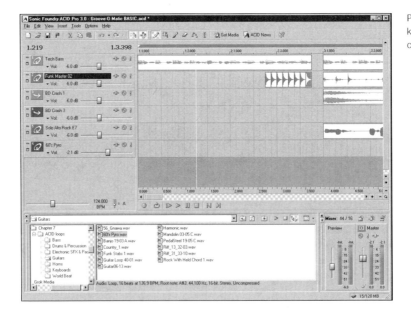

Press and hold down the Ctrl
key and click and drag the
clip to duplicate it.

6 Right-click any of the instances and select Insert/ Remove Envelope > Volume from the context menu.

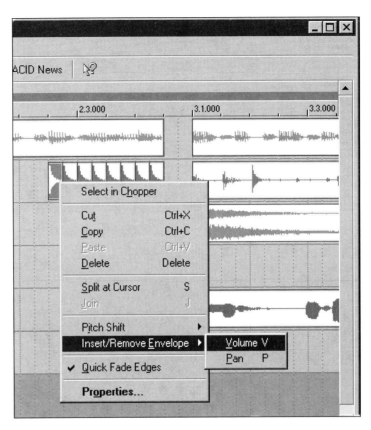

Right-click an instance in the drum track. Select Insert/Remove Envelope > Volume from the menu.

7 Right-click the red line and select Add Point from the context menu. Add several points and drag them to create a volume envelope (much like you can in Flash) to change the dynamics so that the 16th note pattern increases in volume as it plays.

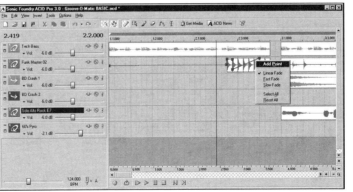

Right-click the volume indicator (red line) where you'd like to change volume. Select Add Point from the menu and drag the points to change the volume.

PLAYING THE MUSIC

To see this effect in action, let's open a different version of the file.

1 Open **Groove-O-Matic THREE.acd**. Notice that several tracks now have volume envelopes added, and a second track for Funk Master 02 has been added.

The second track for Funk Master 02 was added to use two different portions of the audio clip simultaneously—the snare hit and a bass drum/hi hat hit. The only way to do this is to drag the clip from the Explorer window onto the work area a second time to create an additional track.

Notice that a different kind of envelope has been added for the alto sax and keyboard tracks—a stereo pan envelope. Keep in mind that—within Flash, anyway—stereo tracks are usually a luxury. However, there might be situations in which you'd like to use stereo sound. It's nice to know that it's possible to do so.

The differences between what you have now and what you'll end up with have to do with layering sounds. It's that "subtext" thing again. In paintings, you rarely have a single subject—you usually find the main subject within the context of a background scene, with a number of objects in the painting that help establish scale, setting, or some other aspects of the work. Music works the same way. You have the groove established by the bass and drums that serve as a backdrop for the soloists. The soloists are in the foreground and function like the subject of a painting. It's the other instruments—keyboards, rhythm guitars, and so on—that hold everything together, supplying the subtext and populating the work with some interesting characterizations.

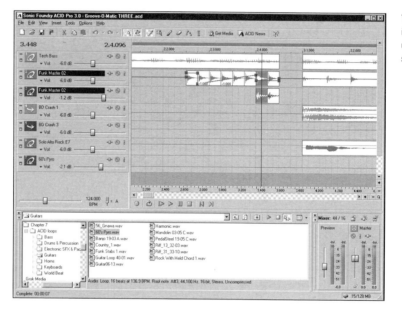

You can add a second instance of the drum track to use different portions of the same clip simultaneously.

2 Open **Groove-O-Matic FINAL.acd**. The + and – buttons enable you to adjust how many tracks you can see in the work area and how much time you can see without scrolling. Dragging the edge of a scrollbar is another way to zoom the time and/or track views in or out.

Listen to this track. Wow. *Big* difference. Let's analyze what's different in this track as compared to the previous version. First of all, two keyboard tracks (Church 1 and Church 2), a rhythm guitar track (Funk Stabs 1), and a horn section (memorably titled 043 r&b riff [a] unison) have been added.

Notice that the keyboard, guitar, and horns each "take turns" playing, filling the holes in the piece and providing some subtle punctuation for the phrases. Direct your attention to the horn track (number 11, also known as 043 r&b riff [a] unison for those of you keeping score). Note that there is a very small + superimposed over the first instance in the track. This indicates that the instance has been transposed into a different key. To see more, use the + button to the right of the horizontal scrollbar to zoom in. Essentially, all this means is that the pitch has been changed. Here's how it works:

3 Click the instance. Press the + key to raise the pitch one semitone (half-step, or from one note to the next note on the scale). Press the (you guessed it) – key to lower the pitch one half-step.

You might have no idea just how *cool* a feature this is. Back in the days of analog reel-to-reel tape decks, if you wanted to change the pitch of something, you sped up or slowed down the motors. This had the unfortunate side effect of changing both the pitch and the speed of the piece.

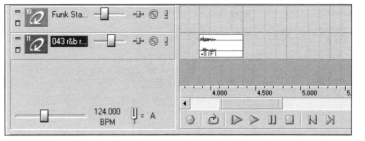

Open the Groove-O-Matic FINAL.acd file. Click the – button next to the vertical scrollbar to see more of the tracks in the work area, if necessary.

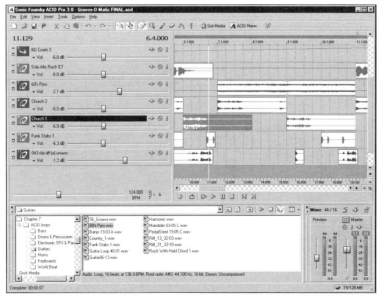

Click an instance to select it. Press the + key to raise the pitch a half-step. Press the – key to lower the pitch a half step.

In the digital age, tools like ACID Pro enable you to change the pitch but not the speed or vice versa. This is phenomenally useful in a variety of situations.

Along this same theme, notice the horizontal slider in the lower-left corner of the ACID client area. Next to the slider, you'll see 124.000 BPM and a tuning fork with = A next to it. Let's say you're working on a piece that needs to be exactly 30 seconds long. No more. No less. Despite your best efforts, your song is just a little over. You could try to cut a beat or two, but that would destroy the symmetry of the song and would violate the 8-bar form you've worked so hard to use. ACID offers you a better way. Simply move the slider and you'll see the total playing time of the tracks compress and expand as the bottom Timeline (which indicates not bars of music but actual playing time in seconds) remains the same. This enables you to change the overall tempo as necessary. Be aware that you can change the tempo only so far before it becomes painfully obvious that you have been jacking with the speed of the piece. If you click the tuning fork icon, you can transpose the entire piece without changing the tempo. Again, you can go only so far before it becomes obvious to even the casual listener that you've modified the original samples beyond what makes sense.

Note: The archetypical example of playing with tape-recording speed is the classic recordings of Alvin and the Chipmunks. Dave Bagdasarian (using the nom de artiste Dave Seville) took a recording of pop song—sans vocals—and slowed it down to half the normal speed. Using a multitrack tape deck, he layered his own voice singing harmonies. When he played the tape back at the normal speed, his voice(s) sounded like chipmunks. (Actually, there was some debate at the time as to what animal sounded like people under the influence of helium, but I digress.) Their first novelty recording—"Witch Doctor"—was a huge hit in 1958 and spawned several albums, two animated cartoon series, and several animated specials. It just goes to prove that it's possible to take some unfortunate limitation in technology and use it to create a very successful career.

Note: No matter what key your song is really in, the tuning fork in ACID has a default setting of A. There is a simple reason for this. A is the international tuning standard. Specifically, A = 440 (meaning the pitch of A is equal to 440 vibrations per second). It wasn't until 1939 that the International Standards Organization (ISO) settled on A = 440 as a universal standard for pitch. In Baroque music, A could be anything from 415 to 435 vibrations per second. Keep in mind that the tuning fork wasn't invented until 1711, and the concept of a universal standard pitch reference was not proposed until 1838. By having a universal standard, however, musicians the world over can rest assured that their instruments can be tuned to play harmoniously with everyone.

HOW IT WORKS

ACID is nothing short of an amazing application. It enables virtually anyone to create original musical compositions by dragging and dropping loops and other sound clips onto a Timeline-driven work area and then arranging them at will. Still, ACID's tools do not do away with the need to understand the form and function of music.

This project supplies a generous assortment of clips that cover a variety of musical styles. If you decide to purchase one of the retail versions of ACID, you'll acquire a library of clips along with the application. Sonic Foundry, of course, sells libraries of loops on CD-ROM in addition to giving away an assortment of clips each month to all registered users via its free online service. A significant number of third-party firms also sell commercial collections of clips and loops in a wide range of musical styles. Additionally, you can record your own sounds and convert them into loops using the tools in both Sound Forge and ACID. With all these tools at your disposal, there really is no reason to limit yourself to canned audio clips or dull and boring loops.

I encourage you to experiment with the clips on the accompanying CD-ROM and to visit Sonic Foundry on the web (**www.sonicfoundry.com**), where you'll find a significant number of free samples from each of the company's commercial libraries.

"The music really became a

cast member."

—JOEL AND ETHAN COEN,
ON THE *O BROTHER, WHERE ART THOU*
SOUNDTRACK

USING BACKGROUND
SOUND IN FLASH

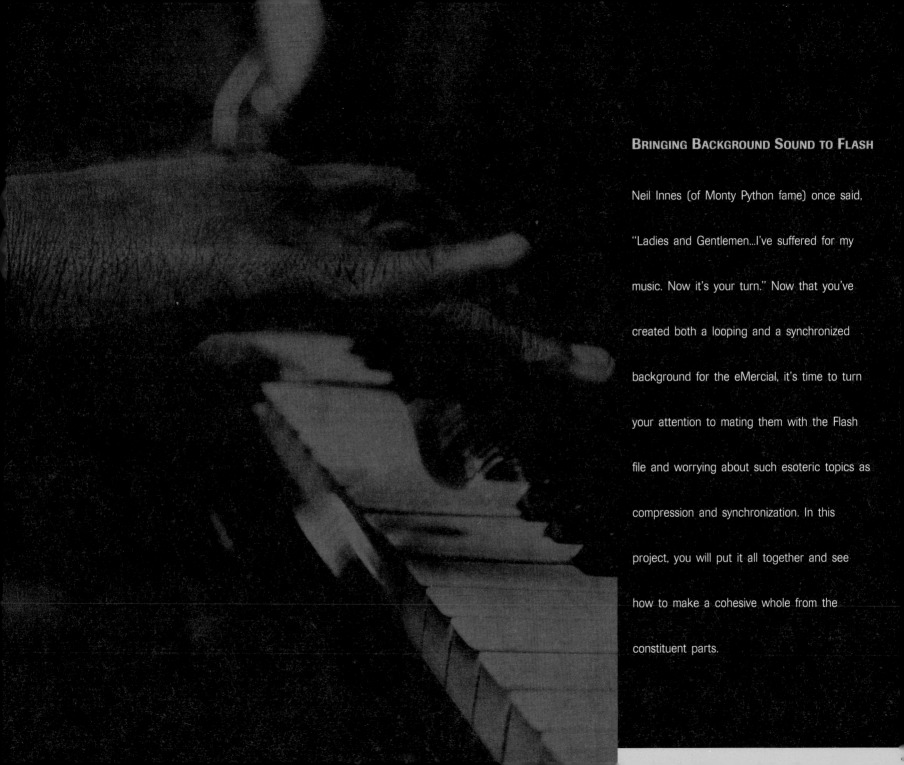

BRINGING BACKGROUND SOUND TO FLASH

Neil Innes (of Monty Python fame) once said,

"Ladies and Gentlemen...I've suffered for my

music. Now it's your turn." Now that you've

created both a looping and a synchronized

background for the eMercial, it's time to turn

your attention to mating them with the Flash

file and worrying about such esoteric topics as

compression and synchronization. In this

project, you will put it all together and see

how to make a cohesive whole from the

constituent parts.

Project 8

Using Background Sound in Flash

by Brad Kozak

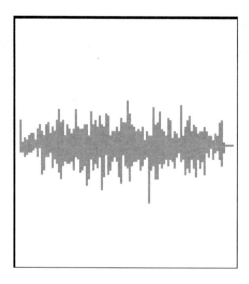

GETTING STARTED

Copy the Project 8 folder from the accompanying CD-ROM to your hard disk for speed and easy access. Install Sound Forge from the accompanying CD-ROM if you haven't already.

OPTIMIZING SOUNDS WITH FLASH COMPRESSION

This section takes a look at the subject of compression and the effect it will have on your Flash SWF file size and playback quality.

Flash is a marvelous tool. In fact, it has literally revolutionized online graphics as we know them. As wonderful as Flash is, however, it still has to contend with the mundane limitations of physics. Yes, sports fans, Flash does have its limits, especially when it comes to things like file size and audio fidelity. What it comes down to is really a numbers game. There are certain limitations that the physical world imposes on you when using audio, and you must learn to live—and work—within those limitations.

Take file size, for instance. No matter what you do, if all other factors are equal, a stereo sample is always going to be twice the size of a mono sample made from the same source material. For a long time, the best you could expect was to use a few simple algorithms to try to eke out a few kilobytes in each clip. Then the MPEG-3 format (popularly known as MP3) was standardized. MP3 compression is by far the best solution for audio today. It is the audio equivalent of one of those machines that turns a car into a small, very dense cube of metal, rubber, and plastic. With the introduction of Flash 4, MP3 became the compression tool of choice within Flash. In fact, you should use MP3 for all your work unless you plan to publish to a CD-ROM for a kiosk or for other such work in which you have absolute control over the playback environment. (In that case, you actually need just enough compression to fit all your files on the disc and in the RAM of the host computer.) For most people, however, Flash movies are destined for the web, and on the web, MP3 is the compression algorithm of choice.

The best way to figure out how compression will affect your movie is to test the actual sound file you want to use with a variety of settings.

1 Go to File > Import and change to the Project 8 folder on your hard disk. Import the **Groove-O-Matic FINAL.wav** file. Press Ctrl+L to open the Library panel. You will see the audio file listed in the Library.

You are going to try to determine two important things: the effect that compression has on sound quality and the effect it has on SWF file size. Because you won't be using the file for anything but testing, you can just drag the sound clip onto the Stage. This will put it into the main Timeline.

2 Drag an instance of the audio clip from the Library onto the Stage. This will make it appear in the first frame of the main Timeline. Click on the fifth frame and press the F5 key to add frames to the movie. Click on the Insert Layer icon (the one that looks like a page with a + symbol on it) to add a second layer.

3 On the last frame of the new layer, add a keyframe (press F6), open the Frame Actions panel (Window > Actions), click the + button, and choose Actions > Movie Control > Stop. Save your movie to the Project 8 folder as **test.fla**.

Congratulations! You now have a movie that, once started, will play the entire sound clip and then stop.

4 Hold down the Ctrl key and press Enter. This enables you to preview your movie within Flash.

If you have the bandwidth profiler turned on while you preview the movie (Ctrl+B), you'll see that you have a fairly significant memory hit on the first frame. (Because you've not built a preloader, this is exactly what you should expect.) On my system, the SWF file ends up being just over 60KB (60.7KB, if you're keeping score).

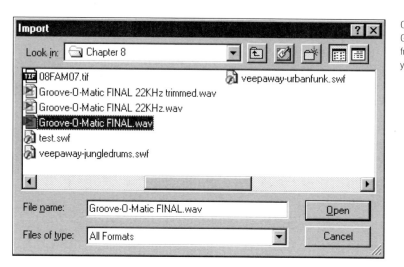

Open Flash and load Groove-O-Matic FINAL.wav from the Project 8 folder on your hard disk.

Now let's see what kind of diagnostic help Flash offers so that you can optimize the audio as much as possible.

5　Go to File > Publish Settings. Select the Flash tab and check Generate Size Report. Note that the default audio stream and event settings are for MP3, 16kbps, Mono. Make sure Override Sound Settings is *not* checked.

The size report will tell you a great deal about the inner workings of the SWF file. The original Groove-O-Matic Final.wav file was saved from ACID Pro (as you will recall from the work you did in Project 7, "Creating Synchronized Backgrounds") as a 44KHz, 16-bit, Mono file.

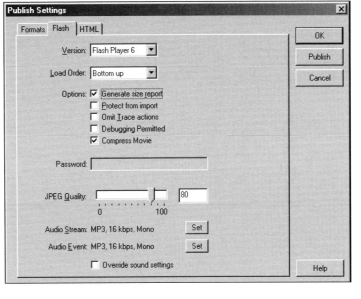

Open the Publish Settings dialog box and turn on Generate Size Report.

6　After making sure that the Generate Size Report option is selected in the Publish Settings dialog box, publish your movie. Open the file **test Report.txt** in Notepad or the text editor of your choice.

If you've never looked at a Flash report before, it can be an eye opener. You'll see a cumulative total of each frame and what it adds to the SWF file in bytes. Even better, you'll find out what Flash has done to your audio files. You can see that the sound file did not keep its original factory showroom settings; in fact, it was resampled automagically by Flash into an 11KHz, 16-bit, Mono MP3-formatted file. This is not necessarily a bad thing, but you do need to know about it. The reason this has happened is that you've not told Flash to do anything but maintain its default configurations for audio.

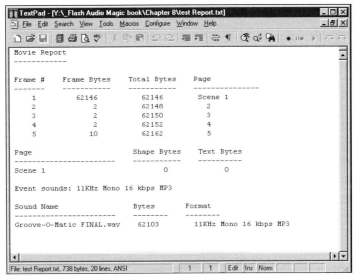

Open a text editor (like Notepad) and open the test Report.txt file.

7 Open the Library panel (if it's not already open) by pressing Ctrl+L and right-click on the icon of the audio file. Select Properties from the context menu.

Notice that the Compression setting is Default. Remember what the Publish Settings panel told you? Now you see why your audio has been unceremoniously changed into an 11KHz, 16-bit file.

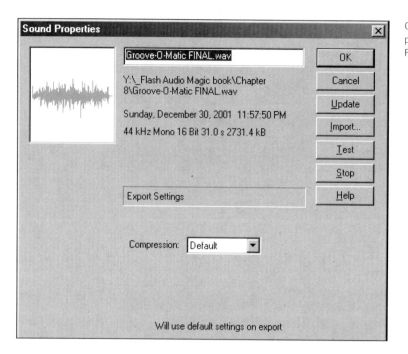

Open the Sound Properties panel for the Groove-O-Matic FINAL.wav sound.

8 Change the compression type to MP3. Click on the Test button to listen to the file.

Listen to the audio. The Test button will rock your world if you've not tried it before. You are likely to discover that there can be a huge difference between the sound qualities of different bit-rate settings in this preferences dialog box. Aside from making changes to the source WAV file in a sound editor such as Sound Forge, this is the one place where you can make a huge difference in the way sound works in Flash.

After you click the Test button, notice the line that appears at the bottom of the dialog box. This provides you with two very important numbers—the size of the audio file after it's been compressed and the relative size (in percent) as compared to the original.

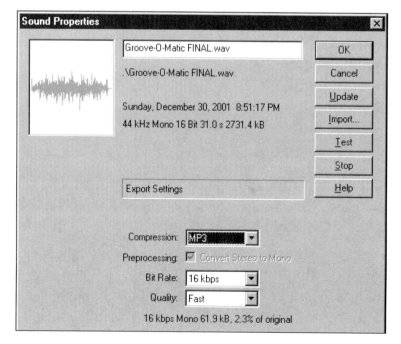

Change the compression setting to MP3. You can safely ignore the other settings for now.

Now you might want to fire up Sound Forge and listen to the original version of the file. You should notice a dramatic difference over your killer speakers and state-of-the-art amplification system. Now listen to both the original file and the compressed file over what can be generously referred to as the entry-level speakers. You will hear some difference, but it probably won't be as dramatic a difference as it was when using the better speakers. The point is that you need to take speaker quality into account when choosing a compression ratio for your files. Sound quality is (usually) just one of the factors you must consider when building a Flash project. It is easy to say "Oh, I want to work with CD-quality audio," but when it's time for your customers to play your work over the web, that CD quality is gonna cost you big time when visitors leave because it took too long to download your magnum opus.

Let's experiment with different settings in the Sound Properties dialog box. The first thing to monkey with is the bit rate.

9   Just for grins, let's shoot for the moon and change the Compression setting to 128K. Click the Test button and see what happens.

Okay, the file quality *is* better, but the file size has gone from a relatively svelte 61K to a mammoth 495.5K. Ouch! It's not bad for a file that was originally 2.6MB, but you're never gonna get anyone to wait around to download a 500K file over a modem. Let's try 24K and 48K settings and hear what *that* sounds like.

10   Change the Compression setting to 24K and click the Test button. Repeat this process with the 48K setting.

Tip: If you're like me, you've taken advantage of the dramatic drop in computer prices over the last few years and bought a PC that has a pretty decent set of speakers. Maybe you've even opted for surround sound or at least a serious woofer. Congratulations. The problem with this kind of setup is that you have no idea what your audio will sound like for the rest of the world that hasn't yet shelled out for audiophile-quality PC sound. For that, you either need to keep a crummy pair of cheap speakers around, or you can go with the ultimate test for sound: a laptop. Laptops might have come a long way in the past 10 years—active-matrix screens that rival desktops, multigigabyte drives, built-in CD/CD-R/DVD/DVD-ROM drives—but I've yet to see a laptop with speakers any better than a $5 transistor radio. Why? I have no idea. I guess it's due to the same reason why most TVs have crummy sound. The manufacturers think consumers don't care and can't tell the difference. This is again another opportunity for you to get to know your audience and design your sound for it.

Note: As I sit here in my lonely writer's garret, I find that there isn't much discernable difference between any of the settings when I play the file over my Sony laptop. (Geez...if there's any company that should know something about audio, you'd think Sony would come up with a laptop that sounds better than two tin cans and a piece of string. But I digress.) If your target audience has better sound systems and expects higher fidelity, you are going to have to either balance the need for better audio against the download times for larger files or hope that they all have DSL or cable modems.

FIXING IT *BEFORE* THE MIX

One interesting thing to try is to see what kind of difference it makes to start with a file that isn't quite so large to begin with.

1 Open Sound Forge. Load the file **Groove-O-Matic FINAL.wav**. Select Process > Resample. Change the Preset to Resample to 22,050 Hz with anti-alias filter. Click OK. Go to File > Save As and name the file **Groove-O-Matic Final 22KHz.wav**.

If you check file sizes between the two audio files (in Microsoft Windows Explorer), the new file is exactly one-half the size of the original. (Math is funny that way.) Now let's see what this does to your Flash movie.

2 Cancel the settings in the Sound Properties dialog box and go to File > Import to load the **Groove-O-Matic FINAL 22KHz.wav** file. Double-click in the main Timeline on the waveform that represents the original sound file. This will call up both the Frame Actions dialog box (which you can close for now) and the Sound panel. In the Sound drop-down selection box, change the sound from Groove-O-Matic FINAL.wav to Groove-O-Matic FINAL 22KHz.wav. Press Ctrl+Enter to test the file.

You'll see that this change has made not one bit of discernable difference in the SWF file. The overall file size is exactly the same. The only place where it *will* make a difference is in the source (FLA) file. If you are working with a very large FLA file, you might want to think about optimizing your files before you import them, just to save on the overall file size for your Flash source. On the other hand, if you feel as if you might be called on to output your Flash movies to SWFs that have higher-than-normal

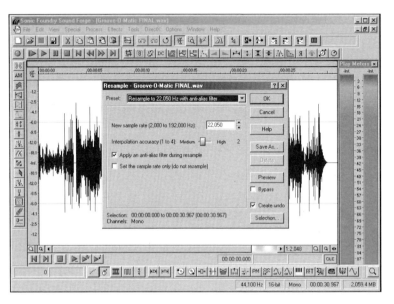

Resample the file from 44KHz to 22KHz.

124

audio fidelity, by all means import the higher-resolution files. In any case, you should always keep your original files—the original loops, ACID files, and original WAV source. This is such an important concept that I'm going to reiterate it as a Tip. (For those of you who get the importance of this concept, skip the Tip and meet me on the other side.)

Okay, now that you've finished your visit from Obvious Man, let's get back to optimizing. What are some other ways of minimizing the hit you get from adding audio? Well, you should always get rid of dead air at the beginning and end of each audio file. Go back to Sound Forge and take a look at your audio file.

3 In Sound Forge, zoom in vertically and horizontally (using the magnifying glass buttons on either end of the horizontal scrollbar). Move to the end of the waveform. Go to Process > Auto Trim/Crop. Select Trim Silence From Ends from the Preset drop-down list. Click OK. Save the file as **Groove-O-Matic FINAL 22KHz trimmed.wav**.

I know we used Auto Trim/Crop back in Chapter 3, but we didn't really touch on just how useful this is. Getting rid of the silence at the beginning and end of files is HUGE. On this file we went from 1,334KB down to 1,290KB, just by losing the dead air at the end. Not too shabby. I've seen audio-heavy Flash files lose a megabyte or more just by using Auto Trim.

Tip: No matter what happens, what you have planned, or what anyone tells you, *always* keep your original files—the original loops, ACID files, and original WAV source. After you have destroyed your source material, there is often no way to change, reconstruct, or rebuild your files. If you're lucky, you'll be able to start over and duplicate them, but even that is not a sure bet. Be wise and back up the source files.

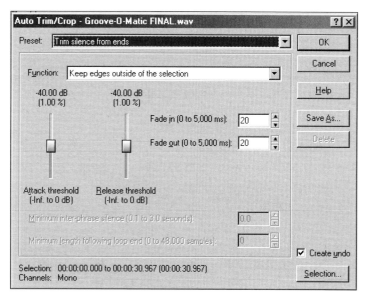

Trim the excess silence from the beginning and end of the audio clip using the Auto Trim/Crop tool in Sound Forge.

Okay, so you have efficient original samples. Now what? Well, let's get back to the discussion regarding compression.

I've found that choosing the right compression scheme is as much objective art as it is subjective science. You might reasonably assume that a 24K compressed file will always sound better, for instance, than a 16K file. Sadly, that is not the case. Particularly when using spoken-word files in Flash, I've found that there is no standard answer. Frankly, I'm stumped about this. (Probably not what you want to hear from an author when you've just shelled out money for this book, but you probably need to know this.) I've done some extensive testing of different kinds of audio files, and I've yet to see the rhyme or reason as to why some compression settings work better for some files and not for others. My best guess is that it has to do with both the volume level of the sample (which gets into sound pressure levels and all sorts of other nasty technical jargon) and the sonic frequencies of the file. What I can tell you is that there is no substitution for experimenting firsthand with your files.

USING AUDIO ON THE TIMELINE

I've compared Flash to an onion—as you get more familiar with the application, you'll discover more sophisticated ways of using it. Audio is no exception. The most obvious way to use audio is on the Timeline—usually the main Timeline because if you are trying to coordinate animations to the sound, this is the most direct way to do it.

In this project, you've seen samples and learned techniques that take the audio off the main Timeline completely and throw it into its own Movie Clip, where you can trigger it just like any other object. In the next two parts of this book, you'll see how you can use ActionScript to control audio that resides only in the Library and never even makes it into a Movie Clip on the Stage. So that begs the question, "which method should I use?" Think back to that onion analogy. Remember the layers? Now let's compare and contrast it to human development and how it relates to using Flash. Think of attaching sound directly to the main Timeline as your first baby steps. It's easy and it works, but it's somewhat limiting. As you're need to create more sophisticated movies develop, you start to think in terms of Movie Clips that can be controlled via ActionScript commands. Now you're walking. Because by this point you're comfortable with ActionScripting, you can start to think programmatically and control all your sound via ActionScripting. Realistically, even though I create a lot of advanced Flash projects, there are times that I don't take the time and effort to code every sound clip with ActionScript. What's important, though, is that by understanding the three ways of controlling sound in Flash, I have the ability to use the method that works best in a given situation.

CHOOSING A SYNC METHOD

When you first crack open Flash and get around to examining the audio features, you immediately gravitate toward sync sound. (I know. I did the same thing.) This is a mistake because sync sound has some real "gotchas" associated with it.

First of all, setting a sound to "sync" means that it is tied to the frames of the Timeline on which it sits. That means you must have a frame for every part of the waveform—no triggering the wave in a "fire and forget" mode. If the sound runs 400 frames, your Timeline has to run 400 frames. If it's any shorter, the sound will automatically stop playing when it runs out of frames. Even worse, many users report a strange effect when using the sync setting on some (but not all) sound clips in that it noticeably distorts the sound when exported to a SWF. To understand why, you must learn how sync sound really works.

The geniuses (and I mean that literally) who developed Flash had a difficult problem to solve. When audio plays, it is instantly obvious when there is something that interrupts the flow of the sound. Video is much more forgiving. Because computers first exhibited multimedia capabilities, this has been a problem—how to keep audio and video in sync. Most schemes revolve around keeping the audio as a constant, dropping frames of animation to ensure that the visual and audible content remain synchronized. Flash accomplishes this by slicing the synched audio file into small pieces, each the exact duration of one frame. If you have a sound file that should take up 400 frames, Flash dices it

up into 400 tiny sound files, bonding each to an individual frame. For some reason, some sound files take exception to this and tend to react in a noticeably noisy fashion.

One other nasty little gotcha is the sync mode's propensity to increase your file size—dramatically. If you have a looping sound, be sure to avoid sync mode because it will slice your file up for each frame it's on, and you will lose all the economies of scale you thought you were getting from using a looped sound. (Why you would need to synchronize something to a loop is another issue for another time.)

So what do you do if you must sync your audio and animations? There is a trick (I've mentioned elsewhere in the book, but it bears repeating here) that you can use to get around the limitations of sync sound. Simply create an empty (silent) sound file that is the same duration as a single frame. In other words, if you run your Flash movies at 20 frames per second, you would create a silent file that is 1/20 of a second long. Then you would import that file and place it on the main Timeline, setting it to loop for as long as you need and specifying sync as your setting of choice. Once Flash goes into sync mode, it synchronizes everything—but slices up the file that is configured to sync mode. This is an elegant workaround that I hope survives in future versions of Flash (even if they fix sync so that it never distorts even one audio file).

HOW IT WORKS

Remember the original version of the VeepAway! eMercial created in Project 6, "Creating Looping Backgrounds"? If you look in the Project 8 folder, you'll see two versions of the file—one with the drum background and one with the urban funk background created in Project 7. Open both files and export them to SWFs. Play them both and see which one you like. Both work in a similar fashion as far as the sound effects go, but the drum version uses Flash to create the overlays, whereas the urban funk version relies on ACID to build a ready-made background. Which works better? It depends on your project, your goals, and your work preferences. From here on out, though, you need not be limited to using canned sounds or short, annoying loops ever again.

CONTROLLING SOUNDS
WITH ACTIONSCRIPT

"Music is moral law—It gives wings

to the mind, a soul to the universe,

flight to the imagination, a charm to

sadness, a life to everything."

—PLATO

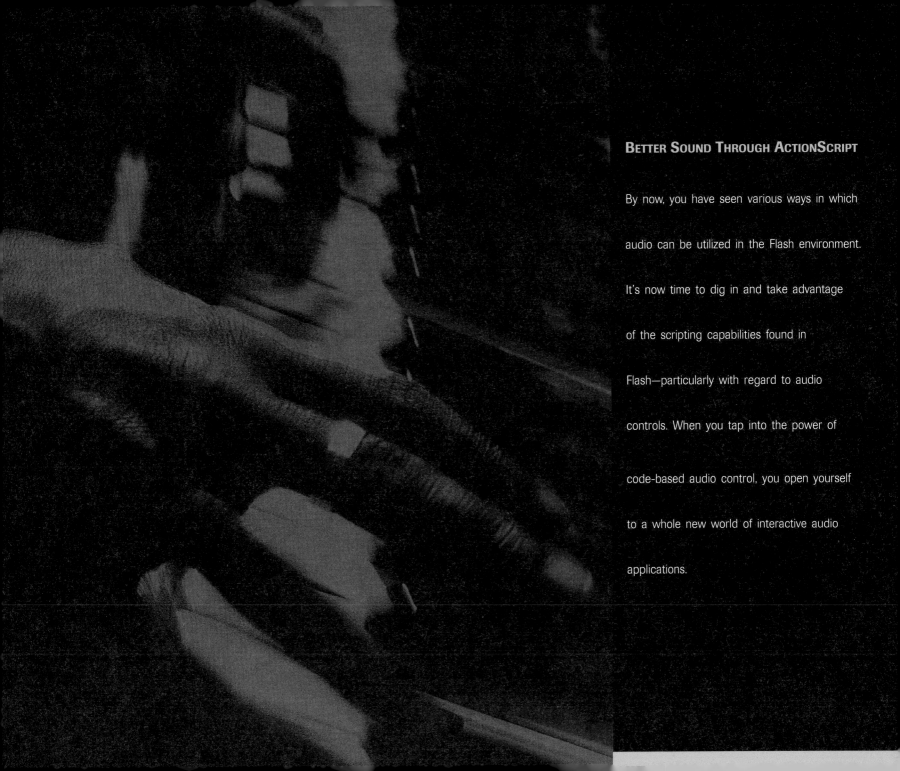

BETTER SOUND THROUGH ACTIONSCRIPT

By now, you have seen various ways in which

audio can be utilized in the Flash environment.

It's now time to dig in and take advantage

of the scripting capabilities found in

Flash—particularly with regard to audio

controls. When you tap into the power of

code-based audio control, you open yourself

to a whole new world of interactive audio

applications.

Controlling Sounds with ActionScript

by Craig Swann

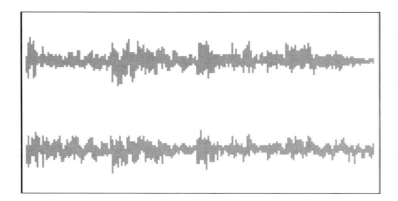

GETTING STARTED

Copy the Project 9 directory from the accompanying CD-ROM to your local hard drive. It contains two files: soundObject.fla and soundObject_final.fla. Notice that soundObject.fla is empty. It contains no symbols or Movie Clips and no frame actions in the main Timeline. It does, however, contain a sound file called s1.wav and two Movie Clips (upButton, dnButton), all of which you'll use in this project. If you want to view the completed project, open soundObject_final.fla.

ACCESSING SOUNDS THROUGH ACTIONSCRIPT VIA THE SOUND OBJECT

Controlling sound through code is obviously a little different than doing so through Movie Clips. When you trigger sound with ActionScript, you do not target Timelines, frames, or labels. Instead, you target methods and properties of sound objects directly.

The sound object was added to Flash 5 and extended through Flash MX to offer developers better control over interactive audio integration. It is only through the creation of sound objects that you can access properties such as volume and pan to affect the sonic experience. So let's quickly prove how easy all of this is!

1 Open the file **soundObject.fla** from the Project 9 directory on your hard drive.

2 Make sure your Actions panel is open (F9) and in Expert mode (Ctrl+Shift+E) and click the first frame in the ActionScript layer. Insert this code:

Here you have instantiated a new sound object and given it the name s1. Although your sound file in the Library is called s1.wav, don't be fooled into thinking that you have somehow linked the sound in the Library to your code. When using sound objects, you must attach sounds from the Library to the objects you create using the Linkage Properties dialog box.

```
s1 = new Sound();
```

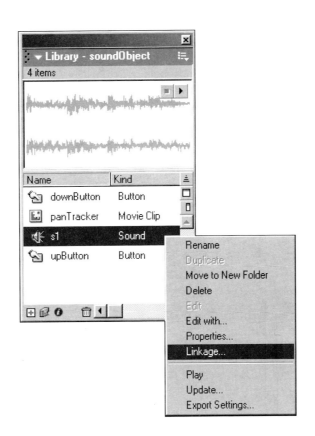

Right-clicking (Ctrl+clicking) your audio file will bring up the Linkage option.

3   Right-click (Ctrl+click on a Mac) the s1.wav symbol in the Library and choose Linkage. Select Export for Actionscript from the Linkage options. In the Linkage Properties dialog box, give the sound an Identifier of **s1**.

Now that you have exported this sound and have given it an identifier, you can attach the sound to your newly created sound object.

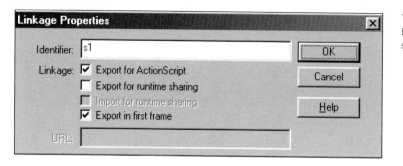

The Linkage Properties dialog box is where you identify your sounds for export.

> **Note:** The attachSound and attachMovie commands—by default—do not work with shared libraries. For this reason, you cannot attach sounds directly through a shared library.

4   Return to your frame action and add this line of code below your newly created sound object:

```
s1.attachSound("s1");
```

Now you have successfully attached the WAV file from your Library to your s1 sound object and can begin to control it through ActionScript. The first thing you'll want to do is actually start the sound so that you can hear it!

5   In the same frame action, place this code to start playing your audio:

```
s1.start(0,9999);
```

6   Test your movie to make sure you've entered everything properly. You should now be bobbing your head to some actual sound!

Before you go on and start manipulating your sound, you need to quickly learn what this last line of code is doing. Here you have the sound object's start() method, which is responsible for getting your s1 sound object to start playing. This method takes the following two parameters:

- **secondOffset.** A number indicating the time, in seconds, from which the sound should start playing. Here you used 0 to start the sound from the beginning. Had you set the argument to 2 seconds, the sound would have looped from 2 seconds into the end.

- **loops.** An integer used to represent the number of times the sound is to continue looping. If you want the sound to play just once, you set the argument to 1. Here you set it to 9999 to ensure that it continues to loop for a good period of time and does not stop on the user.

It's important to know that this start action doesn't need to be placed on a frame action. You can just as easily place this same line of code on a button action, or some other function could start the sound based on any number of criteria, such as a user submitting certain information or two Movie Clips colliding. As you continue to explore the sound object, think of interesting ways in which you can utilize sound in your projects.

Now that you've got your sound playing, you can start having some fun controlling it through some simple ActionScript.

PUMP UP THE VOLUME

The first thing you'll look at controlling is the volume. Like other methods of the sound object, volume can be controlled through different inputs. There are two methods related to the sound's volume:

- **getVolume()** does just what you might think; it gets the volume of the referenced sound object. This method is needed to control sound dynamically because you will often want to adjust the sound based on its current volume.

- **setVolume()** is another cleverly named method. You use this method to change the value of the sound object's volume.

In this exercise, you will address controlling sound with buttons, using the getVolume() and setVolume() methods.

1 In the same frame action where the rest of your code resides, add this trace statement to test the current volume level of the sound that is playing:

```
trace (s1.getVolume());
```

2   When you test the movie now, the Output window should display 100. This is the default level at which sounds begin playing. You can override this, of course, by using the setVolume() method. Insert this code before the previous trace action:

```
s1.setVolume(20);
```

When you test the movie now, you'll notice that the sound is audibly much lower, and your same trace statement is outputting a value of 20, as you just set it. Let's try utilizing these two volume methods in conjunction with some button actions.

3   Create a new layer in the movie and call it **buttons**. On this layer, drag an instance of both Movie Clips (upButton, dnButton) from the Library onto the Stage, and give them instance names the same as their Library names.

4   Select the upButton Movie Clip, give it the instance name **upButton**, and insert this code in your ActionScript frame:

```
upButton onPress = function() {
s1.setVolume(s1.getVolume() + 10);
}
```

5   Copy and paste this code in the same ActionScript frame, changing "upButton" to "downButton," as well as making sure to change "+10" to "-10" to drecrease the sound level.

If you test your movie, you'll notice that you can now control the volume of your new sound object with these buttons. But try repeatedly hitting the downButton until you hear nothing—and keep pressing. Notice that the volume begins to swell back up again! That's because Flash interprets the value of the volume as an absolute value, so a volume of –60 is the same to Flash as 60 would be. To eliminate this, you need to set up some conditionals to check the volume level and only affect volume if it is between 0 and 100.

6 Create a new layer in your movie called **textFields** and place a dynamic text field on the Stage, making sure to label it **s1volume**. You'll use this to visually display the level of your sound's volume. Replace the trace command in your Frame1 action with this line of code to display the value of the sound volume in your movie instead of the Output window:

```
s1volume = s1.getVolume();
```

7 Now you'll add a conditional if statement to your upButton action to detect the level of your volume and only increase it if it is less than 100. You'll also update your s1volume value to reflect the new volume level:

```
on(press){
if (s1.getVolume()  <100){
s1.setVolume(s1.getVolume() + 10);
}
}
```

8 Because Flash treats volume levels as absolute values, it is more important to place this same conditional code on your downButton, making sure to decrease your volume and test that your volume does not dip below 0 and cause the negative values to increase your volume:

```
downButton.onPress = function(){
if (s1.getVolume() >0){
s1.setVolume(s1.getVolume()-10);
s1volume = s1.getVolume();
}
}
```

When you test the movie now, you'll see that your buttons are properly increasing and decreasing your sound volume between 0 and 100.

FLASH IN THE PAN

Just like with volume, a similar set of methods is available for panning your sound: getPan() and setPan(). These methods enable you to control the position of your sound object in the stereo field from left to right. They work exactly the same as the volume methods, but the range for the pan of a sound is not between 0 and 100; instead, it's between −100 (left) and 100 (right). Thus, a pan level of 0 would mean that the sound is centered in the stereo field.

You could easily adjust the ActionScript you've already written for volume by altering the conditionals and substituting the pan methods in place of the volume methods, but instead, you're going to try something a little different and set your sound object's pan setting to the location of the user's mouse. Here you will learn to use dynamic values to affect your sound objects, all while creating a sonic experience that the user controls.

1   Create a new Movie Clip symbol called **panTracker** by using hotkeys (Ctrl+F8) and create a dynamic textField on its Stage. In the Text options, select Dynamic Text and label your variable as **s1Pan.** This Movie Clip will be used to track and set the pan of your sound and to update you with the pan value through this newly created textField.

2   Create a new layer called **panTracker** and drag your new panTracker Movie Clip to the Stage.

3   Select the Movie Clip and give it the instance name **panTracker** in the Instance panel (Ctrl+Option+I). Switch to Expert mode in the Object Actions panel (Ctrl+Alt+A) and enter this clipEvent code to the Movie Clip:

```
panTracker.onMouseMove = function (){
panTracker.s1Pan = Math.round(_root._xmouse/2.5) - 100;
_root.s1.setPan(s1Pan);
}
```

Here you are creating a handler—via the mouseMove action—that repeatedly calculates the pan value (s1Pan) based on the user's horizontal (_xmouse) mouse position and applies it to the s1 sound object. Notice that by calling your new pan value **s1Pan**, you can view its current value through the corresponding textField you just created.

4   Test the movie and experiment with what you've learned so far. Perhaps try to tie the volume to the user's _ymouse location—or create buttons that will change the pan settings.

How It Works

Through the use of the available sound methods—getVolume(), getPan(), setVolume(), and setPan()—you can now control your sound based on any number of criteria. Whether you use button or frame actions, the user's mouse position, or even some imported XML data, sound control is now at your disposal with the new sound object. You've been presented with the main methods used when controlling sounds. Now let's look at how you can incorporate external sound files.

STREAMING MP3 AUDIO IN FLASH

"Everybody should be able to make

some music…That's the cosmic dance!"

—MAUDE (RUTH GORDON), FROM THE

MOVIE *HAROLD & MAUDE*

IMPORTING MP3s INTO FLASH

The hottest thing in online music, without a

doubt, is MP3s. It's no surprise that Flash has

extended its capabilities in handling them. In

this project, you will look at some new methods

that enable you to dynamically import remote

MP3 files from the web, allowing you to

stream in your favorite MP3s from the web

through Flash.

Streaming MP3 Audio
in Flash

by Craig Swann

GETTING STARTED

So far, so good. You've learned how to access and manipulate sound properties of an internal sound. Well, what if you wanted the capability to load sounds dynamically just as you would with, for instance, a loadMovie command? Thanks to some new features of the sound object available in Flash MX, you can now dynamically load sounds and dynamically control them with ActionScript. Let's jump right in and discover how easy—yet powerful—this new technique is. Before we jump in, copy the Project 10 folder from the accompanying CD-ROM to your hard drive.

UTILIZING REMOTE SOUNDS: LOADSOUND

Before Flash MX, the only way you could import sounds dynamically was to create sound objects in external SWFs and load them using the loadMovie command. Now, however, with the addition of the loadSound method, you can trigger the loading of MP3 files that exist on a remote server and control them with the same properties and methods you have just explored.

1   Create a new Flash MX file and save it as **loadMP3.fla** locally on your machine.

> **Note:** If you want to view the completed file, open **loadMP3_final.fla** from the accompanying CD-ROM.

2   Label your default layer **AS**, select the first frame, and make sure you have Expert mode selected in your Actions panel.

3   Insert this code to create your new sound object:

```
mp3 = new Sound();
mp3.loadSound("http://www.ambientmusic.com/mp3s/DeepSpace.mp3", true);
```

With this second line of code, you have called the loadSound method. This particular method has just two parameters: url and isStreaming. The first parameter is the physical address of the file location you want to load into Flash. The second parameter sets whether the loaded sound should behave as an event sound or a streaming sound. If you select false, the entire file must be loaded before it can be controlled via the sound object. If the isStreaming parameter is set to True, the sound will begin to play after Flash has received sufficient data to start the MP3 decompressor.

The great thing is that you can still control this streaming sound using the volume and pan methods of the sound object.

> **Note:** Although you can now dynamically load in MP3 files, you will find that this is best used for streaming sounds—or small event sounds. It would be nice to be able to load and control looped MP3 files, but due to the compression/decompression techniques used in conjunction with MP3 files, you cannot always produce pure seamless looping.

UTILIZING REMOTE SOUNDS: onLOAD

If you want to stream an MP3 song into your Flash piece, it's as simple as that. But what if you want to have access to an event sound? Well, that's a little different because event sounds need to be entirely loaded before you can access them. Although you could use commands such as getBytesTotal and getBytesLoaded to determine whether the sound has completely loaded, with Flash MX, you now have access to the onLoad event handler, which is a function invoked when the sound has completely loaded.

1   Take a look at this code:

2   Notice that when you set the isStreaming parameter to False to identify the audio as an event sound, you use the onLoad handler to inform you when the sound is completely loaded and available to be controlled via the sound object.

All you've done is place a trace statement that will inform you via the Output window when that is. Ideally, this onLoad function could access other input data from your Flash file—variables from your movie—to determine how the sound will be manipulated, what its volume will be, what its pan settings are, what its starting position is, and so on.

```
mp3 = new Sound();
mp3.loadSound("http://www.ambient-music.com/mp3s/DeepSpace.mp3", false);
mp3.onLoad = function(){
trace ("mp3 loading complete");}
```

CREATING A FLASH-BASED STREAMING MP3 PLAYER

Now that you can see how simple it is to load and play MP3 files with Flash MX, let's add some simple code to create an MP3 jukebox of sorts. First you need the remote MP3 files that you want to access via your interface. In this section, you are going to place these in a playList array where you can easily access them through code.

1 In the same file you have been working with, simply select the code you inserted in the first frame and delete it. You're going to start from scratch. That's how easy this will be! Insert this code:

```
playList = ["http://www.ambient-music.com/mp3s/liquid_morphine_maalstroom.mp3",
            "http://www.ambient-music.com/mp3s/DeepSpace.mp3",
            "http://www.ambientmusic.co.uk/mp3/explode.mp3"];
```

What you've just created is called an array, which is an efficient way to store and access data in Flash. You can reference the third track in your playList by using playList[2]. It's important to know that the first item in an array is referenced as 0, the second item as 1, and the third item as 2, and so on. For this reason, you will set the current track to 0 when you insert this next line of code below the playList array:

```
currentSong=0;
```

It probably makes sense to have your MP3 player loop back to the first track when it has gone through the entire playList.

2 To do this, set the variable maxSongs equal to the number of songs in your playList by entering this code:

```
maxSongs = playList.length -1;
```

Because you want to know what audio you are listening to, you need to store the song titles.

3   Create another array that will store the corresponding songTitles:

Now that you've created your playList and corresponding songTitles, you're ready to start listening to your songs. You're going to use the same code just covered for loading remote sounds, but you're going to place it inside a function so that you have greater control over it.

```
songTitles =[
"Liquid Morphine - Maalstrom",
"Puchi Soundtrack - Deep Space",
"Farfield - Exploding Snowdunes "];
```

4   Create a dynamic textField on Stage and give it the variable name **songTitle**.

This will be used to visually display the audio's corresponding songTitle.

5   Now type this code in your frame action:

Try testing the movie. After the sound has loaded sufficient data to play, you'll hear the music begin. You'll also notice that when the song is over, it does not play the next song in the playList. To add this functionality, you need to access another handler to the sound object that is new in Flash MX: onSoundComplete.

```
function startStreaming(){
        _root.songTitle = songTitles[currentSong];
        mp3 = new Sound();
        mp3.loadSound(playList[currentSong], true);
}

startStreaming();
```

The onSoundComplete handler is called when a sound has finished playing in its entirety. This handy new feature enables you to properly control events based on the 100% accuracy of a sound being complete. You will use this handler to determine where you are in your playList and will use this information to begin loading and playing your next song.

6   Inside of the startStreaming function you just created, insert this onSoundComplete code:

Because this function will be called after your first song is complete, you increase the currentSong variable to move ahead in the playList. You then check to see whether this value is greater than the maximum number of songs, and if so, you set currentSong=0 to represent your first song.

7   Test the movie now and wait for the first song to finish.

Notice that the second song in your playList will begin to play after it has been buffered in Flash. You then overwrite the previous MP3 sound object you created and dynamically set the MP3 file to load by using the currentSong value to reference the URL in your playList array.

```
function startStreaming(){
_root.songTitle = songTitles[currentSong]
     mp3 = new Sound();
     mp3.loadSound(playList[currentSong], true);
}
mp3.onSoundComplete = function(){

          currentSong ++;
          if (currentSong > maxSongs){
               currentSong = 0;}

          mp3 = new Sound();
          mp3.loadSound(playList[currentSong], true);
            }

}

startStreaming();
```

ADDING THE INTERFACE

Now that you have a working prototype of your MP3 player, let's add some simple interactivity to control playback of your songs.

1 Create a new Buttons layer and access the default Buttons Library available in Flash from Window > Common Libraries > Buttons.

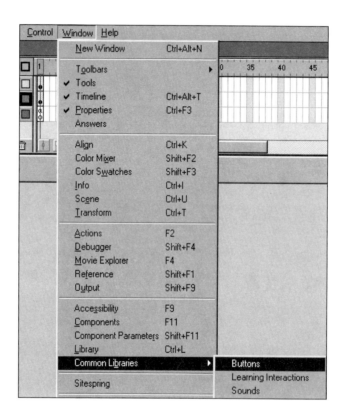

Select Buttons from the Common Libraries menu option.

2 From the Playback folder in this Library, drag the following buttons onto your newly created Buttons layer: gel Fast Forward, gel Rewind, gel Right, and gel Stop.

Select the highlighted buttons and drag them onto the new Buttons layer.

3 Let's first add stop functionality by placing this code on the gel Stop button:

```
on(press){
stopAllSounds();
}
```

4 To start your sounds again, simply call your original startStreaming() function by attaching this code to the gel Right button:

```
on(press){
        stopAllSounds();
        _root.startStreaming();
}
```

You've placed the stopAllSounds() method here to avoid having songs overlap each other if the user decides to repeatedly hit the gel Right button.

5   To control advancing/rewinding through your playList, you will create another function in Frame 1 of your ActionScript layer and insert it below the existing code:

Here your function is receiving a value for the direction parameter to determine whether the user wants to move forward through the playList or backward. The gel Fast Forward button will pass on a positive value of 1, and the gel Rewind button will pass on a negative value of 1 to represent moving backward.

The only other calculation this function performs is the evaluation of currentSong as compared to maxSongs to ensure that when you reach the end of your playList array, you return to the beginning and vice versa.

6   Finally, you call the startStreaming() function to initiate loading and playing your song.

7   Dropping this code on the corresponding buttons (gel Fast Forward, gel Rewind) will complete your interface work for the MP3 player:

8   Give your movie a test.

You'll now be able to skip through the playList as well as start and stop the audio whenever you want.

```
function playDirection(direction){
stopAllSounds();

    if(direction == 1){currentSong ++;}else{currentSong --;}
    if (currentSong > maxTrack){currentSong = 0;}
if (currentSong < 0){currentSong = maxTrack;}
    startStreaming();
}
```

GELFASTFORWARD

```
on(press){
    _root.playDirection(1);
}
```

GELREWIND

```
on(press){
    _root.playDirection(-1);
}
```

HOW IT WORKS

With the new methods included in the MX sound object, you are now able to utilize dynamic MP3s without complicated middleware solutions. Now MP3s can be dynamically imported as sound objects and manipulated just as you did with WAV files in the preceding project. There are a ton of things you could do to improve this player based on what you've already learned. For example, you could create pan and volume controls, which you'll take a closer look at in the next project.

BUILDING A
MULTISOUND MIXER

"There's music in the sighing of a reed;

There's music in the gushing of a rill;

There's music in all things, if men had ears;

Their earth is but an echo of the spheres."

—LORD BYRON

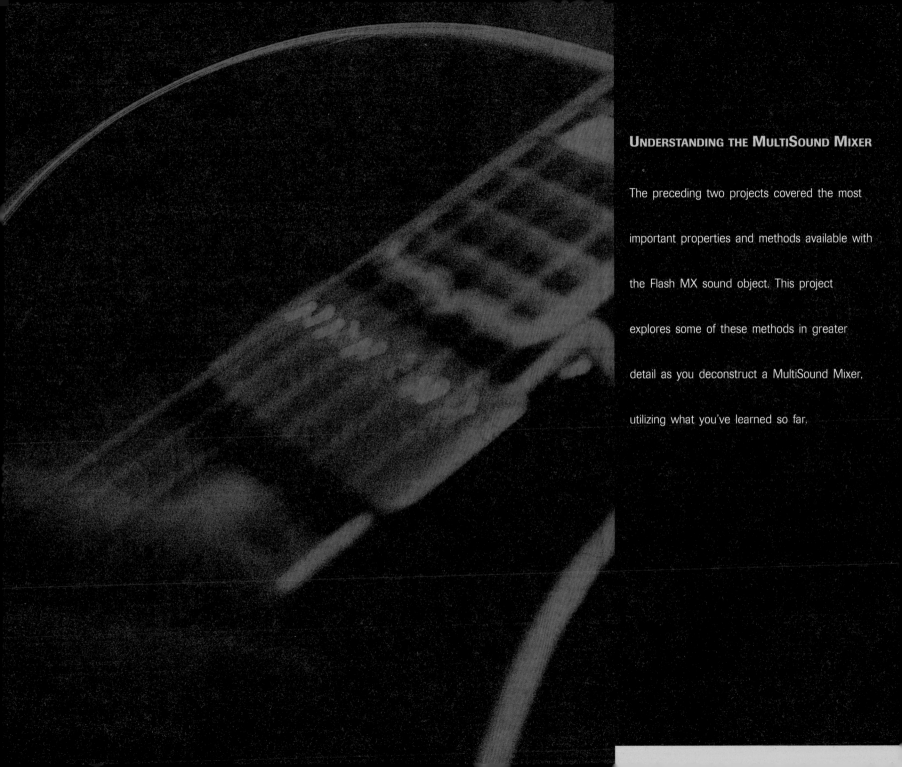

UNDERSTANDING THE MULTISOUND MIXER

The preceding two projects covered the most

important properties and methods available with

the Flash MX sound object. This project

explores some of these methods in greater

detail as you deconstruct a MultiSound Mixer,

utilizing what you've learned so far.

Building a MultiSound Mixer

by Craig Swann

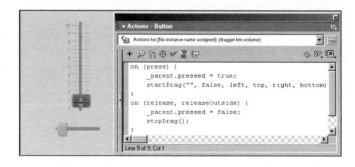

GETTING STARTED

Copy the Project 11 folder from the accompanying CD-ROM to your hard drive for speed and ease of access.

USING MULTIPLE SOUND OBJECTS

Until now, you've only been using single sounds at a time. All the sound objects have been created on the main Timeline in frame actions. In essence, you've been creating *global* sound objects. For instance, if you had added another sound object in either of the examples from the preceding project and performed a setVolume() operation, the same volume would have been applied to both of the sound objects.

Much like targeting Movie Clips with ActionScript, you need to create separate instances of your sound objects. Do this by creating your sound objects inside a separate Timeline, such as a Movie Clip. By doing this, you can separately trigger and control distinct properties of different sound objects, enabling you to create more complex audio applications. The MultiSound Mixer application obviously uses multiple sounds. You'll control them by building Movie Clip controllers.

A Bird's Eye View

Before digging into functions, methods, and clipEvents, open the file and acquaint yourself with the structure of the mixer.

1   Fire up Flash MX and open the **MultiSoundMixer.fla** file from the Project 11 folder on your hard drive.

The movie consists of just two frames and five layers: actionScript, preloader, mixerMC, start/stop btn, and bgGraphics.

The names are quite indicative of the content and purpose of each layer. The first frame is used to place the bg graphics on Stage, set some preliminary functions, and start the preloader. The second frame is where sound elements are created and placed on the Stage.

2   The actionScript layer is where you place global functions to dynamically create and display the mixer controls. You add these functions in frame actions located on the first frame of the actionScript layer, as shown in the accompanying code:

Here you simply set an fscommand to disallow scaling of your movie when it is exported—no big deal. The important piece of code is the variable maxSounds. This variable dictates how many sound objects you are going to build. If you only want to use four sounds, for example, change this value to 4. This variable is needed for the rest of the code in this frame.

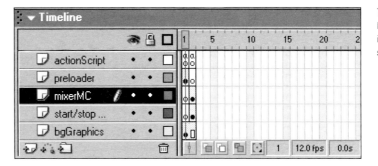

This snapshot of the MultiSoundMixer.fla Timeline illustrates layer and code structure.

```
fscommand("allowscale", "false");
var maxSounds = 6;
```

BUILDING MULTIPLE SOUND OBJECTS

The accompanying function is defined in your first frame and is called in the second frame of the actionScript layer after preloading is complete. It uses duplicateMovie Clip to create new instances of your mixer Movie Clip, which appears on Stage in frame 2 of the mixerMC layer.

1   Notice the variable maxSounds. This value is used here to dictate the maximum number of instances to duplicate. Dynamically set the _x and _y properties of the duplicates as shown and attach an id value, which you later use to independently control your sounds.

You have carefully created your audio files so that they are all running at the same beats per minute (bpm), ensuring they will mix well together.

2   Use this function to simultaneously start these sound loops:

Again, use the maxSounds value, this time to determine the amount of sound to start playing. Set the volume and trigger the sound to start and loop 999 times.

3   The first time this for loop runs, it triggers the sound to start like this, where i = 1:

```
_root.mixer1.loop.start(0,999);
```

Notice that the name of the sound object you are starting is loop, which is located inside the duplicated mixer Movie Clip. To get a better understanding, take a peek at the mixer Movie Clip.

```
function build () {
    for (var i = 1; i<=_root.maxSounds; i++) {
        duplicateMovie Clip ("mixer", "mixer"+i, i);
        _root["mixer"+i]._x = 55+(i-1)*100;
        _root["mixer"+i]._y = 55;
        _root["mixer"+i].id = i;
    }
}
```

```
function startSounds(){
    for (var i = 1; i<=_root.maxSounds; i++) {
        _root["mixer"+i].loop.setVolume(_root["mixer"+i].volume);
        _root["mixer"+i].loop.start(0, 999);
    }
}
```

MIXER MOVIE CLIP

This is where you initialize your sound objects.

1 Take a look at the mixer Movie Clip by double-clicking it in the second frame of the main Timeline. Notice the code attached to its first frame.

2 This function creates the loop object you were just wondering about. It also uses the id variable you set when you duplicated the Movie Clip. This id value dynamically assigns the sound to be attached to the loop sound object. Because the maxSounds value was 6, each duplicate (mixer1…mixer6) will attach a corresponding track (track1…track6). If you take a look at the linkage properties for the WAV file called TRACK1 in the loops folder of the Library, you'll notice that its linkage name is, in fact, track1.

Now that you've taken a look at how sound objects are generated by duplicating Movie Clips, take a closer look at the code associated with this mixer Movie Clip.

```
function initializeSound() {
    loop = new Sound(this);
    loop.attachSound("track"+id);
}
initializeSound();
```

TRACKING THROUGH clipEVENTS

clipEvents are handlers associated with Movie Clips. The mixer Movie Clip uses both the load and enterFrame clipEvents in our example. These actions are not placed *inside* the Movie Clip but *onto* the Movie Clip by selecting it on the Stage.

1 The load clipEvent is executed when the Movie Clip is first instantiated on the Timeline. It contains this code:

```
onClipEvent(load){
//initialize x,y positions
sliderVolume.dragger._x = sliderVolume.box._x;
sliderVolume.dragger._y = sliderVolume.box._y;
sliderPan.dragger._x = sliderPan.box._x+ (sliderPan.box._width/2);
sliderPan.dragger._y = sliderPan.box._y;

//define the ratio for volume(100 units- from 0 to 100)
volRatio = (sliderVolume.box._width-sliderVolume.dragger._width)/100;

//define the ratio for vpan(200 units- from -100 to 100)
panRatio = (sliderPan.box._width-sliderPan.dragger._width)/200;

//reference x
minVol=sliderVolume.box._x;
minPan=sliderPan.box._x;


function setVolumeF(){
        volX=sliderVolume.dragger._x;
        volume = Math.floor((volX - minVol)/volRatio);
        loop.setVolume(volume);}

function setPanF(){
        panX=sliderPan.dragger._x;
        pan= Math.floor((panX - minpan)/panRatio)-100;
        loop.setPan(pan);}

setVolumeF();
setPanF();

}
```

The majority of this code simply establishes initial _x and _y positions for the volume- and pan-related Movie Clips that work in conjunction with the draggable Movie Clips. At a later time, feel free to poke around this code and get a feel for how to grab values from the volume and pan sliders. For now, focus on the two functions you have set:

```
function setVolumeF(){
        volX=sliderVolume.dragger._x;
        volume = Math.floor((volX - minVol)/volRatio);
        loop.setVolume(volume);}

function setPanF(){
        panX=sliderPan.dragger._x;
        pan= Math.floor((panX - minpan)/panRatio)-100;
        loop.setPan(pan);}
```

2 These functions are responsible for translating the position of the volume and pan sliders of the mixer Movie Clip into volume and pan settings using setVolume and setPan. After these functions have been declared onLoad, you can trigger them through the enterFrame handler.

```
onClipEvent (enterFrame){

        if(sliderVolume.pressed){
        setVolumeF();}

        else if(sliderPan.pressed){
        setPanF();}
}
```

3 These if statements are performed continually during every frame of your movie, even if you have a stop() action on a frame. You can see that if either sliderVolume or sliderPan is pressed, the functions from onLoad are called to modify the volume or pan.

4 The pressed value is determined by a button inside of a dragger Movie Clip within sliderVolume and sliderPan that contains this code:

These simple actions toggle the functions set earlier, controlling sound volume and pan as the user is interacting with the controls.

You can see that the complexity in creating audio applications doesn't lie so much in working with the sound object itself but in deriving creative ways to manage and control the properties of sound. Check out **www.looplabs.com** if you are interested in seeing some other possibilities.

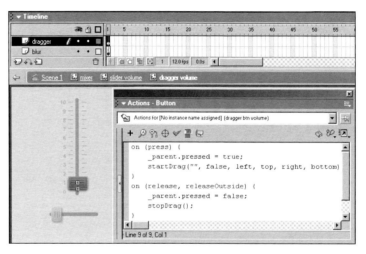

This shows the dragger Movie Clip and actions that control volume and pan.

```
on (press) {
     parent.pressed = true;
     startDrag("", false, left, top, right, bottom);
}
on (release, releaseOutside) {
     _parent.pressed = false;
     stopDrag();
}
```

HOW IT WORKS

This project covers a lot of ground, and although it deconstructs the manipulation of the sound object, if you are new to ActionScript, you might want to just take a peek around—particularly in the mixer Movie Clip—to see how it all comes together. Most importantly, take this opportunity to reflect on what you have learned here and

to imagine what is now possible with audio. Think of creative ways in which audio can be controlled—by user input, dynamic data, or just plain randomly. Experiment! Audio is perhaps the most powerful stimulus we have as multimedia developers. Have some fun with it!

DESIGNING GAME ARCHITECTURES

"Advertising is to art what the banjo is

to an orchestra."

—MARTIN MULL

MEMOSCILLATION

Games are applications designed to entertain
and challenge. Most people can probably recall
long hours spent on a console or computer trying to resolve a clue or learn all those fighting
moves and special attacks. Creating a successful video game is like lighting a never-ending
campfire; an unlimited number of joyful people
will gather around over and over, keeping it
alive. The better the game is, the longer people
will keep it in their memory. Your video game
will also be an eternal representation of a year,
of a period of time—related not only to the
world but also to the person's life.

This game project is called *memoscillation*. It is
made of two words: memory and oscillation.
(An oscillation is a sound's vibration, the basis
of all sounds.) It's designed to challenge and
train people's musical memory, just like the
classic game of memory but with sounds
instead of images. Each level is a different
musical instrument, with six different sentences
I quickly improvised on my keyboard.

Project 12

Designing Game Architectures

by Manuel Clement

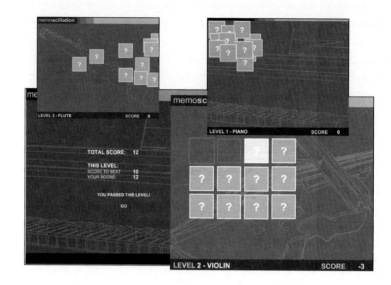

GETTING STARTED

To play memoscillation, the player presses buttons and hears different musical phrases.
To win, two identical sounds need to be matched in one turn; a turn is two clicks.
There are six sounds to match on a grid of 12 buttons. When the six sounds are found,
the score of this level is calculated. If the score is higher than or equal to 10, the player
wins and passes to the next level. Players need to memorize the location of the different
musical phrases to get back to them after finding their match.

In this project, you will design the foundation and architecture of the game. The game
engine uses ActionScript to do everything, from building the interface dynamically to
starting and stopping sounds. You will keep track of which buttons are pressed and
which sounds are triggered. This game can be played at **www.mano1.com** with new
levels and a database-driven high-scores table. Before you start, copy the contents of
the Project 12 folder from the accompanying CD-ROM to your hard drive.

A Look into the Concept

The game is made of several Flash movies. The first one, memoscillation.swf, contains the game engine and the graphics. The others (level1_sounds.swf, level2_sounds.swf, and so on) contain the sounds for each level. The ActionScript engine will load them as needed. This sort of architecture eases the process of adding levels to the game. Each important phase of the game (the levels, the score-calculation screen, the game-over screen, and so on) has a labeled keyframe on the main Timeline that will display as needed. Every piece of script in this project is contained inside individual functions, and the script is called when needed.

I believe that keeping all your actions in the same place, as a Library of reusable functions, is the best way to ensure optimal continuity and consistency in a Flash project. Although this first part of the project is not entirely focused on audio, it is very important to cover these concepts of application design and programming.

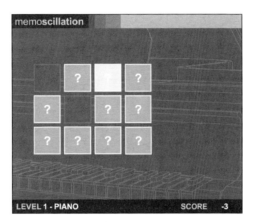

A typical level screen.

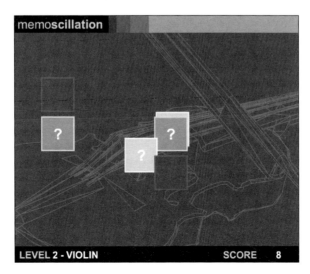

Another level. When two sounds are matched, the squares fly away.

THE ROLE OF IMPORTANT ELEMENTS

It is important for you to learn a bit more about the different elements of the game. Some are visible on the Stage when you open the exercise source file (**12_start.fla** for our exercise); others are visible only in the Library.

Look at the image containing the Library symbols. As you can see, I am using folders to organize my assets—grouping background graphics, interface symbols, various layout graphics, and so on. Folders enable you to make sure anyone (including you) will understand what your project contains when opening the .fla source file.

As you can see, the interface folder contains one symbol called button. This is not a button symbol but a Movie Clip with a text field to display a ? character on the buttons and a square graphic in the background. Inside it, a few keyframes are labeled light and dark, which will be used to make your buttons lighter or darker as needed during a game. This button symbol is the most important item of the Library, and it will be reused for the whole interface.

This figure contains the four Library elements.

DECLARING VITAL VARIABLES AND ARRAYS

The first step is to declare a few variables and create a few arrays. These will store values used by the game engine.

1   Open the file **12_Start.fla** from the Project 12 folder on your hard drive.

As you can see, this file contains a few labeled keyframes, and for each frame, the graphics on the Stage change. Here is an explanation of each main keyframe:

A: The first frame of the movie where you will write all the functions.

B and C: On these frames, you will call the function that checks whether the whole movie is loaded.

D: Checkpoint. This is where the engine checks whether the user has enough points to go to the next level and shows the total score.

E: Init. This is where the game interface and the sound container are built. Again, an ActionScript function will be called.

F: Pass. When the user passes a level, you'll calculate the number of the next level and load it.

G and H: Another loading loop. This time you check whether the new level is loaded.

I: Loaded. No action will be set here. It is just the frame that is played when a level is loaded.

J: Here you'll change the color scheme and the background image.

K: After providing some time for the background to fade in (between J and K), you finally start the level and stop the playback.

L: Game over. You will call the gameOver( ) function, which will end the game and display the final score.

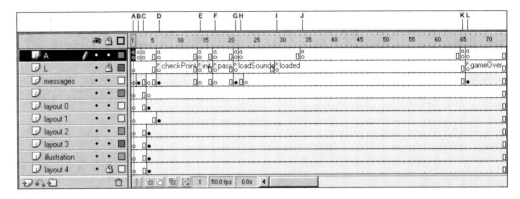

The Timeline. The letters A to L are here to highlight the important keyframes.

2 Click on frame 1 on the layer labeled A (A is for
   Actions). Insert this code to declare a few important
   variables:

   globalButtons is the number of buttons (12).
   globalSounds is the number of sounds (globalButtons
   divided by 2, or 6). globalLevels is the number of
   levels (4 in this exercise). Finally, minScore is the
   score that the user needs to beat to pass a level.

   Now that the variables are declared, you need to
   create a few arrays. Arrays are lists of items that the
   engine can access later. They're like variables with an
   unlimited number of slots to store values.

```
// IMPORTANT VARIABLES
globalButtons = 12;
globalSounds = globalButtons / 2;
globalLevels = 4;
minScore = 10;
```

Important variables are declared. You will use these values later in the project.

3 Insert the instruments array code. This array contains all the instruments featured in the levels of the
   game. In this example, there are four levels and thus
   four instruments: piano (level 1), violin (level 2),
   flute (level 3), and French horn (level 4).

```
instruments = new Array("PIANO", "VIOLIN", "FLUTE", "FRENCH HORN");
```

4 Create two new empty arrays: sndHistory and
   btnHistory. The sndHistory array will be used to
   store a history of the sounds triggered during the
   game. btnHistory array will store the list of buttons
   pressed. Creating these arrays will enable you to
   make the engine know the preceding sounds, detect
   when the user matches them, and make the buttons
   fly away, lighten, or darken as needed.

```
sndHistory = new Array();
btnHistory = new Array();
```

5 Insert the code to declare the xArray and yArray
   arrays. They contain the x and y coordinates for each
   of the 12 buttons that form the interface. To come
   up with these numbers, I previously placed the 12
   squares on the Stage by hand and used the Info panel
   to find the x and y coordinates.

```
xArray = new Array (90, 169, 248, 327, 90, 169, 248, 327, 90, 169, 248, 327);
yArray = new Array (160,160, 160, 160, 239, 239, 239, 239, 318, 318, 318, 318);
```

6 Create the scoreList array. Each time the user passes a level, the score he makes is stored in this list. It enables you to check whether the last completed level's score is enough to pass to the next level. It also enables you to calculate the total score by adding all the levels' scores together.

```
scoreList = new Array(0);
```

7 Create a new array element to control the color scheme, which changes each time a new level starts. This is the list of objects (Movie Clips by their instance name) that should be colored by the engine.

```
elements = new Array("layoutTop", "layoutBottom", "layoutBackground",
"interface.pad1", "interface.pad2", "interface.pad3", "interface.pad4",
"interface.pad5", "interface.pad6", "interface.pad7", "interface.pad8",
"interface.pad9", "interface.pad10", "interface.pad11", "interface.pad12");
```

8 Save the file as **12_Middle.fla**.

INITIALIZING THE GAME

You need to create a function, init(), that will be triggered every time the player starts a new game. It will build the interface: a Movie Clip and 12 buttons inside it, plus the sound engine (a Movie Clip and an ActionScript sound object assigned to it).

1 Return to frame 1, layer A (the Actions layer), where you previously declared the vital variables and arrays of the game engine. Insert this code. This is just the beginning of the init() function.

```
function init(){
    illustration.gotoAndStop(1);
    level = 0;
```

illustration.gotoAndStop(1); tells the illustration Movie Clip containing the level background graphics to go to frame 1. On frame 1 of this Movie Clip, nothing is visible. Basically, you are clearing the background in case a level illustration was visible. level = 0; tells the engine what level to load next. Because this is the initialization, you want to set it to 0. You might wonder why you are not setting it to 1. The reason is that the engine automatically increments this variable by one before loading a new level; thus, the first level that the engine will load is 1.

2 Insert this new code:

The first line creates an empty Movie Clip on the Stage with the instance name interface. The depth where it will be placed using createEmptyMovieClip() is 2. This useful new Flash MX method avoids the need to create and store empty Movie Clip symbols in the Library. By default, you want your interface to be invisible—use Interface._visible = false for this purpose.

```
createEmptyMovieClip("interface", 2);
interface._visible = false;
```

3 Insert this code:

This code creates 12 buttons (the value of the globalButtons variable) inside of the empty interface Movie Clip. You are using a for loop construct to dynamically attach and name the buttons. Each button of the interface is a copy of the button Library symbol whose export name is button. Notice that here you call each button pad + i. In fact, i is a number which changes from 1 to 12 as the for loop is executed. The Movie Clips will be called pad1, pad2, pad3, and so on up to pad12.

The next 4 lines of code define event handlers on each button. onEnterFrame (meaning at every frame), you call the function move(); onRelease (after the user clicks on the Movie Clip), you call the engine() function; onRollover, you scale up the Movie Clip; and onRollOut, you scale it down again. The functions mentioned here will be created and explained later in this chapter. This way to remotely define actions for event handlers is extremely powerful; it was introduced in Flash MX.

```
for (i=1; i<=globalButtons; i++){
    interface.attachMovie("button", "pad" + i, i);

    interface["pad" + i].onEnterFrame = function (){move(this); }
    interface["pad" + i].onRelease = function (){engine(this.sound, this._name);}
    interface["pad" + i].onRollOver = function (){this._xscale = 110; this._yscale = 110;}
    interface["pad" + i].onRollOut = function (){ this._xscale = 100; this._yscale = 100;}
}
```

4 Create another empty Movie Clip, and name it **container**. This Movie Clip will contain the Sound object, used to start and stop sound.

```
createEmptyMovieClp("container",3);
```

5 Finally, a new sound object, sounds, is created inside
   the sound container, and you close the function with
   a }. The sound object enables you to start, stop,
   control the volume, and more on *any* sound located
   inside the specified target (in this case, _root.
   container). The function is closed with a right
   curly brace.

   Your final init( ) function code should look like this:

```
        sounds = new Sound("container");
}
```

```
function init()
{
        illustration.gotoAndStop(1);
        level = 0;

        createEmptyMovieClip("interface", 2);
        interface._visible = false;

for (i=1; i<=globalButtons; i++){
        interface.attachMovie("button", "pad" + i, i);

        interface["pad" + i].onEnterFrame = function (){ move(this); }
        interface["pad" + i].onRelease = function (){ engine(this.sound, this._name);}
        interface["pad" + i].onRollOver = function (){ this._xscale = 110; this._yscale
        ➥= 110;}
        interface["pad" + i].onRollOut = function (){ this._xscale = 100; this._yscale =
        ➥100;}
}
// build sound container
        createEmptyMovieClip("container", 3); // build sound container
        sounds = new Sound("container"); // create sound object in container
}
```

6 The init( ) function needs to be called to trigger the actions contained inside it. On the Timeline, click on the empty keyframe on the Actions layer (A) on frame 14 and add this line of code:

This is a basic function call. It means that when this frame is played, the init( ) function will be called, triggering all the actions inside it. The game will be initialized.

```
init();
```

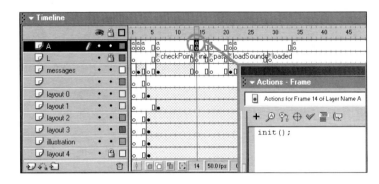

The init( ) function is called on frame 14. The action is placed on the Actions layer (A), circled in red.

MOVEMENT WITH ACTIONSCRIPT

The init( ) function, among other things, creates the interface, made up of one Movie Clip (_root.interface) containing 12 other Movie Clips (_root.interface.pad1 to _root.interface.pad12), which are the buttons. You want to be able to tell the buttons to fly on the screen (forming the interface grid) or to fly away from the screen when needed.

To create this programmatic movement, you will proceed with two steps.

First, you will define a new function, move(), which will constantly be called from each button Movie Clip (onEnterFrame event). This function will calculate the distance between the actual position of a square and a new destination coordinates set by the engine, and it will move the square to this destination.

1 Go back to the actions on frame 1 of the Actions layer (A). Type this code:

A new function is declared. The word target is an argument. When this function is called, a value will be sent as well. This value will be reused inside the function.

```
function move(target){
```

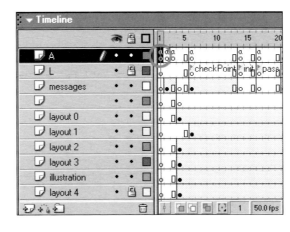

For this step, you will add more actions to frame 1 of the Actions layer (A), circled in red.

2 Add these two lines of code:

The distance between the actual position of the square and a possible new position set by the engine is calculated every time the function is called. distX is the distance horizontally, distY vertically. NewX and newY will be set by the engine if you want a square to move to a new position.

```
target.distX = (target.newX - target._x);
target.distY = (target.newY - target._y);
```

3 Now that you've calculated the distance you can move the square toward the new position, insert these new lines:

This will move the square gently in the direction of the new position. The square will seem to slow down as it approaches its destination because you only move the square by a fraction of the distance each time. Finally, the function is closed by a right curly brace.

The moveSquare() function is being created. You will now call it constantly from every square of the interface. Thanks to the modular architecture, it will be very easy to achieve this.

```
        target._x += target.distX / target.inertia;
        target._y += target.distY / target.inertia;
}
```

169

LOADING THE NEXT LEVEL

You have created the function that initializes the game, and the one that makes the interface buttons move. The next one to create is called passLevel( ). This function, when called, will calculate which level should be loaded next and loads it (for example, level1_sounds.swf for level 1). It also checks to see if no more levels are available. If this is the case, it goes back to level 1.

1   On the main Timeline, edit the actions of frame 1 on the Actions layer (A) and insert this new code:

    Our passLevel() function is created. The if action increments the level variable by 1, as long as globalLevels (the number of levels) is not reached. If it is reached, it sets the level to 1. loadMovie() loads the new level into the sound container. Look at the way the name of the file is constructed: "level" + level + "_sounds.swf", where level is replaced by a number.

```
function passLevel(){
        if (level < globalLevels){    level += 1 } else {level = 1}
        loadMovie("level" + level + "_sounds.swf", container);
}
```

2   Now that the passLevel() function has been created, you just need to call it from a frame. Edit the actions of keyframe 17 on the Actions layer (A) and insert this code:

```
passLevel();
```

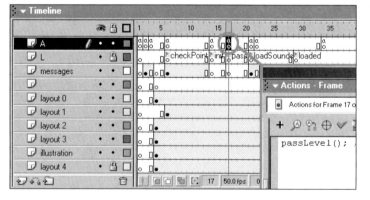

The function passLevel() is called on frame 17.

170

GENERATING A RANDOM COLOR SCHEME

When a new level has been loaded, the engine will trigger a new function called visuals( ). It displays the background image of the new level (for example, a violin for level 2), and it also generates a random color and assigns it to a list of elements.

1   Add this code to frame 1 on the Actions layer (A) with the other functions:

The beginning of the visuals( ) function is created, and three variables—rb, gb, and bb—are declared as random numbers between 0 and 49 (red, green, and blue). Because you are using var, these values will be removed from memory after the function is executed.

```
function visuals(){
        var rb = random(50);
        var gb = random(50);
        var bb = random(50);
```

2   Insert this code to declare the variable myColorTransform:

This variable will be used to feed the Color object with the new random color. The random variables rb, gb, and bb are used to format a value (myColorTransform) that can understand the Color object.

```
var myColorTransform = { ra: '100', rb: rb, ga: '100', gb:
➥gb, ba: '100', bb: bb, aa: '50', ab: '255'}
```

3   Add this code to create Color objects for all the elements you want to colorize (from the elements array) and to assign them with the random color that was previously generated and formatted. To do so, you are using setTransform( ) and a for loop.

```
for (i=0; i<= (elements.length -1); i++){
        c = new Color(elements[i]);
        c.setTransform(myColorTransform);
}
```

4   Finally, add this code to display the new background image for this level:

Backgrounds are contained inside the illustration Movie Clip. For example, the background for level 2 is on frame 3 of this Movie Clip. This is why you tell it to go to frame (level + 1) and stop. The function visuals( ) is closed by a right curly bracket.

```
        illustration.gotoAndStop(level + 1);
}
```

5 The visuals( ) function needs to be called now. Edit the actions of frame 34 on the Actions layer (A). Enter the code to call the function:

```
visuals();
```

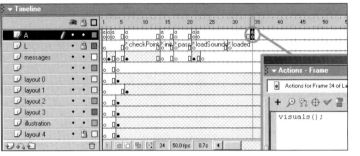

The function visuals( ) is called on frame 34.

STARTING THE NEW LEVEL

The game has been initialized, the new level number has been calculated and loaded, and the level's color scheme and backgrounds are ready. What's next? You need to create a function assigning random sounds (from the 6 sounds available) to each of the 12 buttons. Finally, the function will tell all the buttons to form the interface grid, feeding them with a new destination. The move( ) function will move the squares to reach these new coordinates. This new function is called newLevel( ).

1 Edit the actions of frame 1 of the Actions layer (A). Add this code:

```
function newLevel(level){

        interface._visible = true;
        textLevel._visible = true;

        textLevel.score = 0;
        textLevel.level = level + " - " + instruments[level - 1];
        won = 0;

        prevBtn = null;
        currBtn = null;
```

This is the start of the newLevel( ) function. Because later on the game makes some layout elements invisible, here you need to make sure they are visible. Using the _visible property, the function sets some elements (the interface, the text displaying the level, and the score) to be visible. Next, the score of this level is set to 0, and the title is changed to show the new level number and which instrument it features (for example, 2 – VIOLIN). Both text fields are contained in the textLevel Movie Clip on the Stage. To pull the instrument's name, you access the instruments array. The won variable is set to 0, which makes the engine understand that the user has not matched a sound yet. Finally, both the prevBtn and currBtn variables are set to null. These variables are used by a function that will be added later in this project.

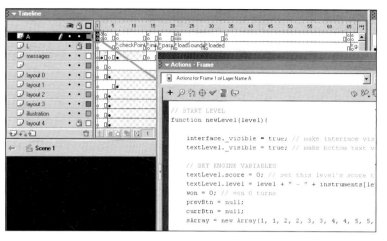

For this step, you will add more actions to frame 1 of the Actions layer (A), circled in red.

2 Insert this code to assign sounds to the 12 buttons randomly:

First a new array, sArray, is created containing 12 values. Because there are 6 sounds and 12 buttons, you have to assign each sound twice. The for loop executes a piece of code 12 times (globalButtons = 12). It grabs one of the values from the array and assigns it as the variable sound inside the padX Movie Clips (X being 1 to 12). A ? character is displayed on the squares. Finally, the value randomly pulled from the array is removed from it using splice( ) so that, after the 12 loops, all of the values stored in the array are used and removed. splice( ) removes values from an array. In this case, you are removing the value that is stored on position *r* (where *r* is a number) of the sArray array. Because you only want to remove one element of the array, the number 1 is specified.

```
sArray = new Array(1, 1, 2, 2, 3, 3, 4, 4, 5, 5, 6, 6);

for (i=1; i<=globalButtons; i++){

        var r = random(sArray.length);
        var result = sArray[r];

        interface["pad" + i].sound = result;
        interface["pad" + i].text = "?";

        sArray.splice(r,1);
}
```

3   Insert this code to tell all the squares to move to a new position, forming the interface grid:

The for loop executes its code 12 times, telling each button to show its frame 1 (resetting its aspect), sets newX and newY as the destination coordinate, and sets a random value for the inertia variable. The bigger the inertia is, the slower the square will move to its new destination. The newX and newY coordinates are pulled from the xArray and yArray arrays. For example, pad5 has xArray[5-1] as its newX value (-1 is used because arrays begin with position 0, not 1). The newLevel() function is closed with a right curly bracket.

```
for (i=1; i<=globalButtons; i++){
    interface["pad" + i].gotoAndStop(1);
    interface["pad" + i].newX = xArray[i - 1];
    interface["pad" + i].newY = yArray[i - 1];
    interface["pad" + i].inertia = random(25)+8;
}
```

4   Edit the actions of frame 65 on the Actions layer (A). Add this code to call the newLevel() function. This time, you are sending an argument to the function. The argument is the variable level. stop() is used to stop the playback on this frame.

```
newLevel(level);
stop();
```

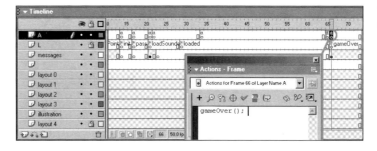

The function newLevel() is called on frame 65.

MAIN GAME ENGINE

Now comes the most important part of this project. The game engine is written as a function, engine(), called each time the user clicks on one of the interface's buttons. The button calls the function, sending two arguments to it: the button's name (pad1 to pad12) and the sound value (randomly assigned by the newLevel() function and going from 1 to 6).

1   Put this function code with the other functions, on
    frame 1 of the Actions layer (A):

    First, this code opens a new function, engine(), which
    will be triggered with two arguments: id and btn.
    Finally, the values prevBtn and currBtn are switched
    so that prevbtn is the button that used to be the cur-
    rent button and the new button is set as the current
    button. This is done so that the engine understands
    what is clicked and what was clicked previously.

```
function engine(id, btn){

    prevBtn = currBtn;
    currBtn = btn;
```

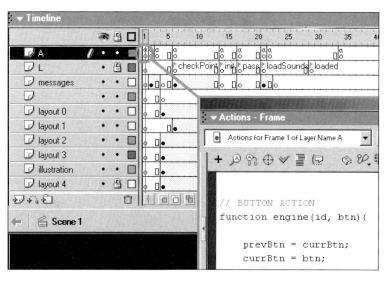

For this step, you will add
more actions to frame 1 of
the Actions layer (A), circled
in red.

2   Insert this code:

    Read the comments (lines with //) to understand the
    code in detail. First, make sure not to trigger actions
    if the user clicked the same button twice. Second,
    remove 1 from the score every time a button is
    pressed. Third, the object sounds is told to stop
    its current playback. Then you play the new
    sound. Look carefully. Here you are using
    gotoAndStop(id+1) to play a sound. This is a
    bit unusual, but it enables you to use the sound
    object and its features without having to use
    the linkage option.

```
if (prevBtn != currBtn){

    textLevel.score -= 1;

    sounds.stop();

    // play the sound!
    container.gotoAndStop(id + 1);

    // reset sound container
    container.gotoAndStop(1);

    // add sound to sound history array
    pSnd = sndHistory.push(id);

    // add button to button history array
    pBtn = btnHistory.push(btn);
```

The level movie previously loaded contains seven keyframes. The first one is just a stop action, and the six others contain sound events with the six sounds of this level. The engine tells the container Movie Clip (which contains the Timeline of the loaded movie) to go to frame (id+1). For example, if you trigger the button that has sound 3, it will tell the container Movie Clip to go to frame 4 and trigger sound 3. After playing the sound, the sound container is asked to go to frame 1 of its Timeline to reset itself. Finally, the sound is added to the sound history array (sndHistory), and the button is added to the button history array (btnHistory) using push( ). push( ) is used to add a new value to an array.

3   Insert this code:

First it checks whether the user is clicking the second (and last) button of the turn, and finally it checks whether the last two sounds are the same (if so, the user won the turn!). This is how you check whether the user is clicking the second (and last) button in the turn: The variable pSnd represents the number of sounds that were triggered from the beginning of the game (including the button currently pressed). If this number can be divided evenly by 2 (2, 4, 6, 8, and so on), you know that the turn is over and that the last button pressed is the second in the turn. To check whether the last two sounds are the same and the user has won the turn, do the following: With the array sndHistory being the list of all the sounds triggered in the game, compare the last two items stored inside it. The latest item is sndHistory[sndHistory.length −1] and the one before that is sndHistory[sndHistory. length −2]. sndHistory.length returns the number of items in the list. You are using −1 and −2 because arrays start with zero. For example, the 10th item of an array will be accessed at position 9 (arrayName[9]).

```
//check if button is second pressed in the turn
if ((pSnd/2) == int(pSnd/2)){
// check if the last 2 sounds are the same
if (sndHistory[sndHistory.length - 1] ==
➡sndHistory[sndHistory.length - 2]){
```

4   Add this script:

You've just checked whether the user won the turn. The actions you are adding now will be triggered if he did. Because the user won the turn, you first add 6 points to the score (the score variable in the textLevel Movie Clip). Second, new coordinates are given to the last two buttons pressed so that they fly away from the screen. Then the last two buttons are told to go to their frame labeled light. They will be lighter than the other buttons are. The won variable is increased. Because won represents the number of turns the user has won on this level, an if statement checks whether at least 6 turns were won (meaning that the level is over). If the level is over, the engine goes to the checkpoint label and stops. The += operator is used to add something to an existing variable. Typing score += 6 is a shortcut of score = score + 6. Use this kind of shortcut as much as possible when you write ActionScript. As you can see, you are giving a newX and a newY value to the two last buttons pressed. To access them, you simply access the btnHistory array, which contains the list of all the buttons pressed since the beginning of the game. random() generates a random number. For example, random(50) would generate a random number between 0 and 49. In this case, you also add +700 as a minimal value for the function.

5   Insert this code:

What happens if the sound was not matched? These actions will be triggered: First, it removes the ? character on the buttons and darkens them. Then it tells them to go to the frame labeled dark. Finally, it closes the last if statement with a }.

```
// WON THE TURN!
// adds 6 to the score
textLevel.score += 6;

// make the 2 last button pressed fly away lighten them
interface[btnHistory[btnHistory.length - 1]].newX = random(300)+700;
interface[btnHistory[btnHistory.length - 1]].newY = random(550);
interface[btnHistory[btnHistory.length - 1]].gotoAndStop("light");
interface[btnHistory[btnHistory.length - 2]].newY = random(300);
interface[btnHistory[btnHistory.length - 2]].newX = random(500)+700;
interface[btnHistory[btnHistory.length - 2]].gotoAndStop("light");

won++; // add a won turn to the engine
// check if all sounds are found
if (won == globalSounds){
     gotoAndStop("checkPoint");
}
```

```
} else { // else (if the sounds are not matched)
     // remove the ? sign on buttons
     interface[btnHistory[btnHistory.length - 1]].text = "";
     interface[btnHistory[btnHistory.length - 2]].text = "";

     // darken buttons
     interface[btnHistory[btnHistory.length - 1]].gotoAndStop("dark");
     interface[btnHistory[btnHistory.length - 2]].gotoAndStop("dark");
}
```

6 Insert this code:

If this is the first button clicked for this turn (a turn is two clicks), this code will be triggered. All it does is lighten the button that was clicked. Three curly brackets close the last two if statements and the engine( ) function.

```
} else { // else (if this is the first button pressed in the turn)

// lighten button
interface[btnHistory[btnHistory.length - 1]].gotoAndStop("light");
    }
  }
}
```

CHECKING THE SCORE AND PASSING

When the user finishes a level, this new function, checkpoint( ), sees if the score is high enough (10 per level) to go to the next level.

1 Add this code to the actions of frame 1 on the Actions layer (A):

The Movie Clip displaying the level title and the score is made invisible, and the last level's score is added to the scoreList array and is set as a variable (levelScore). Then the totalScore variable is reinitialized using null and is calculated a new time. This is done by adding all the level scores from the scoreList array. Finally, an if statement checks to see if the user passes. The success variable is displayed on the screen in a text field. The boolean variable pass is set to true or false.

```
function checkPoint(){

        textLevel._visible = false;
        scoreList.push(number(textLevel.score));
levelScore = scoreList[scoreList.length - 1];

        // calculate the total score
        totalScore = null;
        for ( var i= 0 ; i < scoreList.length ; ++i) {
            totalScore = number(totalScore) + number(scoreList[i])
        }

        // see if user passes or not
        if (levelScore < minScore){
            success = "NOT ENOUGH POINTS TO PASS";
            pass = false;
        } else {
            pass = true;
            success = "YOU PASSED THIS LEVEL!";
        }
    }
```

2 Now that the checkPoint( ) function is created, you are going to call it. Edit the actions of frame 6 on the Actions layer (A) and insert this code. This will call the function checkPoint( ) and stop the playback.

```
stop();
checkPoint();
```

You should see some text on the Stage, at the same frame as the one you've just edited. This is the checkpoint screen. It displays the total score, the score made during the level just completed, and a success or a failure message. This data is fed by the checkPoint( ) function. You should also see a button that appears as a transparent green square because it is a button with only a hit area (the technique often used). You are going to add some action to this button, grabbing the boolean value of pass and redirecting the user either to the next level or to a game-over screen.

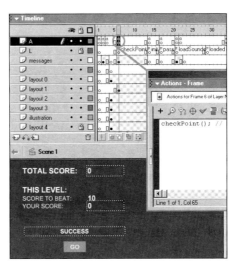

The function checkPoint( ) is called on frame 6.

3 Edit the actions of the button at the bottom of the checkpoint screen on frame 6 and insert this code:

When the button is released, an if statement checks whether the pass boolean variable is true or false. If it is true (if the user passes to the next level), the playback will go to the label pass, where the pass( ) function is called. If it is false, the playback will go to the label gameOver.

```
on (release){
    if (pass == true){
        gotoAndPlay("pass");
        pass = false;
    } else {
        gotoAndStop("gameOver");
        pass = false;
    }
}
```

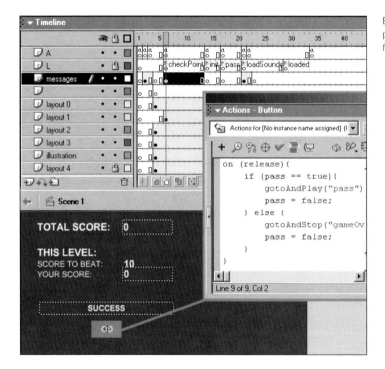

Edit the actions of the button placed on the Stage on frame6.

THE GAME-OVER SCREEN

You are going to add a new function called gameOver( ). This is simply going to make a few elements invisible and display a message on the screen.

1 Edit the actions of frame 1 on the Actions layer (A) and type this code:

First, it masks the illustration Movie Clip (background image) and the textLevel Movie Clip (level number and title, level score). Finally, it displays a game-over message with the totalScore variable.

```
function gameOver(){
    illustration._visible = false;
    textLevel._visible = false;
    msg = "GAME OVER \n YOUR FINAL SCORE IS \n" + totalScore;
}
```

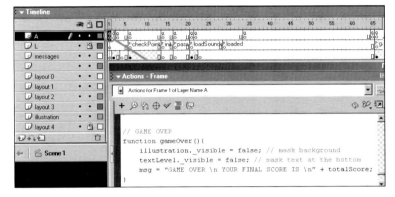

For this step, you will add more actions to frame 1 of the Actions layer (A), circled in red.

2 Edit the actions of frame 66 on the Actions layer (A) and insert this code to call the gameOver() function:

```
gameOver();
```

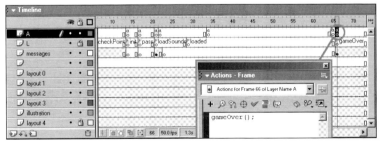

The function gameOver() is called on frame 66.

THE FINAL TOUCH: ACCURATE LOADING

The game is almost perfect. The last thing you need to do in this project is create the functions to check the loading status of both the main game file and the level files. These functions will be called mainIsLoaded() and levelIsLoaded().

1   Add this code to the actions of frame 1 on the
Actions layer (A).

First, the function returns the variables loaded
(how many bytes are already loaded) using
getBytesLoaded( ) and total (the total number of
bytes in the movie loading) using getBytesTotal( ).
Then a message is displayed on the screen showing
the number of kilobytes remaining to load (a kilobyte
is 1,024 bytes). Finally, it checks whether all the
bytes are loaded (if loaded, it is the same as total). If it
is loaded, the frame labeled init will be played (where
the init( ) function is called).

```
function mainIsLoaded(){
      loaded = getBytesLoaded();
      total = getBytesTotal();
      message = "LOADING - " + int((total - loaded)/1024) + "K REMAINING";

      if (loaded == total){
            gotoAndPlay("init");
      }
}
```

2   Edit the actions of frame 2 on the Actions layer
(A) and type this code to call the mainIsLoaded()
function:

```
mainIsLoaded();
```

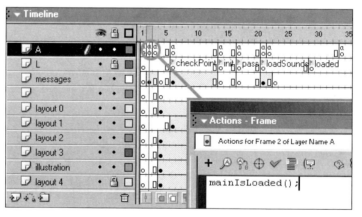

The function mainIsLoaded( )
is called on frame 2.

3   Now edit the actions of frame 3 on the Actions layer
(A) and add this code:

```
gotoAndPlay(_currentFrame - 1);
```

It plays the previous frame a new time, which will call mainIsLoaded() again. This loop will stop when the mainIsLoaded() function tells Flash to bypass frame 3.

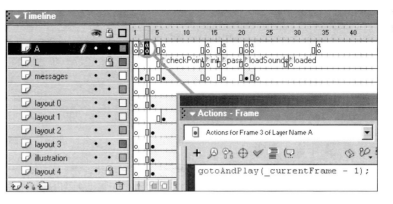

This tells Flash to go back to the previous frame and play.

4   Add this new function, levelIsLoaded(), to the actions of frame 1 on the Actions layer (A):

This one is similar to the previous function, but it checks the movie loading inside the sound container (_root.container). If the level movie is loaded, the frame labeled loaded is played.

```
function levelIsLoaded(){
    loaded = container.getBytesLoaded();
    total = container.getBytesTotal();
    message = "LOADING NEW LEVEL - " + level + " - " + instruments[level - 1]
➥+ " - " + int((total - loaded)/1024) + "K REMAINING";

    if (loaded == total){
        gotoAndPlay("loaded");
    }
}
```

5   Edit the actions of frame 21 on the Actions layer (A) and add this code to call the levelIsLoaded()function:

```
levelIsLoaded();
```

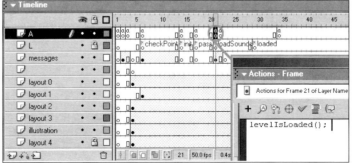

The function levelIsLoaded() is called.

6 Now edit the actions of frame 22 on the Actions layer (A) and add this code, which plays the previous frame a new time and calls the levelIsLoaded( )again:

```
gotoAndPlay(_currentFrame - 1);
```

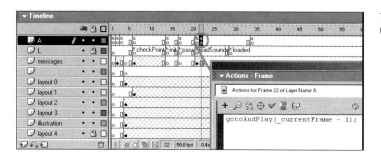

This tells Flash to go back to the previous frame and play.

HOW IT WORKS

The game is ready! To see how levels are made, open the file **12_start.fla** and use it as a model. There is also a template file called **12_level_template.fla** from which you can make your own levels. By studying this project, you are training yourself to use audio in a gaming project, and you will also increase your skills in ActionScript and application architecture. Try creating your own game with the same philosophy of gathering all your actions on one frame as a Library of reusable functions and calling them as you need. May your game touch the heart of millions of people, and may it be a part of their lives and their memories.

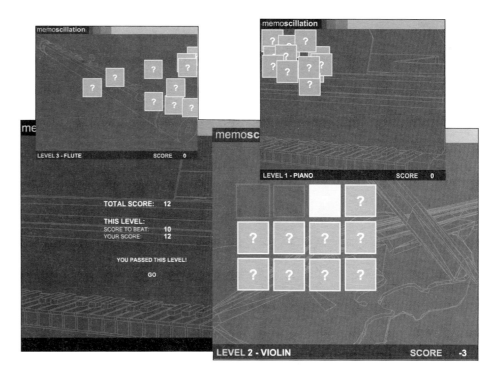

The game in action.

FINDING SOURCE MATERIAL

"Writing about music is like dancing

about architecture."

—THELONIUS MONK

GENERATING OR FINDING MUSIC

To create the sound effects of the game

memoscillation (which was created in Project

12, "Designing Game Architectures"), I

recorded myself while improvising a few notes

on my studio keyboard. You don't have to do it

this way. If you don't own a music studio with

racks of sound modules, you might have to

operate differently. If that is the case, you can

use Sound Forge to generate your own sounds.

In this project, you will learn how to generate

your own sounds using Sound Forge and how

to use online resources and sample CDs.

Project 13

Finding Source Material

by Manuel Clement

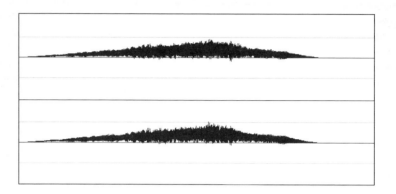

GETTING STARTED

Copy the Project 13 folder from the accompanying CD-ROM to your
hard drive. If you haven't already installed Sound Forge from Sonic Foundry
(**www.sonicfoundry.com**), install the demo version from the accompanying
CD-ROM before you start this project.

CREATING A BUTTON SOUND WITH SOUND FORGE

Sound Forge features a great tool called Synthesis. This tool enables you to generate
basic tones, which can be perfect when you need button sounds for an interface or
need any other clicks or beeping sounds. It means you can create your own sounds
from scratch without buying expensive equipment. In this example, you will create a
quick button sound and use it in a simple Flash project.

1 Open Sound Forge and choose File > New to create a new sound document.

Create a new sound document.

2 The New Window dialog box will appear. Set the Sample Rate to 44,100, the Bit-Depth to 16-bit, and the Channels to Mono. Click OK.

The Sample Rate is the quality of the sound. A higher number results in better definition and quality. CD quality is 44,100Hz (or 44.1KHz). The value in Hertz (Hz) represents the number of cycles per second.

Bit-Depth is the number of bits available to describe the sound when it is recorded or played. With 16-bit, 65,536 possible levels of audio are available. Adding more bits increases the possible accuracy (24-bit, 32-bit).

Finally, the Channels setting determines whether the sound will be mono or stereo. A mono sound has one channel; a stereo sound has two (left and right).

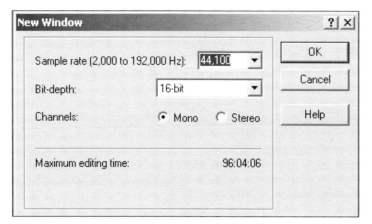

The settings for your new sound document.

3 Look at the new Sound window. This is your empty canvas where the sound you are going to generate will be contained. It is a Timeline, like in Flash.

Now it's time to use the Synthesis tool.

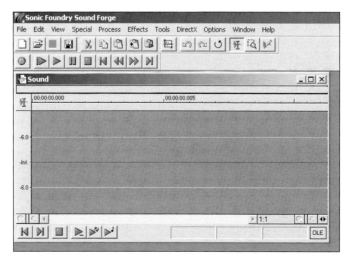

The empty Sound window.

4 Select Tools > Synthesis > Simple, and have a look at the Simple Synthesis tool.

The Amplitude is the level (volume). Be aware that a value of zero does *not* mean the sound will be off; it actually means the sound will be at a *maximum* volume.

The Waveform Shape is the shape of the vibration that will be generated by the Synthesis tool. For example, a sine shape will produce a soft sound, and a saw shape will produce a harder sound.

The Length parameter is simply the duration of the sound generated, in seconds.

Finally, the Frequency parameter enables you to decide whether your sound will be a low or high note. The higher the number, the faster the oscillation will be and, thus, the higher the note will be. For example, if you want to produce a deep sub-bass sound, 50Hz will produce a good result.

Even though you might think the Simple Synthesis tool is complicated, you will quickly understand how to use it, and it will help you a lot when you need to generate simple sounds for your Flash projects. Several other Synthesis tools are available, including DTMF/FM Tones and FM Synthesis. In this particular exercise, you are using the Simple Synthesis tool; you will use the FM Synthesis tool in the next exercise. You will not use DTMF/FM Tones.

Select Tools > Synthesis > Simple.

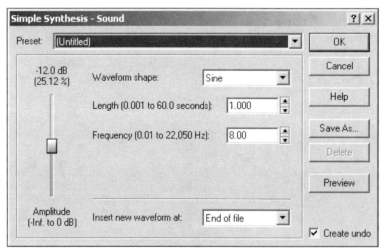

The Simple Synthesis tool.

5 Set the Waveform Shape to Saw with −17.0dB of Amplitude, a Length of 0.050 seconds, and a Frequency of 3,500.00.

The Amplitude setting is set to −17.0dB to make sure you are not going to break your speakers (or the viewer's ears!). A common mistake is to set the amplitude high (around 0dB) when generating a new sound.

The Frequency is set so that the note produced is high enough, perfect for your button sound.

Click OK.

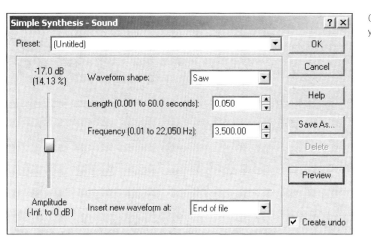

Custom settings to generate your sound.

6 Look at the sound produced in step 5.

The sound is high, short, and hard. It is not perfect yet. You need to add an envelope effect to change the way the sound starts, remains, and fades. Currently, the sound starts right away at full volume and cuts suddenly at the end. You are going to change this.

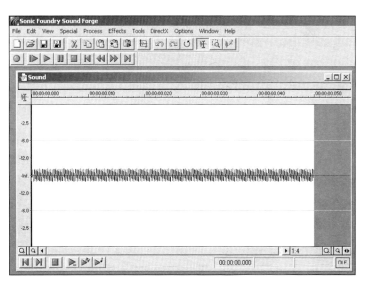

The sound as generated by the Synthesis tool.

7 Select Effects > Envelope to open the Envelope dialog box.

The main thing to look for in the Envelope dialog box is the Level curve. There are drag points you can position to adjust the level (volume) of your sound at different points of its playback. By default, you will see two drag points: one at the beginning of the sound and one at the end.

Select Effects > Envelope.

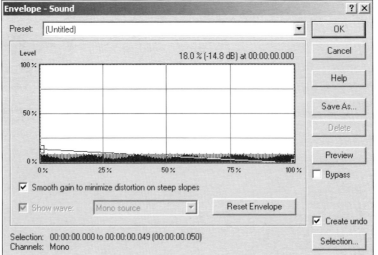

8 Move the first drag point down to 15% and the second one to 0%. Check the Smooth Gain to Minimize Distortion on Steep Slopes option. This will prevent the gain (sound level) from changing too quickly. Click OK.

The Envelope dialog box with your custom settings.

9   Press Play to listen to the sound.

The envelope effect applied in step 8 has softened both the beginning and the end of your sound.

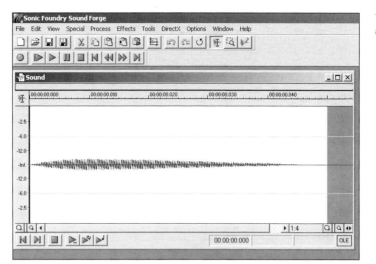

The sound as displayed after applying the envelope effect.

10 Let's work a bit more on the character of your sound. Select Effects > Chorus.

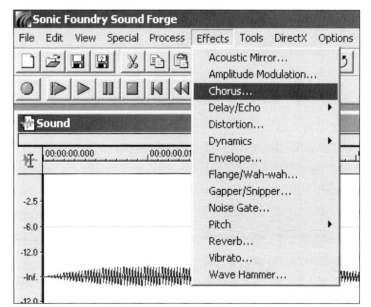

Select Effects > Chorus.

11 In the Chorus dialog box, select Fast Flange 1 from the Preset drop-down list. Click OK.

This dialog box features several parameters, from Input Gain to Feedback and Modulation Rate.

For this exercise, you will use a preset, but feel free to experiment with all these parameters on your own. Increasing Modulation Depth will expand the effect range; Modulation Rate will accelerate or decelerate the effect.

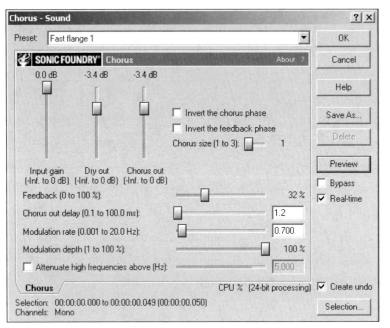

The Chorus dialog box.

12 Press the Play button to preview the sound.

You will notice the chorus effect. A chorus effect adds a pitch-modulated and delayed version of the input signal to the unprocessed input signal. The effect simulates the variances in pitch and timing that occur naturally when two or more people try to play or sing the same thing at the same time.

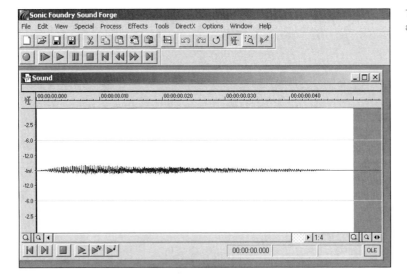

The sound as displayed after applying the chorus effect.

13 Select File > Save As to save the sound file in your project folder.

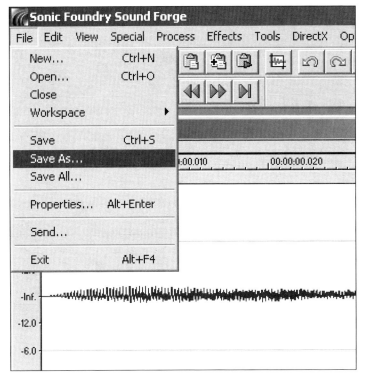

Save the sound.

14 In the Save As dialog box, enter the File name **button_1.mp3**, change the Save as Type parameter to MP3 Audio (*.mp3), and choose the template 128Kbps, CD Quality Audio. Click Save.

A message will appear, asking whether you want to reopen the file. Click Yes. Sound Forge will display the compressed (MP3) file.

Your sound is ready to be imported into Flash and used in any Flash project. It is good to experiment with the Synthesis tool because it enables you to instantly generate sounds. It also helps you understand what sounds are in general.

The Save As dialog box with custom settings.

CREATING A FADING SOUND EFFECT WITH SOUND FORGE

You can use the Synthesis tool in many different ways. In the preceding exercise, you created a short button sound. In this exercise, you will create a long, fading sound effect. This will enable you to create sophisticated ambiance in your Flash projects. From smooth transitions to animated sequences, such sounds will fit perfectly. From heavy distorted noises to smooth pads, the possibilities are endless.

1   Close the sound you created in the preceding exercise and select File > New to create a new sound document.

    The New Window dialog box will appear.

Create a new sound document.

2   Set the Sample Rate to 44,100, the Bit-Depth to 16-bit, and the Channels to Stereo. Click OK.

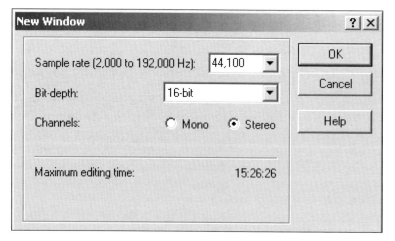

New sound document settings.

A new empty sound document will appear on the screen.

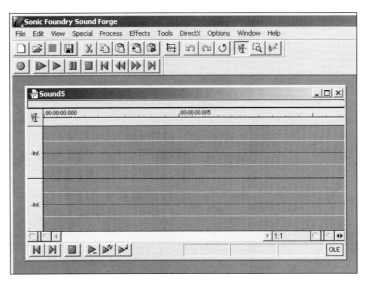

3   Open the FM Synthesis tool by selecting Tools > Synthesis > FM.

Look at the FM Synthesis dialog box. Several new parameters are introduced:

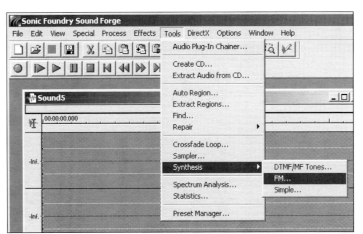

■ Total Output Waveform Length is the duration (in seconds) of the waveform generated. Current Operator (1, 2, 3, 4) selects one of the oscillators to edit its parameters. Up to four operators can be used in tandem when designing sounds with the FM Synthesis tool.

■ The envelope graph enables you to create a level curve affecting the operator's volume.

■ Operator shape features six different oscillation styles, from Saw to Sine and Square.

■ Frequency is the speed at which the selected oscillator vibrates; lower numbers result in a lower note (example: sub bass).

■ Feedback is the amount of the operator's output that is used to modulate itself.

- Amplitude is the operator's output level (volume). Be aware that zero (0) is the limitation (loudest level).

- Configuration enables you to select how many operators you want in your sound. Additionally, it enables you to select the way your operators are arranged. Read the Sound Forge manual to learn more about how complex operator configurations can affect your sound.

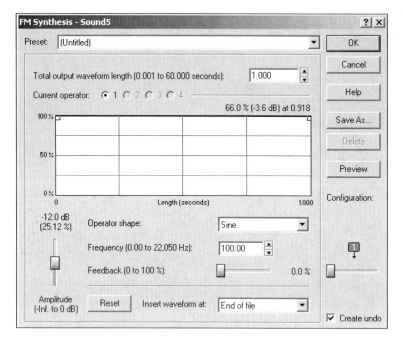

The FM Synthesis dialog box.

4 Set the Configuration parameter to the third position so that two operators are enabled, with operator 2 on top of operator 1.

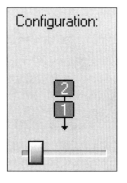

Custom Configuration settings.

5 Set the Total Output Waveform Length to 6.000 seconds.

Total output waveform length (0.001 to 60.000 seconds): 6.000

The Total Output Waveform Length parameter set to 6.000 seconds.

6 Edit operator 1 by selecting 1 in the Current Operator option. Operator 1 is the first oscillator. An oscillator generates an audible waveform. Use the following settings:

- Set the Amplitude to −12.0dB. As in the preceding exercise, this parameter needs to be low to prevent the sound from being too loud.

- Change the Operator shape to Absolute Sine.

- Set the Frequency to 100.00Hz. This will produce a bass tone. Higher frequencies produce a higher note.

- Set the Feedback to 0.0%.

- Manipulate the envelope graph to obtain the same curve as shown in the figure. To do so, drag both beginning and end handles to 0%. Create a new handle along the curve around the middle of the sound and drag it to 75% or so.

- These settings will generate a long and low (100Hz is a bass frequency) sound. For this operator, you are using an Absolute Sine, which generates soft sounds (smooth sinus vibration).

7 Edit operator 2 by selecting 2 in the Current Operator option. This is your second oscillator. Use the following settings:

- Set the Amplitude to −23.0dB.

- Change the Operator shape to Sine.

- Set the Frequency to 150.00Hz. The generated note will be a bit higher than operator 1's note.

- Set the Feedback to 26.5%. This will determine the amount of operator 2's output, which will be used to modulate itself.

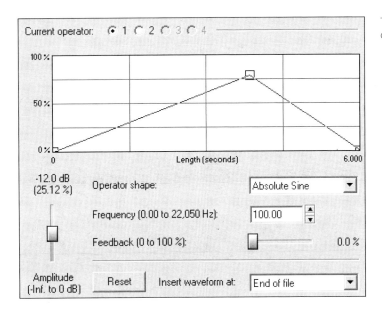

The custom settings for operator 1.

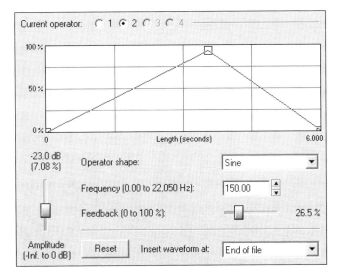

The custom settings for operator 2.

■ Manipulate the envelope graph to obtain the same curve as shown in the figure. Repeat the same process you used to create the envelope curve in step 6. This time, however, drag the middle handle to 90%.

Click OK.

8   Look at the sound after it is generated by the FM Synthesis tool. Press the Play button to listen to it.

Sound after generation.

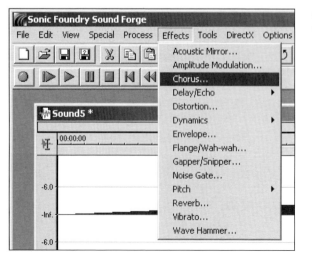

Select the chorus effect.

9   Select Effects > Chorus to add some chorus effect to your sound.

Look at the Chorus dialog box. Several new parameters are featured:

■ Input Gain is the gain applied to the signal before processing.

■ Dry Out sets the level of unprocessed signal mixed into the output.

■ Chorus Out sets the level of processed signal mixed into the output.

- Chorus Size sets how many times the sound is processed through the chorus algorithm.
- Feedback sets the percentage of the processed signal that you want to be reprocessed.
- Chorus Out delay sets the delay time that will be the middle point for the modulation.
- Modulation Rate determines how fast the delay time is modulated.
- Modulation Depth determines the magnitude of modulation applied to the sound.

10 For this exercise, you will use one of the chorus effect's factory presets. Select Chorus 4 from the Preset drop-down list.

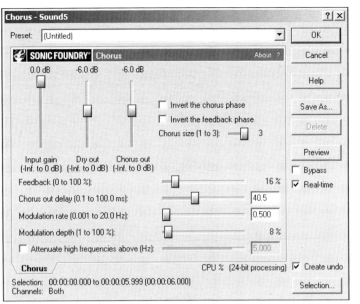

The Chorus dialog box.

11 The Chorus dialog box now shows Chorus 4's preset parameters.

Look at the settings for this preset. In the future, try to create your own presets. Click OK.

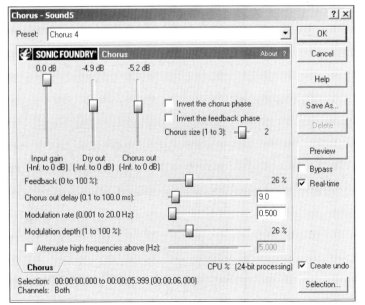

Chorus parameters for the Chorus 4 preset.

12 Look at the sound after you've applied the chorus effect. Press the Play button to listen to it.

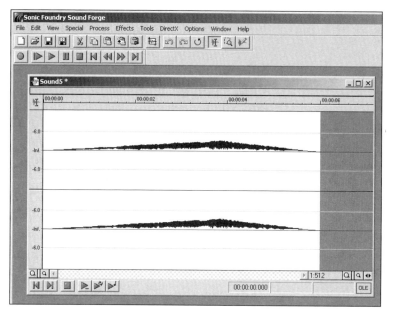

Listen to the sound.

13 Select Effects > Reverb to add a final touch with the reverb effect.

Look at the Reverb dialog box. Several new parameters are featured:

- The Reverberation Mode drop-down list contains the basic types of reverb simulation available to you in the Reverb dialog box. These modes determine parameters such as diffusion and the reflective patterns of the echoes that make up a reverb.

- Dry Out sets the level of unprocessed signal mixed into the output.

- Reverb Out sets the level of processed signal mixed into the output.

- The Early Reflection Style drop-down list contains various options for the first reflections you hear when a sound is created in a space.

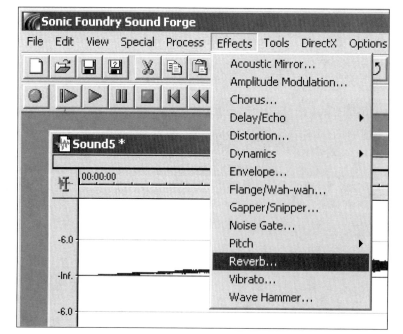

Select the reverb effect.

These reflections typically have bounced only once before reaching your ears. The human ear uses these first reflections to judge the size of the space.

- Early Out sets the level of early reflections mixed into the output.

- Decay Time specifies the length of the reverb. Decay Time is the time it takes for the reverb to decay to –60dB below its initial level. Typically, anything over three seconds is a very long reverb. Most small rooms have Decay Times of less than one second.

- Pre-Delay specifies the time between the initial sound and the start of the reverb. Pre-Delay is another parameter that gives the human ear cues as to how big a space is.

- You can use the Attenuate Bass Freqs. Below option to specify the frequency below which sounds will be attenuated. (Their volume will be lowered.)

- You can use the Attenuate High Freqs. Above option to specify the frequency above which sounds will be attenuated. (Their volume will be lowered.)

14 For this exercise, you are going to use one of the reverb effect's presets. Select the preset Metal Tank from the drop-down list.

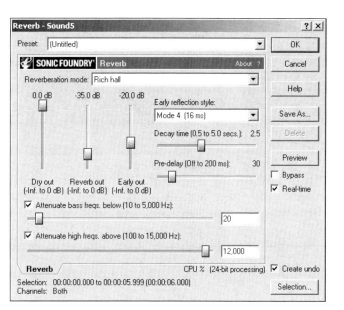

The Reverb dialog box.

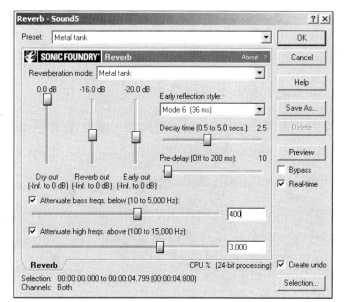

Select the Metal Tank preset.

15 Press the Play button to listen to the sound.

Listen to the sound.

16 Select File > Save As to save the sound.

The Save As dialog box appears.

Select Save As from the File menu.

17 In the Save As dialog box, select MP3 Audio (*.mp3) under Save as Type. Choose the Template 128Kbps, CD Quality Audio and click Save.

The sound is ready to import into Flash. Experiment with the FM Synthesis tool to fully understand and exploit it.

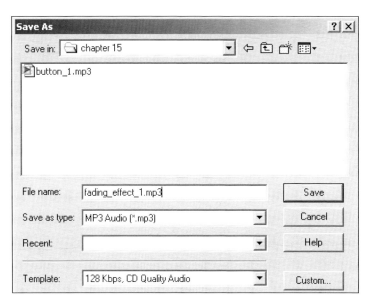

MP3 Audio, 128Kbps.

USING ONLINE RESOURCES

The Internet is an unlimited source of information with several web sites that enable you to download public domain samples. Although you should make sure you are allowed to use sounds you haven't created yourself (as explained later in this project), these online resources can be extremely useful. For example, you will be able to get samples from industry-standard drum boxes and thousands of sound effects. Because you might get lost in the ocean of web sites that are out there, a couple have been selected and reviewed for this project.

- **Sample Arena.** This site (**www.samplearena.com**) is nice and easy to use. All the downloadable sounds are listed on one page. You will find individual drum sounds as well as drum loops, bass and organ sounds, guitars, synthesizers, effects, and several other kinds of sounds. The site also offers a links page featuring dozens of similar sites.

Sample Arena features hundreds of sounds and links.

- **Looperman.** Hundreds of loops and effects are available on this site (**www.looperman.com**), which is focused on various dance music genres. The sounds are organized into categories, including a guest page. The site features an area with thousands of other sounds that are available to members only (in exchange for a subscription fee).

Looperman.

USING SAMPLE CDs

Using sample CDs is one of the best ways to find source material without having to worry about copyrights. Different formats are available, such as audio CD, AKAI CD-ROM, WAV, and SoundFont. Audio CDs and WAV files are probably what you would use if you were not a musician and just want to reuse quick loops without having to compose notes. You can find these CDs at any music store, and their prices range between $20 and $200 per disc. They are the musical equivalent of the stock imagery that designers often get from firms such as Tony Stone and Eyewire.

You are allowed to sample these CDs and reuse the recording anywhere you want, unless some rules are specified inside the CD's booklet. Often the label of the CD will ask you to mention the creator's name in the credits of your project. These CDs are very popular for sound effects in the video game industry, and even the big studios are using them. It is often the best way to have music and sound effects in your project while keeping everything legal.

You can order any sample CD at your local music store. Furthermore, most music stores have kiosks to listen to them.

Here's a list of a few good sample CDs you should try:

- **Distorted Reality 1 and 2 by Spectrasonics.** These sound collections contain dozens of complex textures, ambient drones, and evolving pads. The quality is excellent.

- **Jungle Frenzy 1 and 2 by Zero-G.** This CD features over an hour of percussions and breaks, both loops and individual hits.

- **Drum 'n' Bass Construction Kit by East West.** James Bernard, a New York City–based drum n bass producer, is the author of this CD. It contains complete loops, followed by drum parts, and finally sub elements.

KEEPING IT LEGAL

Let's say you are about to launch this great project. Everything is perfect, but there is one thing you might be pondering: Are all the loops you've recorded from your favorite music albums legal or not? How about the classical music samples in the intro—are they legal? When is it illegal? Confused, you ask your friends, but they don't know much about it either.

For the game memoscillation, I didn't have to license material because I was able to improvise the music myself. In many cases, however, you will want to use a sample from a CD, so it is important to gain the knowledge you might need in such situations.

Just as you own your creations, musicians own theirs. Furthermore, the recording itself might be owned by somebody who is not necessarily the composer (even with classical music). Finally, because you are going to synchronize the piece with images, you'll need to get a license for this as well.

> **Note:** I am not a lawyer or a specialist in copyright law, and the information in this project should not be construed as legal advice or as advocating any specific method of using music legally. Please do not rely on this for your sole means of legal advice. What I am providing is information you need to know when it comes to using music from other sources. Make yourself comfortable with the different legal terms and types of licenses you might run into.

INTERNET MYTHS AND COPYRIGHTS

The Internet is full of myths regarding music copyrights. Some people say you are allowed to use a certain number of seconds from a song or recording (myths range from half a second to 30 seconds); others say you can use four notes or claim that classical music recordings can be sampled without a license.

None of these statements is true.

Basically, unless you possess the appropriate licenses, you are not allowed to use recordings or music that you don't own. Unfortunately, web developers are rarely aware of copyrights, and such rumors often originate with people posting on public message boards.

Web developers have several licenses to consider. Among them are Mechanical (especially Synchronization) and Master Licenses:

- The *Mechanical License* addresses the ownership of the music, not the recording. You will always have to get this license if you use a song composed by somebody other than you. Even if you hire musicians or a producer to reproduce and cover the song or part of the song (or if you do this yourself), you still need to get a Mechanical License for it.

The Mechanical License for our specific example (an animated Internet site) is called a *Synchronization License* (often referred to as a "sync"). This is extremely important for web developers using Macromedia Flash. Websites built with Flash often use sound combined with images and animations; this is where this license becomes crucial. The fee must be negotiated on an individual basis between the copyright owner and the prospective user. The Harry Fox Agency, which is the licensing arm of the National Music Publishers Association (see the following link), acts non-exclusively as an intermediary for many of its publisher principals in negotiations with producers, facilitating communication between the two parties that often leads to the implementation of a license agreement. More than 90 percent of all American licensed songs are handled through the Harry Fox Agency.

If you want to find the forms for Mechanical (including Synchronization) licensing, go to the Harry Fox Agency licensing page at www.nmpa.org/hfa/licensing.html.

- The *Master License* is the right to use an existing recording (such as a CD). Fees to license a song recording can vary tremendously and can range from $200 to $10,000 or more. Note that these numbers are negotiable with the publisher and that you might get a Master License for free if you ask, depending on the project and the record label.

Even though the Internet is new and you might think nobody is going to take action, you should know that the Harry Fox Agency very often cracks down on web sites that use or post unlicensed copyrighted material. For you to use a recording, you have to get licenses for both the music and the recording. If you don't keep everything legal, you might be liable for statutory damages. Fines generally run from $500 to $100,000 for *each* copyright infringement.

Do you remember all the sites that were offering thousands of MIDI files? If you do a search, you will quickly notice that most of the big ones are closed. Many of these MIDI sites have been sued or threatened with legal action by the Harry Fox Agency and others due to alleged copyright infringements. A MIDI file does not contain sound in itself; it is the actual music sheet with the notes of a particular song. If you play a MIDI file, the sounds you hear are the ones from your soundcard or from your MIDI software. This means that the sound of a piano or a drum might be different on somebody else's computer playing the same MIDI file. People thought it was legal to use these files without a license because they were not actual audio samples—another Internet myth. To use a MIDI file in your visual presentation (site, commercial, and so on), you do need to get a Synchronization License.

What happened to the MIDI sites also happened to many lyrics sites before that. This means that the Harry Fox Agency and others could focus on new types of online infringements in the future. Because you build online commercials and sites using sounds, you are directly concerned.

HOW IT WORKS

You should now understand more about oscillators, effects, envelopes, and sample CDs. It is recommended that you use these exercises as templates to train yourself in designing sounds with Synthesis tools. Because the terms explained in this project are common in the music production world, you will start understanding the basics of other tools such as synthesizers and samplers. Tweak all the effect and synthesis settings and experiment with sounds.

To use sounds in a Flash project, use the Import option from the File menu. The sounds you import will be automatically added to your project Library.

"Such sweet compulsion doth in music lie."

—JOHN MILTON

VIDEO PLANNING
AND CREATION

INTEGRATING VIDEO INTO FLASH

Flash is known as the premier medium with
which to design and deploy dynamic and
engaging interactive experiences on the web.
When creating these experiences, don't rule out
integrating traditional video into your projects.
In the world of Flash, vector art rules supreme.
However, Flash's capability to also handle
bitmaps enables it to extend its capabilities
into the realm of sequential bitmap processing
coupled with streaming audio—the basis of
perceived video.

This project is essentially broken into two sections: using Flash 5 and using Flash MX (the
forthcoming Flash 6, which will eliminate the
need for sequential bitmap processing).
Although a single project on this topic cannot
truly do it justice, this project will familiarize you
with the video-integration process and how
things work. You will learn enough so that you
can create and deploy projects of your own
with confidence.

Project 14

Video Planning and Creation

by Eric Dolecki

GETTING STARTED

Copy the Project 14 folder from the accompanying CD-ROM drive for speed and ease of access. This project requires you to access a number of source files, so you'll want them to be conveniently located.

WHY USE FLASH FOR VIDEO?

Although it's true that Flash originally was not meant to natively deliver a true video experience to viewers, it can deliver an experience almost identical to that of traditional streaming video players. Remember that Flash is frame based and not time based, enabling it to incorporate video sequences easily. It also has some advantages over traditional video plug-ins such as QuickTime, RealPlayer, and Windows Media Player.

Flash enjoys a very high level of penetration. Almost everyone can view Flash content, while the streaming video platforms require users to have the correct plug-ins installed. Because streaming video platforms have relatively low penetration rates, you could run into problems deploying your video (setting up detection schemes, providing alternative content, and so on). Flash is your best guarantee to engage the largest audience with your video content.

Also, Flash gives you much more control of the overall presentation of your streaming video. You can add advanced controls, control the user interface, load different content into your player as you see fit, and retain the capability to buffer large files during playback. Plus, the security of your video is all but ensured.

212

ACQUIRING VIDEO ASSETS

When starting a Flash project that will invariably include video footage, you will either be presented with supplied video assets (MPEG, MOV, AVI, digital betacam tape, and so on), or you'll need to plan the footage and have it shot.

How you prepare your assets for use in Flash depends on how you obtain the assets and what format best suits your needs. Video is simply the representation of a quickly displayed series of images that can be synced with audio. Although your video source might be 30fps, you can only reliably deliver 15–20fps for deployment on the web using Flash. You can set an fps of 30, however, targeting viewers with more powerful processors. You'll need to extract the individual frames from your source prior to bringing them into Flash for use. When doing so, you should try to avoid bitmap sequences that are too long or too large. Before getting into some of the guidelines for converting your video assets, let's discuss some of the tools you can use to help you acquire the bitmaps and audio from your source.

Many software packages are available to help you extract frames of video and audio for reassembly into the Flash 5 authoring environment. Some of these include Adobe's After Effects and Photoshop, Apple's QuickTime Player (Pro version), and Discreet's Media Cleaner 5.1.

Depending on what package you use, you should be able to extract individual frames in the video to several formats, including BMP, JPEG, and TIFF. You control the level of compression upon export conversion, and you can also let Flash provide the compression of the images for you. A good rule of thumb is to extract your bitmaps without any additional compression and to set the final compression using the Flash 5 export (publish) settings. My choice is exporting a JPEG sequence.

Note: Extracting video and audio into usable Flash MX assets and importing/publishing those same assets from Flash might require a computer with a large amount of RAM installed. Make sure you have at least 256MB of RAM before attempting any heavy processing. If you have less than 256MB, you could run into problems.

Viewers of simulated Flash video need to have a lot of physical RAM installed as well. Flash processes (uncompresses) the bitmaps for display, and more and more RAM is set aside and acquired by the Flash plug-in. Flash is unable simply to unload material in previous frames it has already displayed. Those bitmaps are cached into memory. For this reason, try to keep your simulated Flash video relatively short.

Tip: In its Knowledge Base Technote 14437, Macromedia documents a frame limit in Flash 5 of near 16,000 frames. In addition to this limit, huge amounts of consumed memory can cause the machine to function slower and can even create stability problems, usually on older operating systems with small amounts of physical memory. This is due to the decompression of the images, and it is unavoidable. You can try to break a large video into smaller segments, or you can reduce the size (in K) or quality (initial compression) of the images in the sequence.

EXTRACTING FRAMES IN A VIDEO ASSET

Of all the formats from which I have extracted source video, it seems that those in a QuickTime-capable format (except for MPEG) are the easiest to work with. QuickTime is a track-based format. This means the contents that build up the video live on their own track, enabling you to strip out the frames one by one and retrieve the audio as a separate file for recombination later. Because QuickTime is track-based, Macromedia and Apple Computer have developed the capability to enclose a Flash track within the QuickTime player, giving you Flash 4–level compatibility within the player. You'll learn more on that aspect in Project 15, "Flash-Tracked QuickTime."

Now that you know some basics about using Flash for video, let's step through the process of acquiring a JPEG sequence of bitmaps that you can use to represent simulated video using Adobe After Effects.

1   Open After Effects and create a new composition by selecting Composition > New Composition. Set the Frame Size by selecting Medium 320×240 in the pop-up settings box.

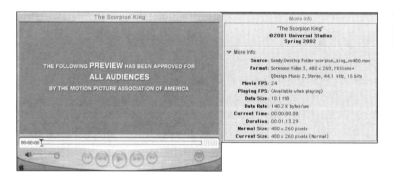

You can determine the frames per second of a video clip using the QuickTime Player.

Note that this setting will vary, and you shouldn't try to resize your video in Flash. If your source is 160×120, set the Frame Size to 160×120. If you scale your source up to 320×240, it's going to look nasty. Set your Frames Per Second to something like 8 to 10. Set your Pixel Aspect Ratio to Square Pixels. (Other pixel-aspect-ratio settings help prepare your video when your final destination is VHS or film.) Also, set your Resolution to Full and your Duration to the length of the Movie Clip. (You can view a video's information by using the QuickTime Player if you have it.) If you need to crop your video, do it in After Effects or a comparable program.

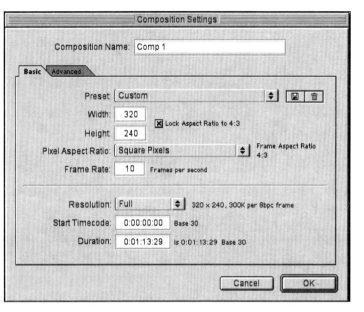

You can adjust your composition in After Effects by using the Composition Settings dialog box.

2 Select File > Import > Footage File to import your movie. Your movie will appear as a yellow square in the Project box. Drag the yellow box down into the Time Layout box.

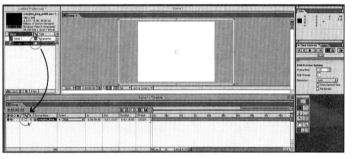

Drag your imported movie file to the Time Layout box.

3 Set the scale by opening the Transform menu in the Time Layout box. Under Scale, click 100%. A Scale dialog box will appear. Select Preserve Current Aspect Ratio. Select % of Source and set the width.

The less you scale, the higher in quality your video will appear. Keep it large even if you need to crop out much of the image.

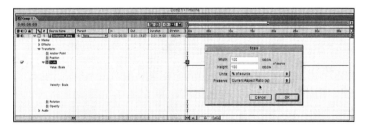

Set the scale in the Transform menu.

4   Set your background color by first selecting
    Composition > Background Color. Click the black
    square in the pop-up window. In the new pop-up
    window, drag the slider bar all the way to the right.

    You won't see changes until the next step. Video
    looks better with brighter images, but if your image
    is washed out, you can set the background to black
    instead of white. Your settings might vary.

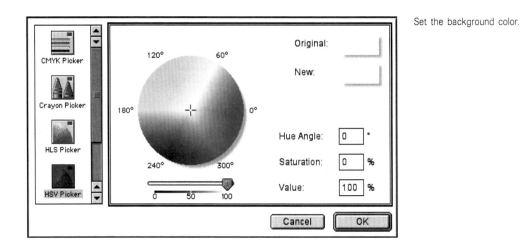

Set the background color.

5   If your movie is a bit washed out or too bright, you
    can make some subtle adjustments by setting the
    opacity of your movie layer (to enable the back-
    ground color previously selected in step 4 to show
    through). From the Time Layout box labeled
    Transform Opacity, click 100%. In the pop-up win-
    dow, set the Opacity between 95 and 100. This will
    enable the previous step's background color to show
    through slightly.

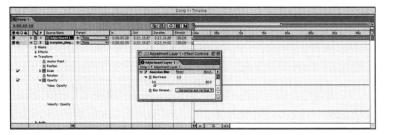

Set the opacity of your movie.

6   From the main menu, select Layer > New
    Adjustment Layer. This will create another layer on
    top of your video. Next select Layer > Mask > New
    Mask to create a mask in the newly created layer.
    With the mask selected, select Effects > Blur >
    Gaussian Blur and set it to a value of 0.3. This will
    reduce the number of pixels that need to be
    processed (slightly).

Apply a Gaussian Blur to your
Adjustment layer.

7 Now it's time to create your movie. Select Composition > Make Movie. A pop-up window will ask you to save the movie. Create a new folder somewhere and name it. Naming the folder something like **Movie 1 JPGs** might be a wise choice. Click Create and then Save.

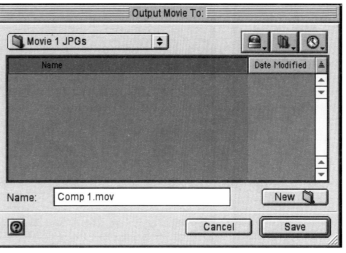

Prepare a folder to hold your processed bitmaps.

8 After saving, the window will ask you for rendering options. Click Lossless to set the compression. Click Format and select JPEG Sequence from the pull-down menu. Click Format Options and set Quality to Maximum-10/Progressive Scans:3, RGB, Millions of Colors, Premultiplied (With Black).

9 This is it! Click Output To and a pop-up window will appear asking how to save the movie. Remove any naming convention in the dialog box to the left of the period (.). It should look something like ".####". Click Save. Click Render to convert the video to a JPEG sequence of images. Rendering might take some time to complete. It's crucial that you save your JPEGs with this naming convention so that Flash can easily import the entire sequence. The resulting export of files will look something like this: 0001.jpg, 0002.jpg, 0003.jpg, and so on.

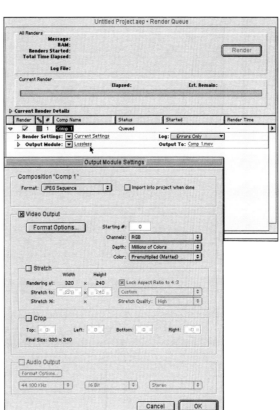

Set your rendering options.

10 Now it's time to create a new file in Flash. Select Symbol > Movie Clip. Now import the first JPEG created with After Effects. Flash will tell you that the JPEG appears to be one in a series of many. Choose Yes to import the series, and Flash will import all the JPEGs on the Movie Clip Timeline, one after the other. Again, this might take some time to complete.

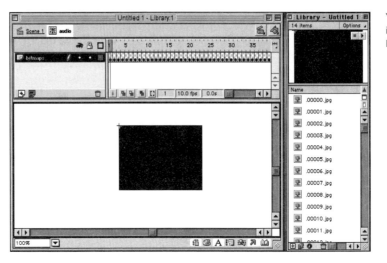

You can see the frames imported and placed on the Movie Clip Timeline.

11 At this point, you're ready to sync your audio. You'll notice that you have captured only the image assets of the video and not the audio. If you have the QuickTime Pro Player or another application, you should be able to save the video's audio track as a separate file (AIF, WAV, and so on). Do this and, on the first frame of your video Movie Clip, import the audio. Set its audio export properties in the Library, set an Event Sound event on that first frame, and set it to the audio you just imported. Set the audio to Stream, and your audio should sync up closely with your video.

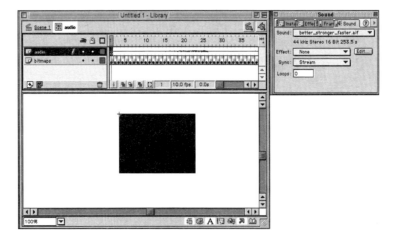

The Flash Timeline showing audio set as an event sound on its own layer and set to Stream to sync it with the bitmaps.

Note: Flash maintains the streaming audio even if it has to sacrifice the display of some frames (visually) in the movie. Therefore, with streaming sound, your video might skip a few frames here and there during playback to ensure uninterrupted audio streaming.

Your Flash file's frame rate should match the exported frame rate of the JPEG sequence (step 1). However, if the source frame rate was quite high (30fps) and you exported at 10fps, your audio might appear to be slightly out of sync with the action in the video (because frames needed to be dropped to match the 10fps target). Try to avoid using video sources with a lot of movement in them; dropped frames will be much more apparent in these cases. If your audio is intensive, it might cause bitmap frames to drop to keep up with the audio.

Tip: Try to avoid converting video sources containing more than three minutes of video. If you have a long video source, you should consider breaking it up into pieces. Because Flash renders the individual frames, it consumes a lot of RAM on the viewer's machine. Too many frames of video can result in unpredictable playback. Generally, a resulting SWF of 5MB or less is a good target to shoot for. Also, a high frame rate in your base SWF can cause problems in the current ActiveX control and with the Netscape plug-in. To ensure proper playback, you should also employ a preloader.

THE MPEG FORMAT AND RESOLUTION

The MPEG video format uses a single audio/video track. Although this might produce a smaller video product in general, if you need to work with video that has already been compressed to MPEG, you will run into a proverbial brick wall when it's time to extract the audio and video frames separately. Because the audio and video are intertwined, you won't be able to extract the audio separately as its own track. This is an extremely important step (unless you will be placing audio that's different from the original audio over the video). You'll be able to circumvent this problem and continue with the authoring process by using the following options:

- Have a third-party video-production house provide you with a native QuickTime file from the supplied MPEG footage. This usually takes a few days and won't come cheaply. It's very important in the planning stages of the project (if you have any kind of control) to acquire the video in a format that is the most flexible.

- Line your audio back into your microphone jack to record the playback with some audio software. This is a hack, but you shouldn't lose too much audio quality, and you will end up with an audio track that you can sync back up to your video.

- Go back to the supplier of the digital video and request the native source files, which you can recompress into a more suitable format. You can use the QuickTime Player or compression software such as Cleaner to get the job done. Also, a new product on the market is called Squeeze. It's made by Sorenson, and it offers a very simple interface for batch processing video assets.

THE REAL PLAYER FORMAT AND RESOLUTION

If you receive Real source video, which was built to stream through a Real Player, you can still extract the audio and frames. However, the still frames might not translate very reliably. It all depends on your video's quality and its importance in your Flash project. If it's not vital, you might be able to get away with using Real source video. You'll need to compress to another format before using it, however. Cleaner Pro is a great way of doing this. Cleaner Pro is a powerful application with a steep learning curve if you are not up to speed with the many options and codecs available to you. However, it does employ an easy-to-use wizard to step you through your options to produce useable and acceptable video.

Personally, I have not run across this format much at all when deploying video from within Flash. There might indeed be other ways of converting Real video, but because I find its quality generally poor, I steer clear of the format when I can. Work with formats with which you are the most comfortable and that you know will retain quality to match your expectations.

Note: That old computer adage of GIGO (garbage in, garbage out) is an important rule to follow when dealing with your video assets. You can never make poor video look better. If your video source has already been compressed badly or shot poorly, you need to pipe up about it right away. The client can recompress based on your specifications or can take a new approach if the video is very poor. If all else fails, sometimes you can simply dress up the video with some Flash effects to get around the poor video and distract the viewer.

VIDEO IMPORT IN FLASH MX

You are going to be hearing a lot of new terms being thrown around in the popular Flash forums on the web, by the water cooler, and elsewhere. You will hear people discussing Sorenson Spark, Sorenson Spark Pro, FLV files, Squeeze, and more. This section will break down the things you'll hear and the things you should know about when working with video in Flash MX. Once you see how Flash MX handles video assets, you won't need to bother with Flash 5 techniques (unless your viewing base doesn't have the MX plug-in yet).

SORENSON SPARK

Sorenson Spark is a streaming video codec developed by Sorenson Media. This motion video codec, included in Flash MX, enables you to add video content to your Flash projects and dramatically lowers the bandwidth required to deliver video while maintaining a very high-quality appearance. This codec allows for compression (via encoder) and decompression (via decoder) while working with Flash. Flash MX contains the encoder, and the player/plug-in contains the decoder.

Sorenson Spark comes in two flavors: Sorenson Spark Standard Edition and Sorenson Spark Pro Edition. Flash MX ships with the Standard Edition encoder that enables single-file processing and good quality for low-motion content. Sorenson Spark Pro ships with Squeeze, which

you can purchase from Sorenson Media. Squeeze is a software application that allows for batch processing of supported QuickTime media. Because it uses the Sorenson Spark Pro codec, your resulting video files will be much smaller while maintaining good quality. It does a better job compressing video to stream than Sorenson Spark Standard Edition does. It can also batch process files, whereas you have to import and compress video files one at a time while using Flash MX.

Embedding video in Flash MX utilizes the Sorenson Spark Standard Edition, and your ability to embed a large range of video formats depends on what codecs are installed on your system. The following are the supported formats if you have QuickTime 4 installed:

File Type	Extension	Windows	Macintosh
Audio Video Interleaved	.avi	x	x
Digital Video	.dv	x	x
Motion Picture Experts Group	mpg, .mpeg	x	x
QuickTime Movie	.mov	x	x

If you have DirectX 7 or higher on a Windows PC, you have support for the following:

File Type	Extension	Windows
Audio Video Interleaved	.avi	x
Motion Picture Experts Group	.mpg, .mpeg	x
Windows Media File	.wmv, .asf	x

One thing to remember is that Spark mixes the audio from a video source into the audio stream of a SWF. If you want to have control over the audio in your resulting SWF (volume, panning), you should extract the audio track and import it separately. You can then use MP3 compression on it and link the audio from the Library (as mentioned in previous projects).

> **Note:** You can set the compression rate for embedded video in your Publish settings to tweak your resulting audio quality.

SORENSON SQUEEZE

Using Sorenson Squeeze with Spark Pro (the encoder it uses) enables you to take advantage of batch processing and to output your video to MOV, FLV, and SWF formats. Batching uses what is called a Watch Folder. While Squeeze is running, any video file placed in the Watch Folder is automatically queued for compression at the user-defined settings. This is very handy if you are going to process music videos for an artist to put online, process digital video (.dv) from a field camera for placement on a news site, and so on.

Spark Pro is capable of much smaller file sizes at a higher quality than the Standard Edition. This is because of a technology called 2-pass VBR (variable bit rate). An example of the capabilities of Spark Pro can be summed up like this: a 422MB video compressed to about 1.5MB while maintaining good quality. This is perfect for use with Flash, but you can also use it to deliver QuickTime MOVs on CD-ROMs and DVDs if you want. It just rocks!

You can find out more about Sorenson Spark and Sorenson Squeeze by visiting the web site at **www.sorenson.com**.

FLV

A FLV is a video file whose video has been compressed but whose audio remains untouched. If you are importing a FLV file into Flash, you'll notice that it imports very quickly because compression has already been applied to it. You will be informed of how many frames the video is going to need to display it in its entirety. Follow these steps to create a FLV file in Flash:

1 Import any supported video to your Library or Timeline. (You might need to change your selection to All Files before your assets can appear in the directory.)

2 Select the new movie in the Library. From the Library, select Properties of the new movie.

3 Select Export. Your only option will be to export the video as a FLV. Name it, save it, and you're done.

If you use a supported video format (one that's QuickTime compatible), importing video into Flash is now incredibly easy. Upon importing like any other Flash asset (like a JPEG or audio file), two choices are available to you: embed the video into the FLA, or make a reference to the video for exporting to QuickTime. You'll want to embed the video in this case.

Based on your criteria in the Embedding Options dialog box, your movie could result in something that looks very good but ends up producing a large SWF, or it could result in a lower-quality overall appearance but a smaller SWF size. This is a tightrope walk. Find settings that work best for you.

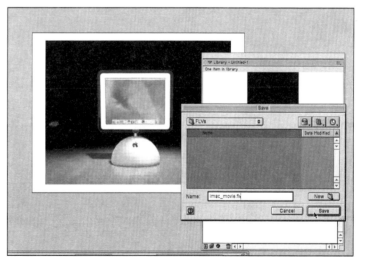

The dialog box you see when exporting a FLV from the Library.

ACTUAL IMPORT OF VIDEO AS AN EMBEDDED FILE IN FLASH MX

When importing a video clip into Flash MX, you can choose to embed it into Flash. The video will become a part of the Flash file just like any other kind of asset (audio, bitmaps, and so on). You can synchronize the frame rate of the embedded video to match the frame rate of your main movie Timeline. Also under your control is the capability to adjust the ratio of the video frame rate.

Just like when you externally update a bitmap or audio file, you can also edit your external video file and update the embedded video symbol. You can use multiple instances of the video without adding any additional size to your resulting SWF.

You can import a video as an embedded clip by importing directly to the Stage (select File > Import), by importing the video into your Library (select File > Import to Library), or by using the Import Video dialog box (select Embed Video in Macromedia Flash Movie). Regardless of the method you use, you'll see the following parameters:

1   An Import Video Settings dialog box will appear with several options for how to import your video file. The first parameter is for Quality. This controls the amount of compression applied to your imported video. A lower Quality setting produces a smaller SWF but compromises the overall appearance.

2   The next parameter is your Keyframe Interval. This controls the frequency of keyframes (keyframes containing complete data) in the video. If you choose a high keyframe rate—say, 30—every 30th frame in your video will be stored complete, and the frames in between will be represented by changed data in those frames. If you choose a keyframe rate of 1, every frame in the video will be represented with complete data, resulting in a better-looking SWF but ballooning its overall size.

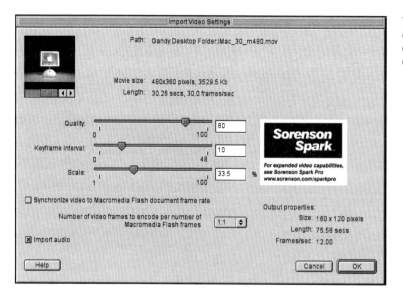

The Import Video Settings dialog box gives you a lot of control over many aspects of your resulting Flash file.

3   The next parameter, Scale, governs size. A smaller pixel size reduces file size and can produce a better streaming performance. (The amount of data streaming is smaller.) If you do not own video-editing software, digital video from a digital video camera might import at a size of 640×480—very large and hard to stream reliably. You can reduce its size with this parameter setting.

4   You can next select to Synchronize Video to Macromedia Flash Document Frame Rate so that your imported video is set to the same frame rate as your Flash movie. Would you ever not want to select this? Yes. If you are importing a video clip with a frame rate of 15 and are importing it into a Flash file of 30fps, you could run into dropped frames to match the Flash movie fps. Dropped frames = choppy playback.

5   The next parameter enables you to select the Number of Video Frames to Encode Per Number of Macromedia Flash Frames. To play one imported frame per one Flash Timeline frame, a ratio of 1:1 works. To play one imported video frame per every two in the Flash Timeline, choose 1:2. This does not end up slowing down the motion in the video. It merely displays fewer frames per second. If you plan to deploy intense animation to go along with your video, you might require that your FLA be set at a high fps while your video plays at 10fps. This setting enables you to bring that video into Flash at 10fps without sacrificing the playback speed of your base Flash Timeline.

6   You can next select Import audio to include the audio track (if there is one). You can turn this off to prevent the audio from being imported with the video. Sometimes you'll get a warning if the audio codec in the video's audio is not supported on your computer. You can either continue without the audio, or you can go to your external editor and export the clip with a supported codec. After this is done, click OK.

7   If your imported clip contains more frames than currently present on your Timeline, Flash will alert you to this fact, and you can either allow Flash to generate enough frames to accommodate the frames in the clip, or you can maintain your current number of frames. If you add more frames to the Timeline, you'll see more of the imported clip.

Note: You might need to import video assets and publish SWFs several times to find the settings that give you the results you require. Working with video normally requires large amounts of hard drive space while working, especially when working directly with uncompressed digital video. Make sure you have enough space allotted before working with video.

A STREAMING VIDEO PLAYER EXAMPLE

I have created a streaming video player to showcase Flash
MX's capability to deliver video online. As long as you
have the new MX plug-in installed in your favorite
browser, if you find yourself a little impatient, you can
preview it right now at
www.ericd.net/chapter14/chapter14.html.

The player streams a few movie trailer videos I acquired
from the Movie Trailers section of Apple's web site. I did
this because the quality of compression of the source files
lent itself to showcase the technology. (The resulting
quality will be very good.) Essentially, the clips are compressed twice (once to place them online at Apple's site
and again using Spark from within Flash MX). However,
even compressing twice seems to produce fairly decent
image quality using the Spark codec. Please refrain from
using these QuickTime sources for anything other than
experimentation. If you have access to straight digital
video (DV), all the better, because this source will not
have compression applied to it.

The video player I have supplied on the accompanying
CD-ROM takes advantage of the Spark codec upon
import and uses a simple drag-and-drop selection process
in choosing video clips to play. Individual video clips are
contained in SWF files and are loaded and played based on
the user's selection. Playback features are rewind, fast
forward, play, pause, scan forward, scan backward, and a
frame counter; you can even scrub the video feed using
the position marker. It's a system that can be employed in
a number of interesting ways. Because the video is actually
embedded in Flash, you'll find that adding controls and
visual feedback is fairly simple.

The streaming video player in
action. All of the source files
are on the accompanying
CD-ROM.

1   I chose to utilize loadMovie() (targeting an empty Movie Clip) in the player to allow for scalability. (The assets are removed from the player itself.) If you wanted to take things a step further, you could implement an XML document that contained track information, the name of the asset SWF to load, the location of the SWF, and more. Because this project is gauged to get you using video within Flash MX quickly, I chose not to encumber newer users with such a system. However, know that it is available to you.

2   I prepared five SWFs as video assets. (These are the videos you can currently choose from in this sample player.) A few of them contain a mask layer (those assets that are large in pixel dimensions) to prevent them from overlapping the frame display in the bottom right of the video player (that is, "frame 401 of 1400"). I imported the video clips into Flash, added a mask if necessary, and simply set a stop(); action at the end of the file to prevent the movie from looping. The lack of a stop(); action on the first frame of each video file enables it to start playing right away (after being loaded).

So now I have five videos embedded in separate SWF files—assets to be loaded into the player. I will now discuss some of the controls that bring the actual player to life.

3   Open the file **chapter14.fla** in Flash MX and look at the layers. The topmost layer is called **as** (which stands for ActionScript). This level contains some initial scripting that sets up some functions that will be called by user controls.

4   On the as layer, I placed this code:

```
// set up the caption clip and programmatic audio
stop();
// bastardized tooltip function
function caption(string, frame) {
    xmouse = 155;
    // was _xmouse
    ymouse = 80;
    // was _ymouse
    // duplicate caption movieclip
    duplicateMovieClip("_root.caption", "caption1", 1);
    // set argument to caption string
    caption1.caption = string;
    // move the caption to the current x,y of the mouse.
    setProperty(caption1, _x, xmouse);
    setProperty(caption1, _y, ymouse);
    // top-left OR bottom-right ?
    caption1.gotoAndPlay(frame);
}
// define remove caption function
function remove_caption() {
    // remove the duplicated clip.
    removeMovieClip("caption1");
}
fscommand(allowscale, false);
// audio for onpress of selection buttons
s = new Sound();
s.attachSound("hum");
s2 = new Sound();
s2.attachSound("gleam");
```

This code sets up for the display of each navigation ball. It also links two audio files for use with programmatic events. As long as you have linked them, you can call the audio when needed (as seen in previous projects of this book).

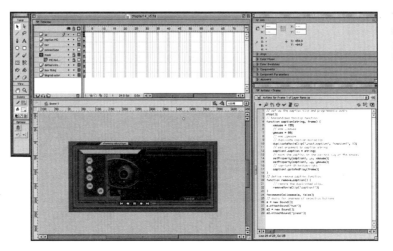

The initial ActionScript in the streaming video player is placed on frame 1 of the as layer.

5   To create the spring-like movement of the draggable navigation balls (Movie Clips), I decided to create a function that could work for each.

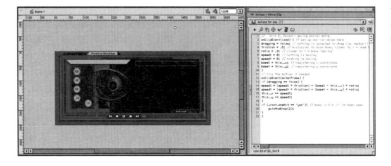

The ActionScript on the first navigation ball (instance one) on the root Timeline.

On each of the draggable Movie Clips (labeled 1 through 5 and with instance names of one, two, three, four, and five), I placed code similar to this (this code is for the Movie Clip with an instance of one):

This code fires when the navigation ball it sits on is released (after having been dragged). It provides elastic movement of the navigation ball when released, putting it back in its place along with the others. Play around with the values of ratio, friction, speedX, and speedY to see how the variables affect the motion.

Note: Notice that placing this code on each element enables you to customize the movement of each Movie Clip independently of the others. You could also set up a single master function to which each Movie Clip would supply variables to control movement, but because this project isn't so much about deploying advanced code, this should serve you well.

6   Below each navigation ball, I placed an instance of a hairline rule Movie Clip set at a 45° angle. On each Movie Clip, you will find code similar to this (this is from the instance named line):

```
onClipEvent(load) { // set up our variables here
    dragging = false; // nothing is selected to drag (ie. navball)
    friction = .5; // multiplier to slow down, closer to 1 = less friction
    ratio = .3; // closer to 1 = more "spring"
    speedX = 0; // nothing is moving
    speedY = 0; // nothing is moving
    baseX = this._x; // registering x coordinate
    baseY = this._y; // registering y coordinate
}
// fire the motion if needed
onClipEvent(enterFrame) {
    if (dragging == false) {
    speedX = (speedX * friction) + (baseX - this._x) * ratio;
    speedY = (speedY * friction) + (baseY - this._y) * ratio;
    this._x += speedX;
    this._y += speedY;
    }
    if (_root.oneHit == "yes"){ // keep it hit if its been seen
        gotoAndStop(2);
    }
}
```

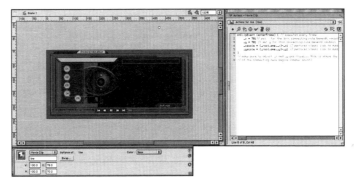

This ActionScript controls the scaling and joining of the first navigation ball (instance one) with its anchor point.

```
onClipEvent (enterFrame) { // executed every frame
    _x = 78;// set x for the thin connecting rule beneath navball
    _y = 70; // set y for thin connecting rule beneath navball
    _xscale = (_root.one._x)-_x; // performs visual link to navball instance "one"
    _yscale = (_root.one._y)-_y; // performs visual link to navball instance "one"
}
// make sure to adjust _x and _y positions... this is where the end
// of the connecting rule begins (anchor point)
```

If you drag one of the navigation balls around the Stage, you'll notice that a thin line is attached to it and anchored to the center of its origin. The preceding code controls this functionality, and selecting each line Movie Clip, you'll see the code change slightly. Each line Movie Clip targets its corresponding navigation ball and each has its own unique _x and _y starting position (the anchor point that does not move). Note that the code is set as an onClipEvent(enterframe). This means the code governing this functionality will fire upon every passing frame of the Flash movie (while the clip remains on the Stage). This all adds up to an enhanced user interface—and it's fun to watch.

The navigation elements are almost completely coded at this point. They move right now, but they do more than just move. They are used to select video clips.

7 Open the Movie Clip with the instance name of one and note the code that sits on the button inside:

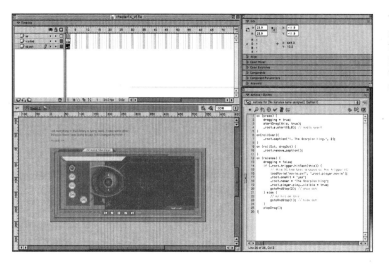

This ActionScript is inside navigation ball one, placed on the button inside. This button provides the bulk of the functionality for this navigational element.

```
on (press) {
    dragging = true;
    startDrag(this, true);
    _root.s.start(0,0); // audio event
}
on(rollOver){
    _root.caption("1. The Scorpion King.", 2);
}
on (rollOut, dragOut) {
_root.remove_caption();
}
on (release) {
    dragging = false;
        if (_root.trigger.hitTest(this)) {
            // this MC has been dropped on the trigger MC
            loadMovie("movie.swf", "_root.player.movie");
            _root.oneHit = "yes";
            _root.namer = "The Scorpion King";
            _root.player.play._visible = true;
            gotoAndStop(2); // show dot
        } else {
            // no hit on this
            gotoAndStop(1); // hide dot
        }
        stopDrag();
}
```

Look at the code closely. The most important thing happening here is that the code performs a hitTest() against a Movie Clip on the Stage with an instance name of trigger—which means a drop has taken place. If the drop has taken place, movie.swf is loaded into the Movie Clip with the instance name of movie, which is nested inside a Movie Clip with the instance name of player. Once the movie is loaded into the Movie Clip with the instance name of movie, it will begin playing because the embedded video in that SWF was previously embedded and streams using the Spark decoder in the MX plug-in.

Continue to look at the code in various elements within the FLA, such as the Movie Clip with the instance name of trigger. Search around to see how the navigation balls are marked as viewed after they have been selected. There is a simple, conditional system that sets a navigation ball as having been viewed (that circumvents the drag-release-hitTest method.)

It's now time to see how the actual controls of the player work (play/pause, frame counter, and so on).

THE STREAMING VIDEO PLAYER CONTROLS EXPLAINED

On the root Timeline, you'll find a layer named Mask and a layer named MC Holder beneath it. The MC Holder layer contains the player Movie Clip.

1   To access the player Movie Clip on the Stage, disable the mask. (Turn the visibility off.) This will enable you to select the player Movie Clip and to see two Movie Clips that appear off the top of the Stage with some reference text beside them (ff/rw code and drag code).

On the instance of the player Movie Clip, you'll notice this code:

```
// hide the play button until something is
selected
onClipEvent(load){
        _root.player.play._visible = false;
}
```

When the Movie Clip is initially loaded, it sets the play button Movie Clip (in the controls) to be invisible. It doesn't make much sense to have the Play button active when no movie is currently being loaded. The Movie Clip is still there, but you can't see it and it won't function.

2   Now double-click the player Movie Clip on the Stage or open it through the Library. The easiest way to edit the player Movie Clip in place is to double-click the VCR-style buttons. Remember to unlock the MC Holder layer first, or you can open the player through the Library by finding MC inside the MCs folder. You should now see four layers labeled bar, target MC, buttons, and code MCs.

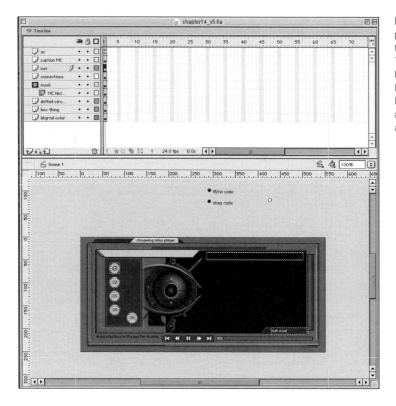

Disable the mask above the player Movie Clip to see all the elements it contains. The mask helps prevent the loaded movie (inside a blank Movie Clip within the player Movie Clip) from obscuring any details...like the eye apparatus.

THE VIDEO SCRUBBER

The bar layer contains, you guessed it, the player progress bar. Double-click it twice until you get to the dragMC (the actual orange marker for the progress bar). On it, you will see this code:

```
on (press) {
        startDrag("", false, 0, 0, 200, 0); //constrain
        _root.player.dr.gotoAndPlay("drag");
}
on (release) {
        stopDrag();
        _root.player.dr.gotoAndPlay(1);
        _root.player.play.gotoAndStop(1);
        _root.player.movie.play();
}
```

Dig through all the referenced Movie Clips in the code to see what's happening and what is providing all of the functionality. Right away, you see that the dragMC contains a button that enables it to be dragged in a constrained space. The Movie Clip with the instance name of dr is the Movie Clip that controls the dragging of the marker. You can navigate to dr through the Library by finding dr inside the MCs folder. Open it and look at the code within. This code controls the scrubbing of the loaded video. After the scrub marker is released, the controls for the scrubbing are no longer active. You make sure the Pause button is visible, and the movie plays from where you let go of the marker.

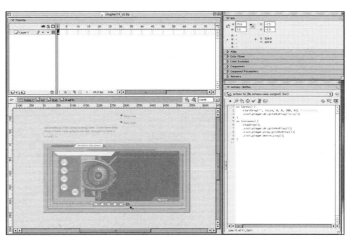

Deep inside the player Movie Clip sits the dragMC Movie Clip. This communicates with other Movie Clips to allow scrubbing of the available video frames to occur.

THE FRAMES COUNTER

The frames counter adds a nice touch to the player, and its functionality is pretty straightforward. Inside the player (named MC inside the MCs folder in the Library), double-click the text box that initially displays "test crud." This is the Movie Clip that displays the frame counter. On the second frame, you'll find this code:

```
fn = _root.player.movie._currentframe;
tf = _root.player.movie._totalframes;
frameNumber = "frame " + fn + " of " + tf;
gotoAndPlay(_currentframe - 1);
```

This simply sets a loop where the current frame of the movie is displayed versus the total number of frames that the movie contains. Remember that you are loading movies into that movie Movie Clip inside the player Movie Clip. You set a string that contains two expressions (variables fn and tn), and the frame counter displays the proper feedback. (A dynamic text field is set that corresponds to the variable frame number.) When the variable for the current frame changes, the change is reflected in this variable. When no movie is loaded and playing, the result should read "frame 1 of 1."

233

THE REWIND AND FAST FORWARD BUTTONS

The player enables a viewer to use buttons to scan forward and backward in the loaded video. Inside the player Movie Clip, you'll see the player buttons. Click the Rewind Movie Clip. This code is revealed:

Now go back to the player Movie Clip and open the Movie Clip with the instance name of ff (found in the Library in the MCs folder). It actually contains the ActionScript for both rewinding and fast forwarding.

```
on (press) {
        ff.gotoAndPlay("rw");
        play.gotoAndStop(2);
}
on (release) {
        ff.gotoAndPlay(1);
        _root.player.movie.play();//play after done scrubbing
}
on(rollOver){
        _root.caption("rewind (scrub)", 2);
}
on (rollOut, dragOut) {
        _root.remove_caption();
}
```

For rewinding, it uses this code:

```
cur2 = _root.player.movie._currentframe - 10;
_root.player.movie.gotoAndStop(cur2);
gotoAndPlay(_currentframe - 1);
```

For fast forwarding, it uses this code:

Each script is set in its own loop inside the Movie Clip. When the buttons are released, the loops stop.

```
cur = _root.player.movie._currentframe + 10;
_root.player.movie.gotoAndStop(cur);
gotoAndPlay(_currentframe - 1);
```

THE PLAY/PAUSE BUTTON

The Play/Pause button actually toggles back and forth. When a loaded video is playing, the Pause icon on the button is visible. When the movie is paused, the Play icon is visible. Initially, the button is set to be invisible. When a movie is selected and playing, the button is visible and its default state is Pause.

Double-click the Play/Pause Movie Clip inside the player Movie Clip. You'll see that the Movie Clip is set up with two frames: one for the Pause button and the second for the Play button. Let's look at the code on the Pause button:

```
on (release) {
    _root.player.movie.stop();
    gotoAndStop(2);
}
on(rollOver){
_root.caption("pause", 2);
}
on (rollOut, dragOut) {
_root.remove_caption();
}
```

This script targets the loaded movie and tells its main Timeline to stop when the button is pressed. It also tells the Pause button to go to and stop at the next frame in the current Movie Clip (the Play button.) Let's venture now to the second frame code on the button (with the play arrow):

```
on (press) {
    _root.player.movie.play();
    gotoAndStop(1);
}
on(rollOver){
_root.caption("play", 2);
}
on (rollOut, dragOut) {
_root.remove_caption();
}
```

This code is very similar to the Pause button code, except now you simply tell the loaded movie's main Timeline to play when this button is released. This is perhaps the simplest part of the whole streaming video player.

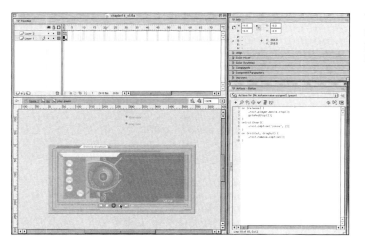

This is the ActionScript found on frame 1 inside the play_pause Movie Clip, on the pause button.

HOW IT WORKS

Although it's possible to simulate video using the Flash 5 environment, Macromedia has stepped up to the plate and belted one over the right field bleachers with its release of Flash MX. If integrating streaming video into your Flash applications has always been a dream of yours, Flash MX now makes this possible—and with relative ease. Everything can be done within the MX authoring environment itself, and with the inclusion of the Spark Pro codec to the plug-in, you need not worry about subjecting viewers to bitmap sequences with almost synched audio. The streaming video player I put together for this project is only a small application. Reviewing it, you can see how relatively easy it was to integrate the streaming video assets.

Soon you'll be seeing various creative uses for streaming video and Flash: live streaming feeds, the capability to record streams through a webcam, delivery on wireless devices, and more. The future of Flash and video has certainly taken many important leaps and bounds with the release of MX. I can't wait to see the great things you do with it!

FLASH-TRACKED
QUICKTIME

"There's nothing remarkable about it.

All one has to do is hit the right keys

at the right time and the instrument

plays itself."

—J.S. BACH

USING FLASH TO TRACK QUICKTIME VIDEO

In the preceding project, you learned some techniques to bring either streaming video directly (Flash MX) or its facsimile (Flash 5) into Flash for deployment. Another technique is available to you that involves using Flash technology, and that technology involves creating a Flash track in an existing QuickTime video asset. This project will discuss some of the key technologies behind this technique, tell you some of the future gains this technology is about to experience, and show you a sample QuickTime video with an embedded Flash track.

Currently, you can use Flash 4 ActionScript in a Flash track in a QuickTime 5 player. A Flash track is a reserved media layer within the QuickTime architecture that allows for the implementation of Flash-based content. It's a fairly cool and mildly useful way to present interactive video.

As of this writing, Apple has not yet released QuickTime 6 (although a preview version is available), but when it does, QuickTime will support Flash 5–level ActionScript. With that, embedding a Flash track into QuickTime will become much more valuable. Flash MX/ QuickTime integration might not be available until QuickTime 7 releases, which is still year or two away.

Project 15
Flash-Tracked QuickTime

by Eric Dolecki

GETTING STARTED

Copy the Project 15 folder from the accompanying CD-ROM to your hard drive for speed and ease of access. Have QuickTime 5 installed and ready (download it from **www.apple/quicktime** if you don't already have it).

QUICKTIME TRACK TECHNOLOGY

QuickTime technology is track based. Everything that's combined to create a QuickTime movie is contained on a separate track. You can think of these tracks in terms of internal layers—much like the layers you build up inside the Flash authoring environment. The following kinds of tracks are available to you as of QuickTime 5:

- **Movie track.** Annotations and general information.

- **QTVR panorama track.** QTVR information for panorama movies.

- **Chapter track.** A type of text track that divides the movie into randomly addressable chapters.

- **Text track.** Text imported into QuickTime for titles, subtitles, credits, and more.

- **Streaming track.** A reference to a live stream or a movie on a streaming server.

- **3D track.** 3DMF (QuickDraw 3D Metafile). These tracks are textured.

- **Sprite track.** One or more small objects with animatable, programmable behaviors.

- **Video track.** Digitized video, rendered 3D animation, or other compiled image sequences.

- **HREF track.** A text track containing interactive or automatic URL links.

- **Flash track.** SWF animation. This track is what this project revolves around.

- **Music track.** MIDI music with QuickTime instruments.

- **Hint track.** Information that enables a streaming server to deliver a media track as a real-time stream.

- **Audio track.** CD-quality audio or other audio formats.

WHY USE A FLASH TRACK IN QUICKTIME?

With the release of Flash MX by Macromedia, there are fewer reasons to use a Flash track in a QuickTime asset. However, knowing the basics of QuickTime deployment might prove to be an alternative to using Flash MX to deliver interactive video (when QuickTime 6 and QuickTime Streaming Server 4 are both finally released to the public). QuickTime Streaming Server 4 might prove to be a better solution than a soon-to-be-released Macromedia streaming media server product, depending on your needs. You can read more about QTSS 4 at **www.apple.com/quicktime/products/qtss/**.

Some benefits (right now) of Flash tracks in QuickTime are as follows:

- The capability to deploy media skins (for breaking the movie out of the standard Player interface in a standalone application)

- Sorenson Video 3 Codec (a very capable video codec that features high compression while maintaining high image quality)

- QuickTime VR integration (the capability to manipulate a scene within QuickTime that enables you to pan/zoom 360 degrees around an environment/virtual space)

- QdesignAudio 2 Codec (which is actually better than MP3 compression)

- Credits (the capability to embed your name, copyright information, and so on right into the video as an annotation; viewable through Get Info in the Player)

The features available will only become more numerous after QuickTime 6 becomes readily available.

THE SAMPLE PROJECT

I created a sample QuickTime movie (**ch15_ flashtrack.mov**—find it in the Project 15 folder you copied earlier) that has a Flash track embedded within it. It offers a brief glimpse of what a Flash track can do within a QuickTime movie. You can pause/play, navigate through sections of the movie, overlay semitransparent objects over the top, and more.

Note: I wanted to use Flash MX to author and export a QuickTime asset as the sample file for this project, but the beta build I had before going to press contained a few bugs that prevented a reliable QuickTime Export or Publish. Hopefully they will have been addressed by the time Flash MX is officially released. In the meantime, I used Flash 5 to author the FLA and to export the QuickTime movie with the Flash track.

I used some previously shot digital video from Flash Forward 2K1 New York. To edit the footage down to something more usable, I could have used Apple's Final Cut Pro or another video-editing application, but I opted to use Apple's iMovie2. I did this in my hotel room and didn't have another video application installed on my laptop. After importing sections of the video into iMovie2, I edited the pieces together and saved out a complete QuickTime MOV file. I then used Discreet's Cleaner 5 to compress the video so that it would be a smaller asset without losing too much quality.

I then used the QuickTime Pro Player to copy out segments from the single source file, creating two individual movie sources (mainly for the purpose of showing how separate movie sources can be "sequenced" within Flash to result in a seamless integration of different video assets).

1   Using the QuickTime Player, open **ch15_ flashtrack.mov**. Click Movie > Get Movie Properties and use the pull-down menu for Movie.

You'll see two audio tracks, two video tracks, and a Flash track. The two audio and video tracks relate directly to the two different video sequences that I sequenced. You'll see this later in this project.

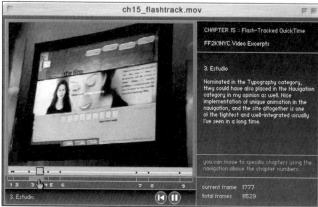

Open ch15_flashtrack.mov with version 5 of the QuickTime Player to view the completed sample project.

2 Whatever video application you have available to you should serve you well if you can directly acquire the DV feed from your video camera. You can also acquire video from Betacam or VHS tape, or you might already have QuickTime footage available for use. In any case, you need QuickTime-compatible footage to bring into Flash.

Tip: Take note of the frames per second setting of your existing or created QuickTime movie(s). You want your Flash movie's frames per second setting to match. If you find that your resulting fps is something like 12.7 (or anything besides a whole number), use some compression software to manually set the fps to a whole number so that you can properly match the fps in your FLA. You can even use the Pro version of the QuickTime Player to do this in a pinch. (Export the movie and change the settings via the Options button.) Set the fps as close to the original source fps as possible to avoid dropped frames.

3 When you import a QuickTime MOV file using Flash MX, it will import just like an ordinary audio asset, bitmap, and so on. However, you will see a pop-up dialog box asking you whether to embed the video or create a link to the asset. Choose Link to External Video File. This creates a reference to your QuickTime video for when you later Export or Publish to Movie.

When using Flash 5 (like I had to do), you won't see this dialog box. Your QuickTime asset will be placed on your Timeline and will display in your Library with a small video camera icon beside it. This is because, in Flash 5, you simply don't have the option to embed video.

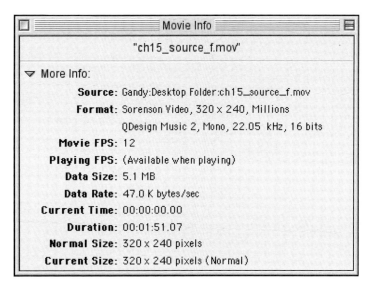

Open your QuickTime movie asset and choose Show Movie Info from the Window > File menu. This will reveal the Movie FPS setting.

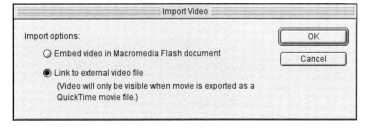

This is the first dialog box you will see after importing a QuickTime asset in Flash MX.

4 When the movie has completed its import to your main Timeline (this will be quick because the import is a reference to the source only), you'll see a representation of it on the Stage. Make sure the movie has enough frames on the Timeline for the complete movie to properly display. If your movie is 28 seconds long and has a frame rate of 15, you'll need 420 frames associated with it on the Timeline.

When your Timeline is longer than the number of available frames in the imported movie, you will see an "X" across your movie asset. If you don't have enough frames associated with the video, all of the video will not be available upon export.

5 When your video is imported and you have the proper number of frames available, you can scrub the video with the frame playhead in the authoring environment, enabling you to see the contents of the video on any given frame.

Although you can scrub the video visually, all audio in the video will not become available until you have exported or published a QuickTime movie. If you need some audio to generally sync to an event in the video, you might be best served by using an Event sound to handle this.

Note: If you add a keyframe to the QuickTime movie, the movie will start over again from the point of the keyframe. Refrain from using a keyframe on the last frame of the video because this will reset the video. Also realize that you can take separate QuickTime movies and sequence them on the Flash Timeline. I have done this in the sample project FLA.

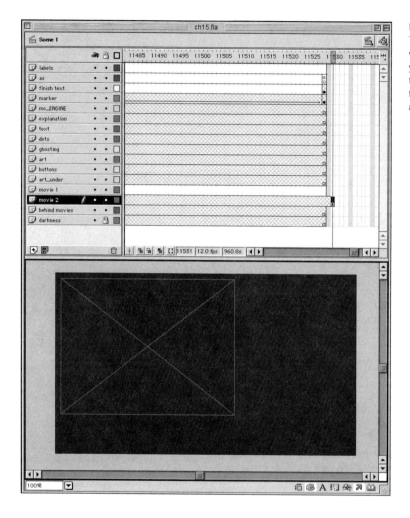

Having more frames in your Timeline than in the imported video results in an "X" across your asset, telling you that there are no more available frames in the video to display at that point in the Timeline.

INSIDE THE SAMPLE PROJECT

What's going on in that project FLA? Open **ch15.fla** from the Project 15 folder on your hard drive. You'll see that I have used many layers to separate individual content. If you take a look at the number of frames used in this FLA, you'll see that it contains 7,245 frames. This FLA contains two separate QuickTime assets (part one and part two) that reside on the bottom two layers titled movie 1 and movie 2. The two imported movies take up quite a few frames, huh? I had to manually set those frames, but you won't have to using Flash MX. Flash MX will ask if you'd like to add the necessary frames to view the movie in its entirety. What a huge timesaver!

An important thing to note in this FLA is that the QuickTime 5 Player will only recognize and execute Flash 4 syntax ActionScript. You might need to brush off your old Flash 4 books to remember the syntax. I can hardly remember much Flash 4 syntax myself, to be honest. The controls for the movie are indeed written with Flash 4 syntax. Take a look at the code on the Play/Pause button Movie Clip. All targeting is done with Flash 4 syntax as well. Remember, though, that when QuickTime 6 is released, most (if not all) Flash 5 syntax will be recognized by the QuickTime 6 plug-in.

1 To show a little of the Flash 4 syntax in action, here is the code that makes the Play/Pause button affect the _root Timeline.

Frame 1 inside the Play/Pause Movie Clip (instance name of play) on the button looks like this:

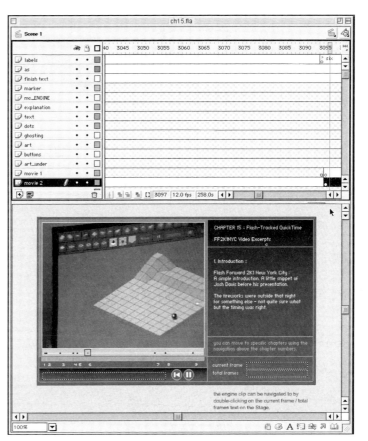

You can sequence two or more video files together within Flash.

```
on (release) {
    gotoAndStop (2); // changes state of this MC
    tellTarget ("../") { // targets the root
        stop (); // pauses the root
    }
}
```

On the second frame on the Play button, it looks like this:

That's basically all there is to it. The Movie Clip changes the state of the button by toggling back and forth between the two frames that make up the Movie Clip, and each button on each frame governs the behavior of the playhead on the _root Timeline. Easy as pie.

2   After I had everything coded and placed the way I wanted (you can peruse the FLA to see how the navigation buttons move the playhead along the main Timeline), I used Export to Movie.

```
on (release) {
    tellTarget ("../") { // targets the root
        play (); // play on the root
    }
    gotoAndPlay (1); // change the state of this MC
}
```

EXPORT SETTINGS

You can use Flash's File > Export Movie option to create your QuickTime movie with the Flash Media handler track. You can also set this up in your Publish settings. You will be given the opportunity to set several properties that govern your resulting movie export. The dialog boxes shown are from the Flash 5 authoring environment.

1   When you are past the Destination Location dialog box, you will be presented with a second dialog box. You can manually enter the dimensions of the resulting movie, but you almost always want to leave Match Movie selected. Alpha and Layer can be left at Auto. You can choose the stacking order of both, but normally I leave these alone.

The Alpha option controls the transparency mode of the Flash track in a QuickTime movie without affecting any alpha settings in the Flash movie. Alpha Transparent makes the Flash track transparent and shows any content in tracks behind the Flash track. Copy makes the Flash track opaque and masks all content in tracks behind the Flash track. Auto makes

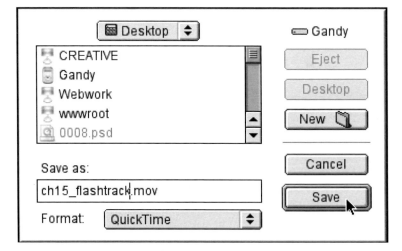

Choose QuickTime in the first dialog box after you select Export to Movie.

the Flash track transparent if it is on top of any other tracks but makes it opaque if it is the bottom or only track in the movie.

The Layer option controls where the Flash track plays in the stacking order in the QuickTime movie. (Remember that QuickTime is track based.) Top places the Flash track on top of all other tracks in the QuickTime movie. Bottom places the Flash track below other tracks. Auto places the Flash track in front of other tracks if Flash objects are in front of video objects within the Flash movie and places it behind all other tracks if Flash objects are not in front.

2   Experiment with these settings and notice how your choices affect the resulting QuickTime movie. Changing the Layer setting affects how the actual movie asset inside Flash will be exported.

3   If you are not using your own means to navigate the QuickTime movie through Flash controls, you can make sure the default QuickTime controller is used.

In my sample, I added Flash navigation, so I left the Controller drop-down box as None. You can then choose whether your movie will Loop, be Paused At Start, or Play Every Frame. For my sample, I left these all unchecked.

4   The last setting is extremely important. You want to Flatten your movie, making it self-contained. This will enable you to distribute it anywhere without the movie trying to reference any of your QuickTime source files. If you uncheck this and then export your movie, then your movie might work great locally, but if it's moved to another machine or server, internal reference links will be broken, and your QuickTime movie will generate an error.

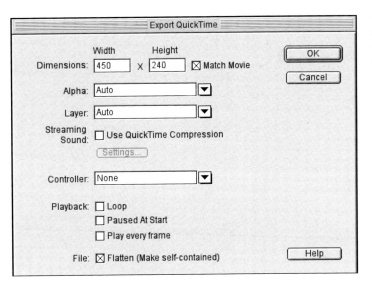

The second dialog box after selecting Export Movie enables you to control several settings that affect the final movie.

HOW IT WORKS

You can do some amazing things with the QuickTime 5 plug-in/player and Flash if you are so inclined. For the even more daring, you can combine QuickTime with a Flash track and even add some additional scripting by using totally hip's LiveStage Pro 3. It allows for tight integration in the design and deployment of some of the more advanced features built into the QuickTime video platform. You can read more about LiveStage at **www.totallyhip.com/lo/index.html**.

Using this project as a guide—and with some experimenting on your part—you'll be able to deliver dazzling and engaging QuickTime movies across the Internet.

APPENDIX

WHAT'S ON THE CD

The CD-ROM that accompanies this book contains source files for each of the book's projects to help you learn how to implement audio and video in your own Macromedia Flash projects.

For more information about the use of this CD, please review the ReadMe.txt file in the root directory. This file includes important disclaimer information, as well as information about installation, system requirements, troubleshooting, and technical support.

Technical Support Issues: If you have any difficulties with this CD, you can access our web site at **http://www.newriders.com**.

SYSTEM REQUIREMENTS

This CD-ROM was configured for use on systems running Windows NT Workstation, Windows 95, Windows 98, Windows XP Home, Windows XP Professional, Windows 2000, Windows ME, or on Macintosh 9.x, OSX.x. You should have the following system requirements in order for this CD and the demos and source files to operate properly:

- Memory (RAM): 128MB minimum
- Monitor: VGA, 800x600 or higher, with thousands of colors or higher
- Storage Space: 10MB minimum (will vary depending on installations)
- Other: Mouse or compatible pointing device
- Optional: Internet connection and web browser

PROJECT FILES

This CD contains all the source files you'll need to complete the exercises in *Flash MX Audio Magic*. These files can be found in the Projects folder. Please note that some of the chapters contain exercises that do not require you to access any project files.

LOADING THE CD FILES

To load the files from the CD, insert the disc into your CD-ROM drive. If AutoPlay is enabled on your machine, the CD-ROM setup program starts automatically the first time you insert the disc. You may copy the files to your hard drive or use them right off the disc.

Note: This CD-ROM uses long and mixed-case filenames, requiring the use of a protected mode CD-ROM driver.

THIRD-PARTY PROGRAMS

This CD also contains several third-party programs and demos from leading industry companies. These programs have been carefully selected to help you strengthen your professional skills in Macromedia Flash.

Please note that some of the programs included on this CD-ROM are share-ware—"try-before-you-buy"—software. Please support these independent vendors by purchasing or registering any shareware software that you use for more than 30 days. Check with the documentation provided with the software on where and how to register the product.

- Macromedia Flash MX (Mac and PC)

- Sonic Foundry ACID Pro (PC)

- Sonic Foundry Sound Forge (PC)

- Sonic Foundry Vegas Audio (PC)

- Musicmatch Jukebox (Mac and PC)

READ THIS BEFORE OPENING THE SOFTWARE

INDEX

assets, video
  acquiring, 213
  audio, syncing, 218-219
  extracting frames, 214-218
audio. *See also* **sounds**
  ACID Pro, 82-86
    auditioning sound clips, 83
    loop controls, 84
    merging loops, 87
    raising pitch, 87
    Solo button, 86
    versions, 83
  background, 15
  files
    compressing, 9-12
    merging, 41-42
  looped audio, 15
  quality, 9
  recordings, dynamic ranges, 22
  sampling, 29
  sound effects, 15
    finding, 17
  soundtrack audio, 15
  syncing in imported video, 218-219
Auto Trim/Crop tool, 44

B

background audio, 15
bandwidth, preplanning, 8-12
bars, 94
batch processing, Sorenson Squeeze, 222
beats, 94

bit rates, selecting, 14
buttons
  associating sounds, 188-195
  creating, 134
  Fast-Forward, 234
  and logic, 54-59
  Movie Clips with animation
    creating, 51-54
  MP3 jukeboxes, 146
  MultiSound Mixers, 157
  Mute buttons, creating, 68
  Pause, 234
  Play, 234
  randomly assigning sounds to
    (memoscillation), 173
  Rewind, 234

C

CD-quality sound, 36
choosing music for projects, 15
Chorus effects, 200
clicks and rollovers, 54-58
clipEvents handlers, 155
clipping, 22
code-based audio control, 129
color
  grayscale, 5
  schemes
    generating random, 171-172
    in memoscillation, 171-172
color schemes (memoscillation), 165

compression (sound files), 119
  allowing for speaker quality, 123
  audio files, 9-12
  determining how compression will affect
    Movie Clips, 119-123
  effect on sound quality, 120
  making adjustments before compression,
    124-126
  MP3, 14, 119
  settings, 122
  sound, 46
  testing, 119-123
compressors, recording sounds, 24
copying loops, 110
copyrights, 16, 208-209
  Master License, 209
  Mechanical License, 208
  Synchronization License, 208
cropping in Sound Forge, 34-36

D

DAT (digital audio tape) recorder, 27
dB meters, 22-23
digital audio tape (DAT) recorder, 27
Distorted Reality, 207
double equal sign (==), 57
dynamic ranges
  audio recordings, 22
  recording sounds, 24-25**

HOW TO CONTACT US

VISIT OUR WEB SITE

WWW.NEWRIDERS.COM

On our web site, you'll find information about our other books, authors, tables of contents, and book errata. You will also find information about book registration and how to purchase our books, both domestically and internationally.

EMAIL US

Contact us at: **nrfeedback@newriders.com**

- If you have comments or questions about this book
- To report errors that you have found in this book
- If you have a book proposal to submit or are interested in writing for New Riders
- If you are an expert in a computer topic or technology and are interested in being a technical editor who reviews manuscripts for technical accuracy

Contact us at: **nreducation@newriders.com**

- If you are an instructor from an educational institution who wants to preview New Riders books for classroom use. Email should include your name, title, school, department, address, phone number, office days/hours, text in use, and enrollment, along with your request for desk/examination copies and/or additional information.

Contact us at: **nrmedia@newriders.com**

- If you are a member of the media who is interested in reviewing copies of New Riders books. Send your name, mailing address, and email address, along with the name of the publication or web site you work for.

BULK PURCHASES/CORPORATE SALES

If you are interested in buying 10 or more copies of a title or want to set up an account for your company to purchase directly from the publisher at a substantial discount, contact us at 800-382-3419 or email your contact information to corpsales@pearsontechgroup.com. A sales representative will contact you with more information.

WRITE TO US

New Riders Publishing
201 W. 103rd St.
Indianapolis, IN 46290-1097

CALL/FAX US

Toll-free (800) 571-5840
If outside U.S. (317) 581-3500
Ask for New Riders
FAX: (317) 581-4663

WWW.NEWRIDERS.COM

Publishing
the Voices
that Matter

VIEW CART   search ▷

▸ Registration already a member? Log in. ▸ Book Registration

OUR AUTHORS

PRESS ROOM

| web development | design | photoshop | new media | 3-D | server technologies |

EDUCATORS

ABOUT US

CONTACT US

You already know that New Riders brings you the **Voices that Matter**. But what does that mean? It means that New Riders brings you the Voices that challenge your assumptions, take your talents to the next level, or simply help you better understand the complex technical world we're all navigating.

Visit **www.newriders.com** to find:

▸ Discounts on specific book purchases

▸ Never before published chapters

▸ Sample chapters and excerpts

▸ Author bios and interviews

▸ Contests and enter-to-wins

▸ Up-to-date industry event information

▸ Book reviews

▸ Special offers from our friends and partners

▸ Info on how to join our User Group program

▸ Ways to have your Voice heard

New Riders

WWW.NEWRIDERS.COM

COLOPHON

Flash MX Audio Magic was laid out and produced with the help of Microsoft Word, Adobe Acrobat, Adobe Photoshop, Adobe Illustrator, and QuarkXpress on a variety of systems, including a Macintosh G4. With the exception of pages that were printed out for proofreading, all files—text, images, and project files— were transferred via email and edited on-screen.

All body text was set in the Bergamo family. All headings and figure captions were set in the Imago family. Code was set in the Letter Gothic family. The Symbol and Sean's Symbol typefaces were used throughout for special symbols and bullets.

Flash MX Audio Magic was printed on 60# Provincial Matte paper at CDS Publications in Medford, OR. Prepress consisted of PostScript computer-to-plate technology (filmless process). The cover was printed on 12pt paper, coated on one side, at Moore Langen Printing in Terre Haute, Indiana.

THE FLASH MX AUDIO MAGIC CD

The CD-ROM that accompanies this book contains source files for each of the book's projects to help you learn how to implement audio and video in your own Macromedia Flash projects. For more information about the use of this CD, please see Appendix A, "What's on the CD."

PROJECT FILES

This CD contains all the source files you'll need to complete the exercises in *Flash MX Audio Magic*. These files are organized by project number in the Projects folder. To load the files from the CD, insert the disc into your CD-ROM drive. If AutoPlay is enabled on your machine, the CD-ROM interface starts automatically. You may copy the files to your hard drive or use them right off the disc.

THIRD-PARTY PROGRAMS

This CD also contains several third-party programs and demos from leading industry companies. These programs have been carefully selected to help you strengthen your professional skills in Macromedia Flash MX.

- Macromedia Flash MX (Mac and PC)
- Sonic Foundry ACID Pro (PC)
- Sonic Foundry Sound Forge (PC)
- Sonic Foundry Vegas Audio (PC)
- Musicmatch Jukebox (Mac and PC)

READ THIS BEFORE OPENING THE SOFTWARE

By opening the CD package, you agree to be bound by the following agreement:

You may not copy or redistribute the entire CD-ROM as a whole. Copying and redistribution of individual software programs on the CD-ROM is governed by terms set by individual copyright holders.

The installer, code, images, actions, and brushes from the authors are copyrighted by the publisher and the authors.

This software is sold as-is, without warranty of any kind, either expressed or implied, including but not limited to the implied warranties of merchantability and fitness for a particular purpose. Neither the publisher nor its dealers or distributors assumes any liability for any alleged or actual damages arising from the use of this program. (Some states do not allow for the exclusion of implied warranties, so the exclusion may not apply to you.)